STANDARD FIRST AID

safety oriented

MODULAR COURSE

WORKBOOK

SECOND EDITION 1988

St. John Ambulance
312 Laurier Avenue East,
Ottawa, Canada K1N 6P6

First Edition - 1986
Second Edition - 1988
First Impression - 100,000
Second Impression - 100,000

Canadian Cataloguing in Publication Data

Main entry under title:

Standard first aid safety oriented modular course :
workbook

2nd ed.1988
Issued also in French under title: Secourisme
   général orienté vers la sécurité : cours modulaire :
   cahier de travail.
ISBN 0-919434-71-1

   1. First aid in illness and injury. 2. First aid
in illness and injury—Problems, exercises, etc.
I. St. John Ambulance.

RC86.7.S82 1988   616.02'52   C88-090028-8

©1988 St. John Priory of Canada Properties
All rights reserved

Printed in Canada

Stock No. 3480

FOREWORD

This self-instruction workbook will help you to learn the first aid theory for the Standard First Aid Modular Course and it will prepare you for the final written examination.

Your Instructor will tell you which workbook exercises to complete and when to do them.

FIRST AID SKILLS AND CPR SKILLS IN PARTICULAR, DETERIORATE VERY QUICKLY UNLESS THEY ARE PRACTISED REGULARLY. ANNUAL RECERTIFICATION IN CPR IS CONSIDERED ESSENTIAL.

COVER ART

The white cross, superimposed on a red maple leaf, was designed to mark St. John Ambulance's Canadian Centenary in 1983. Plans to bring first aid training into its second century with a new look were begun and are reflected in this book.

DANIEL BOULT's airbrush rendition of the logo in medallion form signified, in a tangible way, that this modern approach to first aid is an outstanding achievement that should make us proud to be part of St. John Ambulance.

First Aid Safety Oriented, Second Edition, is the reference manual for this course.

You may use the manual as -

• Supplementary reading during the course, if time permits; or

• Reference material after the course.

CONTENTS

> There is no Workbook Exercise 14

> There is no Workbook Exercise 17

CONTENTS

Addendum A has been designed to enrich your knowledge of basic anatomy and physiology. It will help you to prepare for more advanced first aid training, the National Instructor Training and Development Programme (NITDP), St. John Ambulance Brigade qualifications and child and health care work.

Addendum A is NOT a requirement for certification in Standard First Aid. It is offered as a "stand alone" module or as a voluntary homework assignment.

1-7, 8, 9, 10, 11, 12
18, 22.

NOTES

USE OF THE WORKBOOK

1-1

Before starting Excercise 1, you should have completed the **REGISTRATION FORM** contained in this Workbook and handed it to your Instructor.

Your Instructor will ask you to work through several exercises in this workbook.

Each exercise consists of teaching units called **FRAMES**. Each frame is numbered.

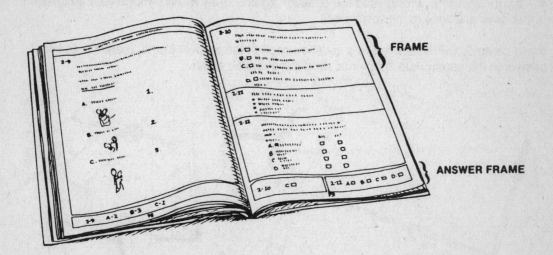

FRAME

ANSWER FRAME

1-2

Each frame in this book contains -

• **INFORMATION** for you to read

  OR

• **A QUESTION** for you to answer

The correct answer to the question appears in the **ANSWER FRAME** at the bottom of the page.

When there is **MORE THAN ONE** question frame on a page, the correct answers appear in separate answer frames.

To use the workbook:

1. Tear off the **CURSOR** attached to the back cover.

2. Use the cursor to cover the answer frame at the bottom of the page until you have marked your answers to the questions.

3. To check your answers, slide the cursor to the **RIGHT** as far as the **SOLID LINE** at the end of the answer frame. The correct answers will be revealed in the answer frame.

4. If your answer is wrong, read the question again. Draw a line through your incorrect answer and write in the correct one.

If you do not know the answer to a question, look at the answer frame, mark the correct answer in the appropriate space and read the question again.

Several types of questions are used in this workbook. Four examples are given below.

True or False Type

Mark each statement true (T) or false (F).

A. [T] Each workbook exercise consists of frames.

B. [F] The answer frame is found at the top of each page.

Multiple Choice Type

Check (✔) the correct statement(s).

A. [✔] Teaching units in this book are called frames.

B. [ ] The frames in each exercise are not numbered.

C. [✔] A frame may contain information or a question.

D. [✔] Question and answer frames have the same number.

NOTE: Multiple choice questions may have more than one correct answer.

Match Type

Write a number in the box to match each word with its meaning.

	Words		Meanings
A. [2]	Exercise	1.	Number appearing at the top of a frame.
B. [3]	Frame	2.	Major division of the book.
C. [1]	Frame number	3.	Teaching unit.

Order Type

Number the following steps in the correct order.

A. [2] Mark your answer in the box.

B. [1] Read the question in the frame.

1-5

FIRST AID is emergency care given to an injured or ill person to -

- **PRESERVE LIFE**

- **PREVENT AN INJURY OR ILLNESS FROM BECOMING WORSE**

- **PROMOTE RECOVERY**

A person who requires first aid is called a **CASUALTY**.

Most casualties who have received first aid will require medical aid as soon as possible.

MEDICAL AID is the professional treatment given by or under the direction of a doctor at or on the way to a medical facility.

1-6

Mark each statement true **(T)** or false **(F)**.

A. `T`   First aid is help that you give to a person who has had an accident.

B. `F`   Medical aid is not necessary when first aid has been rendered.

C. `T`   First aid may keep someone alive.

D. `F`   In first aid, an injured person is called a patient.

E. `T`   First aid may keep a person's condition from getting more serious.

F. `T`   A person has a better chance of healing if first aid is given.

1-6   A. `T`   B. `F`   C. `T`   D. `F`   E. `T`   F. `T`

1

SAFETY ORIENTED FIRST AID TRAINING makes you aware of -

- **WHY** an accident happens

- **WHAT** injuries may result from an accident

- **HOW** accidents and injuries can be prevented

Check (✓) the correct completions of the following statement.

First aid training -

A. [✓] Alerts you to dangerous situations.

B. [✓] Assists you to become safety minded.

C. [✗] Prepares you to provide professional medical aid.

D. [✓] Alerts you to the harm caused by an accident.

First aid training will help you to develop a **SAFETY ORIENTED LIFESTYLE** and to prevent accidents at home, at work and at play.

Among the things you should do to develop a safety oriented lifestyle are the following -

• Make a personal commitment to safety

• Follow safety rules

• Adopt safety practices

• Use protective clothing and equipment

• Learn the safe operation of machinery and equipment

• Read and follow directions when using chemical products

• Recognize and heed the symbols of hazardous products

A. B. D. [✓]

Each picture illustrates a dangerous situation.

Write into the boxes the appropriate number to match each picture with the safety practice that would prevent an accident.

| **Dangerous Situations** | **Safety Practices** |

A.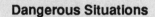

1. Store all medicine out of the reach of children.

B.

2. Wear face and hand protection when working with chemicals.

C.

3. Wear life jackets for boating.

D.

4. Follow rules of safe driving.

E.

5. Handle hazardous products in a safe manner.

1

1-11

Many accidents could be prevented by paying attention to the symbols displayed on the labels of hazardous products.

Each symbol shows the nature of the hazard -

POISON	CORROSIVE	FLAMMABLE	EXPLOSIVE	RADIATION

Each shape indicates the degree of hazard -

DANGER	WARNING	CAUTION

1-12

Match each symbol with the corresponding safety message by placing the appropriate number into the boxes provided.

A. [2]   Danger corrosive

B. [5]   Danger radiation

C. [3]   Danger explosive

D. [1]   Caution flammable

E. [4]   Warning poison

1.

2.

3.

4.

5.

1-12

A.	2	B.	5	C.	3	D.	1	E.	4

1

1-13

In an **EMERGENCY SITUATION** you should use the **PRIORITY ACTION APPROACH (PAA)**.

PAA is the sequence of actions that should be followed by a First Aider at an accident/illness scene to give safe and appropriate first aid for life-threatening conditions. Although circumstances may dictate that the order of the steps in PAA be changed, they should usually be performed in the following sequence -

- **TAKE CHARGE**
- **CALL FOR HELP TO ATTRACT BYSTANDERS**
- **ASSESS THE HAZARDS**
- **MAKE THE AREA SAFE FOR YOURSELF AND OTHERS**
- **IDENTIFY YOURSELF AS A FIRST AIDER AND OFFER HELP**
- **ASSESS THE CASUALTY FOR LIFE-THREATENING CONDITIONS**
- **GIVE FIRST AID FOR LIFE-THREATENING CONDITIONS**
- **SEND FOR HELP**

Make use of any help which is available -

- Bystanders, e.g.   - to get help
  - to make the area safe
  - to assist in giving first aid as directed

- Authorities, e.g.   - police, ambulance, hydro personnel

1-14

Mark each statement true **(T)** or false **(F)**.

A. ☐ It is up to the First Aider to organize onlookers and tell them how they can help.

B. ☐ If there are several people trained in first aid at the accident scene, all take equal responsibility.

C. ☐ The First Aider should recognize the risks and use safety precautions to protect himself, the casualty and bystanders.

D. ☐ On arrival at an accident scene, all injuries should be discovered and treated immediately.

E. ☐ Priority Action Approach is performed in the same order regardless of the type of injury or illness.

1-14   A. T   B. F   C. T   D. F   E. F

1

1-15

The three **PRIORITIES** of first aid are **stopped breathing, severe bleeding** and **unconsciousness**. These are all threats to life and must be assessed in the **primary examination** which is part of **Priority Action Approach**.

The order in which you must give immediate first aid for these conditions is -

FIRST - STOPPED BREATHING

SECOND - SEVERE BLEEDING

THIRD - UNCONSCIOUSNESS

Even if there is more than one casualty, deal only with the life-threatening conditions of each of the casualties first.

1-16

Three casualties are described below. All are found lying on their backs.

Number them 1, 2, 3 according to first aid priorities.

A. ☐ Unconscious breathing casualty.

B. ☐ Unconscious non-breathing casualty.

C. ☐ Conscious breathing casualty with heavy bleeding.

1-16   A. ☐ 3   B. ☐ 1   C. ☐ 2

1

To give appropriate first aid to a casualty, you should know as much as possible about the accident or illness.

You need three kinds of information: **HISTORY**, **SIGNS** and **SYMPTOMS**.

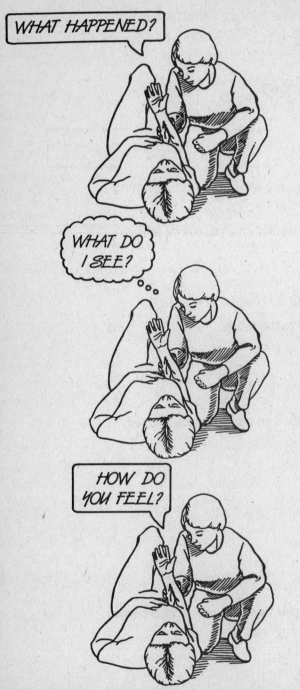

WHAT HAPPENED?

HISTORY

- **ASK** the conscious casualty what happened

- **ASK** bystanders what happened

- **OBSERVE** the scene

WHAT DO I SEE?

SIGNS

- **OBSERVE** the casualty

- **EXAMINE** for indications of injury or illness

HOW DO YOU FEEL?

SYMPTOMS

- **ASK** the conscious casualty how she feels

- **LISTEN** to the casualty's comments

Identify the information in each statement below as History, Signs or Symptoms by writing the appropriate number in the boxes provided.

1	HISTORY
2	SIGNS
3	SYMPTOMS

A. ☐3 A casualty tells you he feels cold.

B. ☐2 There is blood soaking through the sweater on a casualty's arm.

C. ☐2 A casualty's skin is cold and clammy to the touch.

D. ☐1 A man tells you that the casualty slipped on a patch of ice and fell.

E. ☐3 A young boy says he feels sick.

F. ☐1 You see an empty bottle of sleeping pills near an unconscious person.

1-19

Three of the signs which must be observed when giving first aid are called **vital signs**. These provide important information about the condition of the casualty.

The **VITAL SIGNS** are -

- **TEMPERATURE** (warmth of the skin)
- **PULSE** (number of times the heart beats in a minute)
- **RESPIRATION** (number of times a person breathes in a minute)

Assess and record vital signs as a basis for subsequent assessments -

- **FEEL** the forehead and neck for temperature
- **ASSESS** the carotid pulse, noting rhythm and strength
- **CHECK** the quality of breathing, noting rate, rhythm and sound

Vital signs in a normal healthy person remain almost **CONSTANT**. Noticeable changes in any of the vital signs could mean that the casualty's condition is becoming worse.

1-20

Check (✓) from the examples below the observations that could indicate that the casualty's condition is getting worse.

A. ☑ The pulse becomes very slow and weak.

B. ☐ The casualty falls asleep.

C. ☑ Breathing becomes very fast and shallow.

D. ☑ The skin becomes cold to the touch.

E. ☑ The casualty starts gasping for air.

1-20

A.	C.	D.	E.
✓	✓	✓	✓

1

1-21

Valuable information about the **HISTORY** of a casualty can often be found on a **MEDIC-ALERT** device; e.g. a bracelet, necklace or pocket card.

A **MEDIC-ALERT** device is a warning sign which alerts First Aiders and medical personnel that the person wearing it -

- Has a **MEDICAL CONDITION** requiring special treatment

OR

- Is **ALLERGIC** to certain substances (e.g. medications, plants, foods, insect bites)

1-22

Mark each statement true (**T**) or false (**F**).

A. ☐T A person whose arm swells and has difficulty breathing after a bee sting may wear Medic-Alert jewellery.

B. ☐T Important facts about the condition of an unconscious casualty may be revealed on a Medic-Alert tag.

C. ☐T You may find Medic-Alert information in a casualty's wallet.

D. ☐F Medic-Alert information will tell you what first aid to give.

1-22

A. T   B. T   C. T   D. F

1

After you have given first aid for life-threatening conditions, you may have to perform a **SECONDARY EXAMINATION**.

Examine the casualty from head to toe **IN THE POSITION FOUND.**

The examination must be **SYSTEMATIC -**

- Assess the vital signs
- Look and feel for signs of bleeding, swelling and deformity
- Check for loss of muscle power and lack of feeling

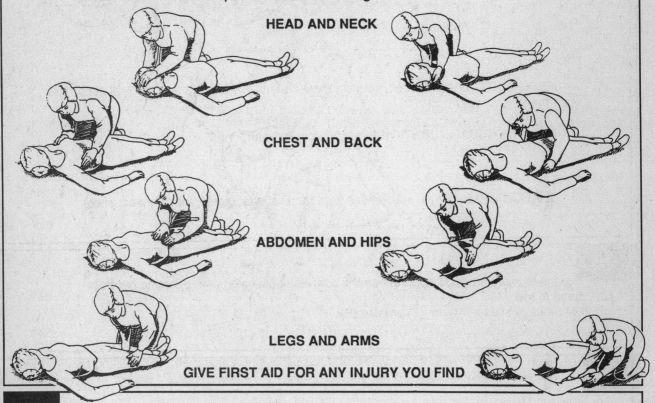

HEAD AND NECK

CHEST AND BACK

ABDOMEN AND HIPS

LEGS AND ARMS

GIVE FIRST AID FOR ANY INJURY YOU FIND

1-24

Check (✔) the correct statements regarding the secondary examination.

A. ☐ A head-to toe examination should be done to discover any immediate danger to the casualty's life.

B. ☑ Each part of the body should be examined carefully for signs of injury.

C. ☐ Place the casualty in a comfortable position to allow a thorough examination.

D. ☑ So that nothing is missed, start by checking the casualty's head and work down the body.

1-24

B. ✓   D. ✓

1

1-25

If the casualty is **CONSCIOUS**, a head-to-toe examination is not always necessary.

You should question her about the **HISTORY** of the incident and her **SYMPTOMS**. This information may lead you **DIRECTLY** to the injury.

WHAT HAPPENED?

If signs of injury are **NOT** apparent on the conscious casualty, then examine her from head to toe.

1-26

You are assessing a conscious casualty for injuries.

What should you do **FIRST**?

A. ☐ Search for Medic-Alert information.

B. ☐ Check the carotid pulse.

C. ☑ Ask her what happened and how she feels.

D. ☐ Systematically examine for injuries.

1-26

C. ☑

1

1-27

With an **UNCONSCIOUS** casualty, you must perform a secondary examination and rely on -

- The history of the incident as told to you by a bystander
- The surroundings of the accident
- An accurate interpretation of physical signs

- **EXAMINE** the casualty from head-to-toe **IN THE POSITION FOUND**

- **CHECK FOR MEDIC-ALERT INFORMATION** which may help you determine the required first aid

- **BE SYSTEMATIC** so that no injury is overlooked

- If a spinal injury is suspected, **DO NOT MOVE** the casualty

1-28

Check (✓) the actions you should perform in the secondary assessment of an unconscious casualty.

A. ☐ Examine for injuries that could cause death.

B. ☐ Listen to the casualty's complaints.

C. ☑ Examine thoroughly and note all abnormal signs.

D. ☐ Look for apparent injuries only.

E. ☑ Perform a thorough examination without moving the casualty.

F. ☑ Look for a device indicating that the casualty has a medical condition requiring special care.

1-28   C. ✓   E. ✓   F. ✓

1

PRECAUTIONS WHEN GIVING FIRST AID

When you offer first aid, you are assuming **RESPONSIBILITY** for the care of the casualty.

Certain **PRECAUTIONS** should be taken -

> **DO NOT** give first aid to an adult or an older child who refuses help
>
> **GIVE** first aid to an unconscious person or a young child who is alone

DO NOT MOVE the casualty except for reasons of safety.

GIVE only that first aid which is necessary.

PROTECT the casualty's belongings.

TAKE detailed notes.

DO NOT leave the casualty until medical aid arrives.

Mark each statement true **(T)** or false **(F)**.

A. ☐ As a First Aider, it is your duty to give first aid to all casualties, even if they insist they don't need it.

B. ☐ Once you have given first aid, wait with the casualty for medical aid to arrive.

C. ☐ To make it easier to give first aid, place the casualty into a more comfortable position.

D. ☐ A written record of facts surrounding the emergency and first aid given should be kept for reference.

E. ☐ Make sure that the casualty's wallet and jewellery are safe.

F. ☐ Give care for all ailments even those which the casualty has had for a long time.

A. F   B. T   C. F   D. T   E. T   F. F

1

As a First Aider, you have the **RESPONSIBILITY** to watch for certain signs which may indicate **CHILD ABUSE**.

These might be -

- **BROKEN BONES** in infants
- Unusually shaped **BRUISES** and **BURNS**
- A child's **OBVIOUS FEAR** of his parent or babysitter

> **INSIST ON MEDICAL ATTENTION FOR ANY CHILD YOU SUSPECT HAS BEEN ABUSED**

If medical aid is not obtained, notify the local child welfare agency.

> **NEVER CONFRONT A PARENT OR BABYSITTER WITH ACCUSATIONS OF CHILD ABUSE**

1-32

Which of the following signs could point to child abuse?

A. ☐ An injured three-year-old who runs from her father in terror.

B. ☐ A six-week-old baby who has a fractured arm.

C. ☐ A six-year-old who has a broken leg following a bike accident.

D. ☐ A five-year-old child who has dark handprints on his back, buttocks and chest.

E. ☐ A four-year-old with several round bruises on her knees.

1-32   A. ✓   B. ✓   D. ✓

1

1-33

After immediate first aid is given, you should **MAINTAIN** the casualty in the **BEST POSSIBLE CONDITION** until hand-over to medical aid.

- **CALL MEDICAL AID** if you have not already done so

- **MONITOR** the casualty continuously

- **PROTECT** and **SHELTER** the casualty

- **PROVIDE** for medical aid a record of the casualty's injuries or illness and the first aid given

> **ENSURE** that the casualty who does not require medical aid is placed in the care of friends or relatives

1-34

Which of the actions listed below should you take to maintain a casualty following immediate first aid?

A. ☐ T   Keep the casualty safe, warm and comfortable.

B. ☐ T   Report on the casualty's condition and the help given to medical personnel.

C. ☐ T   Ensure that medical aid is not delayed.

D. ☐ F   Reassess the casualty's condition every half hour.

E. ☐ F   Send the casualty, who no longer needs first aid, home by herself.

1-34

A. ☑   B. ☑   C. ☑

1

1-35

Mark each statement true (**T**) or false (**F**).

A. T   First aid training teaches us how to develop a safety oriented lifestyle as well as what to do in case of an accident or a sudden illness.

B. T   At the scene of an accident, you must make sure the area is safe for the casualty, bystanders and yourself before giving first aid.

C. F   The three priorities of first aid in order of importance are: bleeding, stopped breathing and unconsciousness.

D. F   The three vital signs give little information on the casualty's condition.

E. T   Recognizing symbols of hazardous products helps to prevent accidents.

F. T   If a casualty is conscious, he may be able to describe his symptoms to assist you in assessing his condition.

G. F   If there are several casualties, give all the first aid that is required to one before moving on to the next.

H. T   The head-to-toe examination of an unconscious casualty must be systematic and thorough.

I. F   As a First Aider you have the duty to care for all casualties, even those who refuse your help.

J. T   You should give first aid to a casualty where you find him, unless your safety or that of the casualty is threatened.

1-35

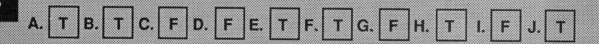

A. T B. T C. F D. F E. T F. T G. F H. T I. F J. T

1

For more information on this topic, refer to: *First Aid Safety Oriented*, Second Edition, Chapters 1, 11

END OF EXERCISE 1

NOTES

INTRODUCTION TO RESPIRATORY EMERGENCIES

2-1

WE BREATHE TO LIVE

The air we breathe **IN** contains oxygen (O_2). The blood carries it from the lungs to all parts of the body.

Carbon dioxide (CO_2), a waste product of the body, is taken from the blood and is in the air we breathe **OUT**.

2-2

Mark each statement true **(T)** or false **(F)**.

A. ☐   When we breathe, carbon dioxide is removed from the blood and oxygen is added.

B. ☐   The lungs allow the oxygen from the air to reach all parts of the body.

C. ☐   Our bodies need oxygen to live.

D. ☐   Carbon dioxide is the vital part of inhaled air.

E. ☐   The blood plays an important role in respiration.

2-2

A. T   B. T   C. T   D. F   E. T

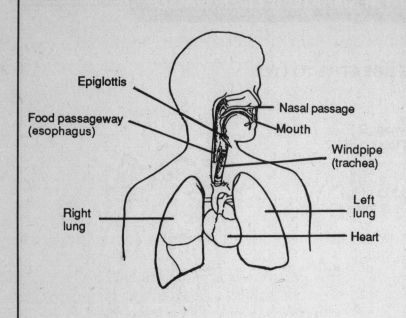

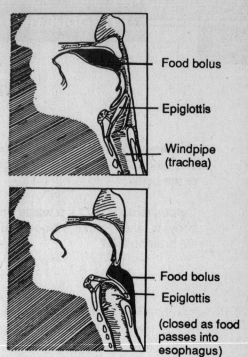

Food bolus

Epiglottis

Windpipe
(trachea)

Food bolus

Epiglottis

(closed as food
passes into
esophagus)

AIR REACHES OUR LUNGS THROUGH THE AIRWAY

The entrance from the throat to the windpipe is protected by a flap called the
EPIGLOTTIS.

The epiglottis closes when we swallow. This keeps food and liquids out of the lungs.

The epiglottis opens when we breathe to allow air into the lungs.

2-4

Check (✔) the correct statements.

A. ☐ The airway ends at the epiglottis.

B. ☑ The function of the epiglottis is to keep the windpipe clear of obstructions.

C. ☑ The air we breathe enters the lungs through the airway.

D. ☐ When we swallow, food passes through the windpipe.

E. ☑ When we breathe, the epiglottis lets air pass into the windpipe.

2-4

B. ☑   C. ☑   E. ☑

2

2-5

A respiratory emergency occurs when breathing stops. The body is deprived of oxygen. This is called **ASPHYXIA**.

After **4 MINUTES** without oxygen brain damage may result.

> **YOU MUST ACT IMMEDIATELY TO RESTORE BREATHING**

2-6

Mark each statement true **(T)** or false **(F)**.

A. ☑ T   A casualty who is not breathing is in a life-threatening condition.

B. ☑ T   The brain's function may be harmed if a person does not breathe for 5 minutes.

C. ☑ T   You must begin first aid for stopped breathing without delay.

D. ☑ F   Death occurs as soon as breathing stops.

E. ☑ F   A casualty who has stopped breathing must be transported to hospital immediately.

F. ☑ T   Asphyxia is a condition in which the body lacks oxygen.

2-6

A. T   B. T   C. T   D. F   E. F   F. T

There are many **CAUSES** of breathing emergencies. These will all fit into one of three main **TYPES** -

- Lack of oxygen

- Obstructed airway

- Loss of effective function of the lungs and heart

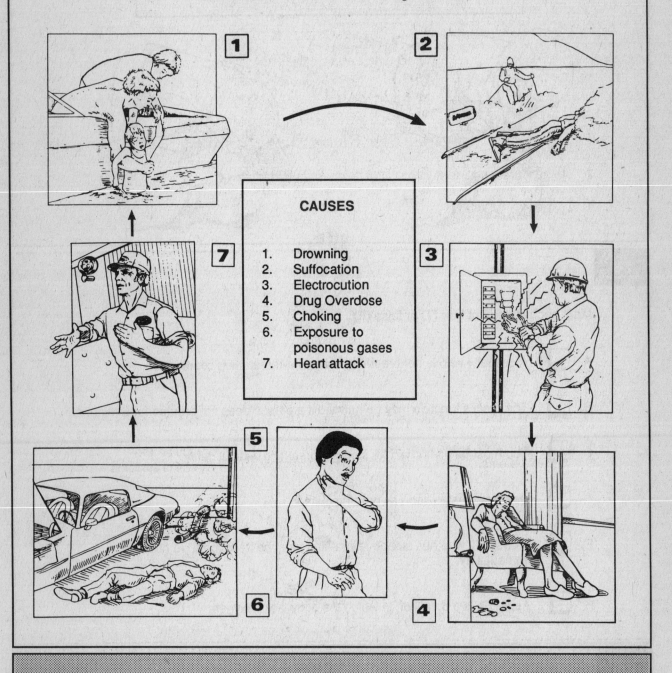

CAUSES

1. Drowning
2. Suffocation
3. Electrocution
4. Drug Overdose
5. Choking
6. Exposure to poisonous gases
7. Heart attack

Check (✓) the correct completions.

The three (3) types of breathing emergencies occur when:

A.   A person is deprived of -

1. ☐   Carbon dioxide.   **OR**   2. ☑   Oxygen in inhaled air.

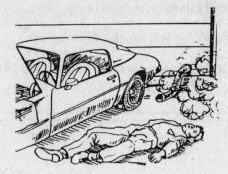

B.   Air is not reaching a person's lungs because of a blocked -

1. ☐   Nasal passage.   **OR**   2. ☐   Airway.

C.   A person has a malfunction or arrest of the -

1. ☑   Respiratory and circulatory   **OR**   2. ☐   Muscular and
           systems.   digestive systems.

A. [2]   B. [2]   C. [1]

2

2-9

Be alert for signs of a respiratory emergency.

Observe the casualty for these changes in breathing -

RATE - irregular, faster or slower than normal breathing

DEPTH - shallow or abnormally deep

QUALITY - noisy, raspy or gasping and struggling for breath

ABSENCE OF BREATHING - air movement cannot be heard or felt and the rise and fall of the chest is not observed

2-10

Which of the following signs could indicate a breathing emergency?

A. ☑ Rapid breathing.

B. ☑ Lack of any signs of breathing.

C. ☑ Natural speed of breathing alternating with very quick and rapid breathing.

D. ☑ Very little or too much chest movement.

E. ☐ Regular, quiet breaths.

F. ☑ Deep, sucking breaths.

2-10 A. ✓ B. ✓ C. ✓ D. ✓ F. ✓

2

Be alert also for changes in -

SKIN COLOUR - lips, ears and fingernail beds show bluish discolouration

When parts of the body look "blue" it means that the body is not getting enough oxygen.

This condition is called **CYANOSIS**.

BLOOD VESSELS - vessels in the head and neck area may stand out (congestion).

2-12

Mark each statement true **(T)** or false **(F)**.

A. ☑ Cyanosis, by itself, is not a dangerous condition.

B. ☑ Cyanosis is a condition in which certain body parts change colour because of lack of oxygen.

C. ☑ If a breathing emergency is suspected, monitor breathing and the appearance of the skin.

D. ☑ During breathing difficulties the veins of the throat may be full and swollen with blood.

2-12

A. F   B. T   C. T   D. T

2-13

The **PULSE** is the regular throbbing of the heart felt at different points of the body. To ensure that blood circulates and carries oxygen to vital tissues, you must assess the pulse.

When giving artificial respiration -

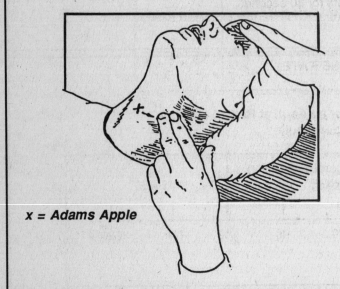

x = Adams Apple

- Check the **CAROTID** pulse

  - following the **INITIAL TWO BREATHS**

  - **AFTER ONE MINUTE** and

  - **EVERY FEW MINUTES** thereafter, until normal breathing is resumed

2-14

Which statements relating to artificial respiration are true **(T)** and which are false **(F)**?

A. ☐ The presence of a pulse indicates that oxygen provided through ventilations is reaching the brain.

B. ☐ Take the pulse at the casualty's wrist when giving artificial respiration.

C. ☐ You should take the carotid pulse following the first two ventilations.

D. ☐ The pulse should be reassessed after one minute and every following few minutes as long as artificial respiration continues.

2-14   A. T   B. F   C. T   D. T

2

The **PULSE RATE** is the number of times the heart beats in one minute.

DETERMINE YOUR OWN PULSE RATE

1.	Feel your carotid pulse.	33
2.	Count the number of beats for 30 seconds.	
3.	Multiply by 2.	x 2
4.	The result is **YOUR PULSE RATE**.	66

Pulse Rates for an Adult at Rest
(beats per minute)

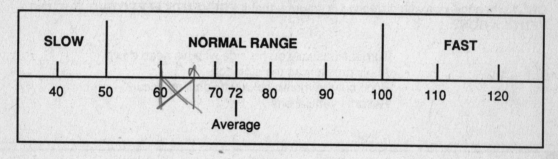

SLOW		NORMAL RANGE			FAST	

40   50   60   70 72   80   90   100   110   120

Average

	Yes	No
Does your pulse rate fall within the **NORMAL** range for an adult?	☐	☐

You are taking the carotid pulse of a resting adult casualty. The count for 30 seconds is 34 beats.

The pulse rate would be considered -

A. ☐ Very slow.

B. ☑ Within the normal range.

C. ☐ Very fast.

B. ☑

2

2-17

GASTRIC DISTENTION occurs when ventilations are given too fast and with too much force, and air enters the stomach. This makes artificial respiration more difficult and increases the risk of vomiting.

To **MINIMIZE** the risk of gastric distention -

- Give slow breaths
- Use just enough air to expand the chest

If the stomach **BECOMES SLIGHTLY DISTENDED** -

- Reposition the airway
- Reduce the rate and volume of ventilations
- Observe the rise and fall of the chest

ONLY when the stomach distention is so great that it **PREVENTS EFFECTIVE VENTILATIONS** -

- Turn the casualty on his side with his head down
- Apply pressure to the stomach
- Wipe out the mouth quickly if vomiting occurs
- Resume ventilations

2-18

Check (✔) the correct procedures that should be followed when the stomach of the casualty becomes distended during artificial respiration.

A. ☐ Give abdominal thrusts immediately.

B. ☐ Avoid excessive speed and pressure when ventilating.

C. ☐ Recheck and ensure an open airway.

D. ☑ Position the casualty for good drainage before applying abdominal pressure.

E. ☐ Rinse the casualty's mouth thoroughly before continuing artificial respiration.

2-18

B. ☑   C. ☑   D. ☑

2

2-19

After artificial respiration, the casualty may gag or vomit.

This could **BLOCK** the airway.

Place him in the **RECOVERY POSITION** to allow fluids to drain from the mouth and the airway to remain open.

2-20

Check (✔) the correct position for a casualty whose breathing has been restored following artificial respiration.

A.

B.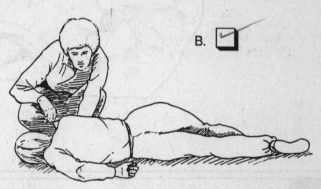

C.

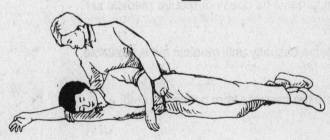

2-20

B.

2

A casualty in the recovery position must receive **FOLLOW-UP CARE**.

You should -

- **MONITOR** breathing closely and resume artificial respiration if necessary

- Keep the casualty **WARM**

- **OBTAIN** medical aid

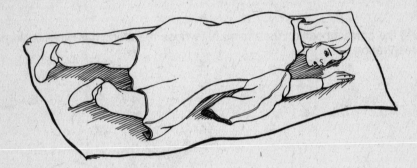

2-22

Choose the correct completions for the following statement.

When a casualty is in the recovery position following successful artificial respiration, you should -

A. ☐   Inform him that he does not require medical aid.

B. ☑   Watch the casualty until medical aid is available.

C. ☑   Prevent the casualty from becoming cold.

D. ☑   Be prepared to ventilate if breathing stops.

2-22

B.   C.   D.

2

2-23

MOUTH-TO-NOSE is another direct method of artificial respiration.

Use this method when -

- A casualty has injuries in or about the mouth

- Your mouth cannot fully cover the casualty's mouth

2-24

For which non-breathing casualty is the mouth-to-nose method preferred?

A casualty with -

A. ☑ Lip wounds.

B. ☐ A suspected neck injury.

C. ☑ Bleeding from the mouth.

D. ☐ A nosebleed.

2-24

A. ☑   C. ☑

The basic techniques for the mouth-to-nose method are the same as for the mouth-to-mouth method except that you breathe through the casualty's nose.

The mouth-to-nose method is modified by using the following techniques -

- Tilt the head back with one hand, but **DO NOT PINCH THE NOSTRILS**

- Lift the chin with the other hand, using **THE THUMB** to **CLOSE** the casualty's **MOUTH**

- **COVER** the casualty's **NOSE** with **YOUR MOUTH** to give ventilations

- **OPEN** the casualty's mouth **BETWEEN BREATHS** to let the air **OUT**

Choose the correct completions for the following statement. When using the mouth-to-nose method of artificial respiration, you -

A. Blow air into the casualty's -

1. ☐ Mouth.   **OR**   2. ☑ Nose.

B. Prevent air leakage by using your thumb to close the -

1. ☐ Mouth.   **OR**   2. ☐ Nose.

C. Allow air to escape between breaths by opening the -

1. ☐ Mouth.   **OR**   2. ☐ Nose.

2-26   A. ☐2☐   B. ☐1☐   C. ☐1☐

2

Special care must be taken when giving artificial respiration to a casualty who may have a neck injury. The neck must **NOT** be moved. To open the airway, use the **JAW THRUST** without **HEAD TILT** method. To ventilate, use your cheek to seal the casualty's nose.

2-28

Check (✔) the correct completions for the following statement. When giving artificial respiration to a casualty with a neck injury -

A. The head must be -

1. ☐ Tilted backward.

2. ☐ Tilted forward.

3. ☑ Not tilted.

B. When ventilating -

1. ☐ The nostrils are sealed by the mouth.

2. ☑ The nostrils are sealed by the cheek.

3. ☐ The nostrils are sealed with the fingers.

C. Use your hands to -

1. ☐ Lift the neck.

2. ☑ Open the mouth.

3. ☐ Straighten the neck.

2-28

A. 3   B. 2   C. 2

CAUTION!

It may be necessary to place a casualty with a suspected neck injury into the recovery position when -

- The casualty is likely to vomit

- You must leave to get help

APPLY A CERVICAL COLLAR FIRST
(commercial or improvised)

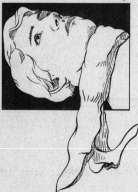 

ANY MOVEMENT OF THE NECK AREA COULD CAUSE FURTHER DAMAGE

Check (✔) the correct completion.

A casualty with a neck injury has been revived by artificial respiration. He must be left alone while you get help.

You should -

A. ☐   Leave him on his back and turn his head to one side.

B. ☐   Roll him gently on his side and then support his cervical spine.

C. ☑   Put on a cervical collar and gently roll him into the recovery position.

D. ☐   Roll him into the face-down position and turn his head to one side.

2-30

C. ☑

2-31

Mark each statement true **(T)** or false **(F)**.

A. [F] The pulse should be checked every 5 minutes during artificial respiration.

B. [✓] A pulse rate of 65 beats per minute is within the normal range for a healthy adult at rest.

C. [F] The carotid pulse can be felt only on the left side of the neck.

D. [T] In artificial respiration to an adult casualty, 2 separate breaths should be given initially and then 1 breath every 5 seconds.

E. [T] After 4 minutes of stopped breathing, brain damage may occur.

F. [T] Stomach distention during artificial respiration can hinder proper inflation of the lungs.

G. [T] Heavy socks or rolled up towels could be used as an improvised cervical collar.

H. [F] To apply a cervical collar, gently lift the casualty's head and turn it from side to side.

I. [T] Placing the casualty into the recovery position maintains an open airway.

J. [T] The mouth-to-nose method of artificial respiration is used for a casualty with injuries around his lips.

2-31

A. [F] B. [T] C. [F] D. [T] E. [T] F. [T] G. [T] H. [F] I. [T] J. [T]

For more information on this topic refer to:
First Aid Safety Oriented, Second Edition, Chapters 5, 6, 7

END OF EXERCISE 2

CAUSES AND PREVENTION OF CHOKING

3-1

CHOKING IS A BREATHING EMERGENCY that occurs when the airway becomes **PARTIALLY** or **COMPLETELY** blocked.

The common causes of airway obstruction are -

- The **TONGUE FALLING TO THE BACK OF THE THROAT** of an unconscious person

- **FOOD** or **SMALL OBJECTS** lodged in the throat

3-2

Choose the correct completion for the following statements.

When a casualty is choking -

	Choice 1			**Choice 2**
A. ☑	His air passage is clogged.	OR	A. ☐	His air passage is clear.
B. ☐	Air flows freely into and out of the lungs.	OR	B. ☑	Air flow to the lungs is impaired or stopped.
C. ☑	His life is endangered.	OR	C. ☐	His life is in little danger.

When a casualty is unconscious -

D. ☑	His tongue may block his air passage.	OR	D. ☐	His air passage opens wider.

3-2

A. 1   B. 2   C. 1   D. 1

CHOKING MAY RESULT FROM -

- Swallowing large pieces of food
- Gulping drinks with food in your mouth
- Eating or drinking while doing something else
- Small objects in an infant's mouth
- Too much alcohol before and during meals

MOST CHOKING INCIDENTS CAN BE PREVENTED BY -

- Cutting food into small pieces and chewing it well
- Avoiding talking, laughing, drinking while chewing food
- Supervising children while they are eating
- Keeping small objects away from infants and young children
- Drinking alcohol in moderation

Listed below are unsafe eating habits and behaviours that could result in choking.

Match each situation with the appropriate safety measure by placing the correct number into the squares provided.

Situations	Safety Measures
A. [4] A ten-month-old puts peanuts into his mouth.	1. Avoid eating and drinking at the same time.
B. [3] A teenager pushes a hot dog into his mouth and eats it quickly.	2. Avoid other activity when you are eating.
C. [1] A woman takes a gulp of coffee while she is chewing on a piece of meat.	3. Cut food into small pieces and chew it well before you swallow.
D. [2] A man is eating a sandwich while he is driving his car.	4. Keep small objects away from infants.

A. [4]   B. [3]   C. [1]   D. [2]

3

3-5

Any or all of these signs may indicate that a person is choking.

PARTIAL AIRWAY OBSTRUCTION

SIGNS

You may observe:

- Forceful coughing and gagging
- Wheezing sound between coughs
- Redness in the face (congestion)
- The person can speak

} **GOOD AIR EXCHANGE**

- Weak, ineffective cough
- High-pitched noise when inhaling
- Increased respiratory difficulty
- Cyanosis (blue discolouration about the lips)
- The person is unable to speak

} **POOR AIR EXCHANGE**

COMPLETE AIRWAY OBSTRUCTION

SIGNS

You may observe:

- Respiratory distress
- Clutching the throat
- Cyanosis in the face
- The person is unable to breathe, cough or speak

Universal Distress Sign

3-6

Which of these conditions would indicate that a person is choking?

A. ☐   He is pale and sweating.

B. ☑   He is coughing and is red in the face.

C. ☑   He cannot make any sounds and his face is turning bluish.

D. ☐   He is holding his throat in apparent panic.

3-6

B.   C.   D.

3-7

If the choking person has a **GOOD** air exchange, **CAN** breathe, cough or speak, the airway is only **PARTIALLY OBSTRUCTED**.

DO NOT INTERFERE with the person's attempts to clear his airway.

You should -

- Encourage **COUGHING**

- **STAND BY** ready to help

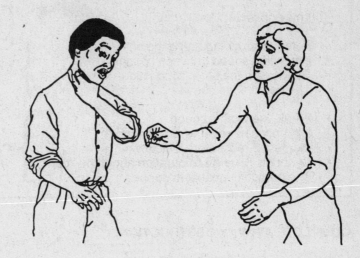

Stand By

3-8

A choking person is coughing and gasping for air but he can still speak.

What should you do?

A. ☐   Call for help and immediately begin first aid manoeuvres for a complete airway obstruction.

B. ☐   Place him at rest and leave at once to obtain medical aid.

C. ☑   Stay with him and urge him to continue his efforts to remove the obstruction.

D. ☐   Calm the casualty and instruct him to lie on his back.

3-8

C. ☑

3

If the choking person is conscious and -

- Shows signs of **POOR AIR EXCHANGE**

  OR

- **CANNOT** breathe or cough

- **CANNOT** answer the question -

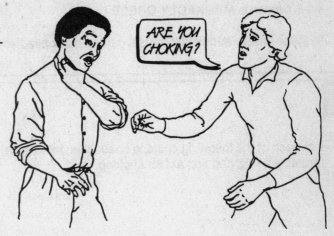

GIVE FIRST AID FOR A COMPLETE AIRWAY OBSTRUCTION

YOU MUST ACT QUICKLY -

- Immediately give **ABDOMINAL THRUSTS** until successful or until the casualty becomes unconscious

When should you begin first aid manoeuvres for choking?

When the choking person -

A. ☐ Is coughing and gagging.

B. ☑ Has an ineffective cough and is starting to turn blue in the face.

C. ☑ Is unable to speak and get air into and out of the lungs.

D. ☑ Has a completely clogged airway.

B. ☑   C. ☑   D. ☑

3

3-11

CHEST THRUSTS may have to be used instead of abdominal thrusts for choking when -

- A woman is in an **ADVANCED STAGE OF PREGNANCY**

    OR

- A person is **MARKEDLY OBESE**

In these cases, abdominal thrusts cannot be applied effectively.

3-12

For each of the following choking casualties, indicate whether it is advisable to use chest thrusts when giving first aid for choking.

Casualties	Yes	No
A. 40-year-old woman who is unconscious.	☐	☑
B. 25-year-old man who is extremely overweight.	☑	☐
C. 20-year-old man who is conscious.	☐	☑
D. 30-year-old woman in her last month of pregnancy.	☑	☐

3-12   A. No   B. Yes   C. No   D. Yes

When a choking person's airway has been cleared, he may not breathe on his own and it may be necessary for you to give artificial respiration.

When normal breathing has resumed –

- Monitor breathing frequently

- Stay with the casualty to ensure that no further breathing difficulties develop

- Place the unconscious person in the recovery position and obtain medical aid

- Advise the conscious person to seek medical aid

CHOKING MANOEUVRES COULD CAUSE INTERNAL INJURIES

A casualty should be advised to get medical attention following –

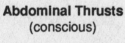

Abdominal Thrusts
(conscious)

Chest Thrusts
(advanced pregnancy)

Abdominal Thrusts
(unconscious)

When an airway obstruction has been removed by abdominal or chest thrusts and normal breathing has been restored, the casualty should -

A. ☐ Require no further medical care.

B. ☑ Be positioned so that the airway will remain open.

C. ☑ Be told to have a doctor check him for injuries.

D. ☐ Be placed on his back in case he requires more chest thrusts.

E. ☑ Be observed until normal respiration has been established.

B. ☑   C. ☑   E. ☑

These questions are based on this workbook exercise, your practical session and the audio-visual.

Mark each statement true **(T)** or false **(F)**.

A. ☐ In the unconscious person the tongue may fall to the back of the throat and close off the air passage.

B. ☐ A choking person with poor air exchange should be given first aid for a complete airway obstruction.

C. ☐ Chest thrusts should be avoided on an extremely overweight person.

D. ☐ Following abdominal thrusts on an unconscious choking adult, finger sweeps are performed to remove dislodged foreign matter.

E. ☐ When a person is alone and choking, he can help himself with self-administered abdominal thrusts.

F. ☐ Choking manoeuvres could cause internal injuries and the casualty may require medical care.

G. ☐ A choking person with good air exchange will require immediate first aid for his airway obstruction.

A. T   B. T   C. F   D. T   E. T   F. T   G. F

For more information on this topic, refer to: *First Aid Safety Oriented*, Second Edition, Chapter 9

END OF EXERCISE 3

3

WOUNDS

4-1

A **WOUND** is any injury to the tissues of the body. It usually results in **BLEEDING**.

Bleeding may be -

- **EXTERNAL**: when blood escapes from a surface wound and **CAN BE SEEN**

OR

- **INTERNAL**: when blood escapes from tissues inside the body and **CANNOT BE SEEN IMMEDIATELY**

4-2

Mark each statement true (**T**) or false (**F**).

A. ☐ Loss of blood usually occurs when there is a break in the skin.

B. ☐ A deep cut on the finger is an example of a wound with only internal bleeding.

C. ☐ Internal bleeding occurs when tissues inside the body are injured.

D. ☐ A wound is any injury in which just the skin is punctured.

4-2

A. ☐ T   B. ☐ F   C. ☐ T   D. ☐ F

There are 6 types of wounds -

- **CONTUSIONS** (bruises)
  - Caused by a fall or blow. Skin is not broken.
  - Little risk of contamination.

- **ABRASIONS** (scrapes)
  - Slight bleeding.
  - Embedded dirt may lead to infection.

- **INCISIONS** (clean cuts)
  - Moderate risk of infection.

- **LACERATIONS** (tear wounds)
  - Jagged wounds.
  - Dirt may cause infection.

- **PUNCTURE WOUNDS** (stab wounds)
  - Caused by sharp, pointed objects.
  - Wounds have small openings, may be very deep.
  - Risk of infection, damage to internal organs.

- **GUNSHOT WOUNDS** (penetrating wounds)
  - Small entry wound, large exit wound.
  - Cause internal tissue damage and severe bleeding.

Choose the correct completion from the choices given below and write the appropriate number in the box provided.

A. ☐ 4 A wound caused by barbed wire is a/an

B. ☐   Loose gravel is more likely to get into a/an

C. ☐ 3 A wound caused by a sharp knife is a/an

D. ☐   Stepping on a long nail will cause a/an

Choices

1. Contusion
2. Abrasion
3. Incision
4. Laceration
5. Puncture wound
6. Gunshot wound

4-4   A. ☐ 4   B. ☐ 2   C. ☐ 3   D. ☐ 5

4

4-5

The sign of **EXTERNAL BLEEDING** is the appearance of **BLOOD**.

BLOOD is not immediately visible with **INTERNAL BLEEDING**.

SEVERE INTERNAL and **EXTERNAL BLEEDING** will be accompanied by some or all of the following -

SIGNS

You may observe:

- Anxiety
- Restlessness
- Paleness
- Cold, clammy skin
- Rapid, weak pulse
- Shallow breathing
- Gasping for air
- Yawning

SYMPTOMS

The casualty may complain of:

- Faintness
- Dizziness
- Nausea
- Thirst

Even SLIGHT BLEEDING may produce any of these signs and symptoms to some degree.

4-6

Which of the following signs and symptoms may appear when bleeding is severe?

A casualty -

A. ☑ Feels light-headed and asks for a drink of water.

B. ☑ Is panting for breath and his skin is cool and moist to the touch.

C. ☐ Has a hot, flushed face and appears restless.

D. ☑ Complains that he is about to vomit.

4-6

A. ☑   B. ☑   D. ☑

4

INTERNAL BLEEDING is not easy to recognize.

A CASUALTY COULD BLEED TO DEATH WITHOUT ANY BLOOD BEING SEEN

Suspect internal bleeding when -

- A casualty has received **SHARP BLOWS, DEEP PUNCTURE WOUNDS** or **CRUSH INJURIES**

- Signs and symptoms of **SEVERE BLEEDING** appear but **BLOOD IS NOT SEEN**

- You observe one or more of the following -

SIGNS

- Bleeding from mouth, ears, nose
- Red, frothy blood coughed up
- Blood in the vomitus
- Blood in the stool
- Blood in the urine

SIGNS AND SYMPTOMS MAY NOT APPEAR IMMEDIATELY

Mark each statement true **(T)** or false **(F)**.

A. ☐ F   A casualty who is bleeding inside the body is not in danger.

B. ☐ T   Internal bleeding may result when a person has been punched in the abdomen.

C. ☐ F   Blood is seen instantly when a casualty is bleeding internally.

D. ☐ T   The oozing of blood from the nostrils may indicate that a casualty is bleeding internally.

E. ☐ T   When blood is seen in the waste products of the body, internal bleeding should be suspected.

4-8

A. F   B. T   C. F   D. T   E. T

4

> **SEVERE BLEEDING IS AN IMMEDIATE THREAT TO LIFE.**
> **YOU MUST ACT QUICKLY!**

To control severe external bleeding, you should -

- Apply **DIRECT PRESSURE** on the wound with your bare hand or over a pad of dressings, if available

- **ELEVATE** an injured limb to help slow down the bleeding

- Place the casualty **AT REST**

- **DO NOT REMOVE** blood-soaked dressings; apply another pad of dressings over them

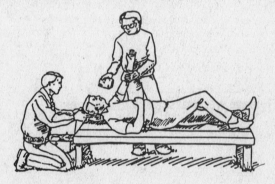

When bleeding is controlled -

- **BANDAGE** the dressings in place to maintain pressure on the wound

- **IMMOBILIZE** the injured part in an elevated position, if injuries permit

- Obtain **MEDICAL AID**

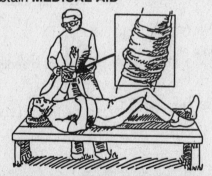

Your co-worker has cut his forearm on a sharp knife and blood is flowing freely from the wound.

Which of the following actions should you take to control the bleeding?

Yes   **No**

A. ☑   ☐   Tell him to press tightly on the wound, raise his arm and lay him down, then go for suitable first aid supplies.

B. ☑   ☐   Place several layers of clean cotton fabric on the wound and maintain the pressure.

C. ☐   ☑   Replace wet dressings with dry ones.

D. ☑   ☐   Use a broad bandage to secure the dressings on the wound when bleeding has slowed down.

E. ☑   ☐   Support the bandaged arm in a sling.

4-10   A. Yes   B. Yes   C. No   D. Yes   E. Yes

4

4-11

There is little a First Aider can do to control internal bleeding.

> **WHEN YOU SUSPECT INTERNAL BLEEDING,
> SEND FOR MEDICAL AID IMMEDIATELY**

The **AIM** of first aid is to -

- **PREVENT** shock from worsening and
- **MAINTAIN** the casualty in the best possible condition until medical aid arrives

Do the following -

- Place the **conscious** casualty at rest with feet elevated 15 to 30 cm (6 to 12 in.), if injuries permit

- Place the **unconscious** casualty into the **recovery position**

- Keep the casualty **warm**
- **Reassure** the conscious casualty
- Give **nothing by mouth**
- Ensure other injuries are treated

4-12

Which of the following would you do for a casualty who you suspect has internal bleeding?

A. ☐ Allow him to sip some hot tea.

B. ☑ Cover him with a jacket to keep body heat in.

C. ☐ Elevate his head and shoulders.

D. ☐ Tell the casualty he is bleeding inside.

E. ☑ Comfort the casualty by giving first aid for any other injuries.

F. ☑ Obtain medical help quickly.

G. ☑ If the casualty's condition allows, raise the legs and feet by placing them on a folded coat.

4-12

B. ☑	E. ☑	F. ☑	G. ☑

4

4-13

CONTAMINATION (dirt, foreign material) in a wound may lead to INFECTION.

All open wounds are contaminated to some degree.

PREVENT FURTHER CONTAMINATION of an open wound by taking these precautions -

- **Wash your hands**, if possible, before giving first aid

- **Flush** any visible dirt from the wound and swab **away from** the edges of **the wound**

- **DO NOT** touch the wound, cough or breathe into it

- **DO NOT** touch the side of the dressing that will contact the wound

- **Cover** the wound promptly with a sterile or clean dressing

- When wound care is completed, **wash your hands again**

4-14

Classify each of the following actions as a GOOD or POOR first aid procedure.

	Good	Poor
A. Blow loose dirt away from a wound to prevent infection.	☐	☑
B. Use your fingers to remove visible dirt from a wound.	☐	☑
C. Use soap and water to clean your hands before applying dressings.	☑	☐
D. Brush off both sides of a dressing to ensure it is clean before applying it.	☐	☑
E. Wipe from the wound with a piece of gauze to remove dirt.	☑	☐
F. Protect the wound with a clean cloth.	☑	☐

4-14

A. Poor   B. Poor   C. Good   D. Poor   E. Good   F. Good

4

TETANUS (lockjaw) is a serious disease characterized by muscle spasms and stiffness of the jaw. It is caused by a wound being contaminated with the tetanus bacillus and **can be fatal.**

The tetanus bacillus is found in **SOIL, DUST** and **ANIMAL FECES.** (Particular caution should be taken with wounds caused by farming and gardening tools.)

ANY OPEN WOUND may be contaminated by the tetanus bacillus. In minor wounds, careful washing can flush away the bacillus before it begins to grow.

Mark each statement true **(T)** or false **(F).**

A. ☐T☐   The tetanus bacillus may be found almost anywhere.

B. ☐F☐   The tetanus bacillus is a threat only if a wound is caused by rusty metal.

C. ☐F☐   The tetanus bacillus can infect the body through the food we eat.

D. ☐T☐   Lockjaw can result in death.

E. ☐T☐   Deep wounds contaminated with dirt should receive medical attention following first aid.

4-16   A. ☐T☐   B. ☐F☐   C. ☐F☐   D. ☐T☐   E. ☐T☐

A person can be **PROTECTED** (immunized) **AGAINST TETANUS**.

As a First Aider it is your duty **TO ADVISE** any casualty with an open wound to protect himself against the threat of tetanus by **SEEKING MEDICAL AID** as soon as possible.

4-18

A casualty has stepped on a long spike while working in a barnyard.

In addition to cleansing and dressing the wound, you should -

A. ☐ Obtain some tetanus toxoid to give to the casualty.

B. ☐ Advise him to soak his foot in an antiseptic solution.

C. ☑ Talk to him about the importance of having a tetanus shot as soon as possible.

D. ☐ Mind your own business.

4-18

C. ☑

4

4-19

An **AMPUTATION** is a complete or partial separation of a body part and requires **IMMEDIATE CONTROL OF BLEEDING**.

4-20

The questions in frames 4-20 and 4-22 are based on the audio-visual *Amputations*.

Check (✔) the correct choice in giving first aid for an amputation.

	Choice 1			**Choice 2**
A. ☑	Stop the bleeding as quickly as possible by using your bare hand.	OR	A. ☐	Go and locate sterile material before you try to stop the bleeding.
B. ☑	Elevate the injured limb.	OR	B. ☐	Leave the injured limb as found.
C. ☐	Leave the casualty standing to allow for quick transportation.	OR	C. ☑	Sit the casualty down to slow the flow of blood to the wound.
D. ☑	Apply dressings and wrap securely.	OR	D. ☐	Ensure air circulation around the wound to help clotting.
E. ☐	Stabilize the wound with padding.	OR	E. ☑	Use a sling to immobilize the limb.
F. ☑	Apply an ice pack to prevent swelling and relieve pain.	OR	F. ☐	Apply a hot water bottle to prevent swelling and relieve pain.

4-20

A. [1] B. [1] C. [2] D. [1] E. [2] F. [1]

4

In many cases amputated parts can be surgically reattached.

The part must be kept dry and cool. **NEVER TRY TO CLEAN OR WASH IT OFF.**

> **A PARTIALLY AMPUTATED PART SHOULD BE BANDAGED IN PLACE**

Select the correct completions for the following statement.

A completely amputated or partially amputated part should be -

A. ☑   Covered with sterile dressing.

B. ☐   Rinsed under running water.

C. ☐   Placed in a container with cool water and sent to medical aid with the casualty.

D. ☐   Cleaned with an antiseptic.

E. ☑   Sealed in a watertight container, placed on ice, labelled and sent to medical aid with the casualty.

F. ☑   Supported in its normal position if partially amputated.

A. ✓   E. ✓   F. ✓

4-23

A **NOSEBLEED** may occur spontaneously or be caused by -

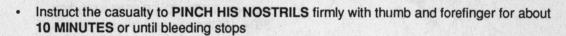

- Blowing the nose
- Injury to the nose or skull

To control a nosebleed, you should -

- Place the casualty in a **SITTING POSITION**, with the **HEAD SLIGHTLY FORWARD**

- Instruct the casualty to **PINCH HIS NOSTRILS** firmly with thumb and forefinger for about **10 MINUTES** or until bleeding stops

- **LOOSEN TIGHT CLOTHING** around the casualty's neck and chest

- Get medical aid if bleeding **DOES NOT STOP** or if bleeding recurs

- When bleeding stops, instruct the casualty **NOT** to blow his nose for some hours

---

DO NOT ATTEMPT TO STOP A NOSEBLEED RESULTING FROM A HEAD INJURY. WIPE AWAY THE EXTERNAL TRICKLING BLOOD AND SEEK MEDICAL AID IMMEDIATELY

4-24

From the following choices, check (✔) the appropriate first aid procedures for controlling a nosebleed.

Choice 1   **Choice 2**

A. ☐ See a doctor before you start with first aid. OR A. ☑ See a doctor if first aid doesn't halt the bleeding.

B. ☑ Sit the person down and lean him ahead slightly. OR B. ☐ Sit the person down and tilt his head back.

C. ☑ Ask the person to press on the soft parts of his nose until there is no blood flow. OR C. ☐ Ask the person to press on the soft parts of his nose for 1 to 2 minutes.

4-24   A. 2   B. 1   C. 1

4

BLEEDING FROM THE EAR may indicate a serious injury.

When a casualty is **BLEEDING FROM THE EAR,** you should -

- **SECURE** a sterile dressing **LOOSELY** over the ear. **DO NOT** put anything into the ear

- **LAY** the casualty down carefully with his head supported in a slightly **RAISED** position, **TURNED TO THE INJURED SIDE.** (If the casualty is unconscious and has no suspected neck injuries, place him in the recovery position with the injured side down.)

- **ENSURE** adequate breathing

- **OBTAIN** medical aid

Check (✓) the correct choice in giving first aid when blood is oozing from a conscious casualty's left ear.

Choice 1		Choice 2
A. ☑ Assist the casualty to lie down in order to assess the injury.	OR	A. ☐ Assist the casualty to sit down in order to assess the injury.
B. ☐ Pack the ear with sterile cotton wool.	OR	B. ☑ Tape a gauze dressing lightly over the ear.
C. ☑ Lay the casualty down, incline his head to the left side and support.	OR	C. ☐ Lay the casualty down, incline his head to the right side and support.

4-26

A. | 1 | B. | 2 | C. | 1 |

4

To control **BLEEDING FROM A SUPERFICIAL SCALP WOUND** you should -

• Clean away loose dirt **WITHOUT PROBING** into the wound

• Apply thick sterile dressings to **EXTEND WELL BEYOND** the edges of the wound

• **BANDAGE** the dressings firmly in place

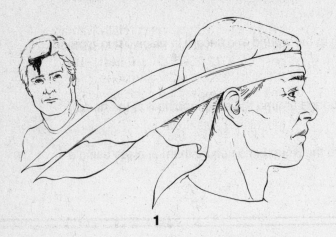

1

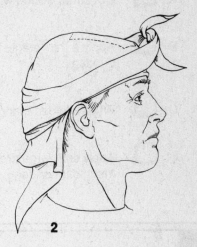

2

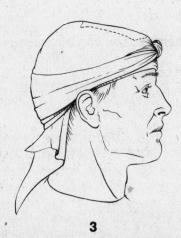

3

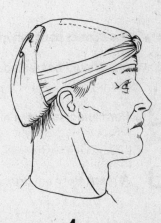

4

Any scalp wound could indicate a serious head injury that may cause unconsciousness and breathing problems.

Therefore, you should -

• **ENSURE** adequate breathing

• **OBTAIN** medical aid

A casualty is bleeding severely from a scalp wound.

Before getting the casualty to medical aid, what method should you use to control the bleeding?

A. ☐ Cover the wound with an adhesive dressing and secure it loosely in place.

B. ☐ Apply a thin, sterile dressing to the wound and secure in place using a broad bandage.

C. ☐ Wrap a folded triangular bandage around the scalp and tie it at the neck.

D. ☑ Apply soft, large dressings to the wound and secure them in place using a triangular bandage.

Check (✓) the correct completions for the following statement.

A scalp wound should be treated as a serious condition because -

A. ☐ Permanent hair loss and scars may result.

B. ☑ A respiratory emergency may develop.

C. ☐ There may be severe damage to the lungs.

D. ☑ There may be severe injuries to the skull.

4-28		4-29		
	D. ☑		B. ☑	D. ☑

4

BLEEDING from the **TONGUE** or **CHEEK** may be very heavy.

There is a danger of the blood -

- **BLOCKING THE AIRWAY**

- **ENTERING THE STOMACH AND CAUSING NAUSEA**

To give first aid for bleeding from the **TONGUE OR CHEEK -**

- Put **pressure** on the wound with your finger and thumb using a sterile dressing or clean cloth

- Have the casualty **lean forward to allow drainage** of the fluids

Check (✓) the correct statements below.

A. ☐ Severe bleeding inside the mouth will usually stop on its own.

B. ☑ Bleeding in the mouth could be a potentially life-threatening situation.

C. ☑ Vomiting may follow a mouth injury.

D. ☑ Pressure will usually stop bleeding from the tongue.

4-31   B. ✓   C. ✓   D. ✓

4

4-32

A **TOURNIQUET** is a device, such as a narrow bandage, which is twisted tightly around a limb **ABOVE THE WOUND** to stop bleeding.

A TOURNIQUET SHOULD BE USED ONLY AS A LAST MEASURE WHEN SEVERE BLEEDING CANNOT BE CONTROLLED BY PRESSURE AND ELEVATION

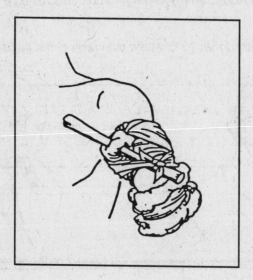

4-33

Which method should you use first to try and control a severe flow of blood from a gaping wound to the lower leg?

A. ☐ Apply a tourniquet just above the wound and elevate the limb, if possible.

B. ☑ Apply direct pressure on the wound, place the casualty at rest and elevate the limb.

4-33

B. ☑

4

TO APPLY A TOURNIQUET -

- Use a triangular bandage folded to a width of 7 to 10 cm
- Wrap the bandage tightly around the limb twice
- Place a stick on a half knot and then tie a full knot
- Twist the stick to tighten the tourniquet until bleeding stops
- Tie the stick in place to keep the tourniquet from loosening

TAG OR MARK THE CASUALTY IN A CLEARLY VISIBLE PLACE WITH THE LETTERS "TK" AND THE TIME WHEN THE TOURNIQUET WAS APPLIED. THE TOURNIQUET MUST ALWAYS BE VISIBLE

Put the steps of how to apply a tourniquet in the correct order by writing the appropriate numbers in the boxes provided.

A. 3

B. 2

C. 4

D.

1.

2.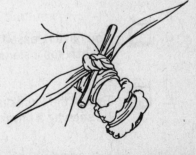

3.

4.

A. 3   B. 2   C. 4   D. 1

4

If **MEDICAL AID IS READILY AVAILABLE, DO NOT LOOSEN** the tourniquet.

If **MEDICAL AID IS NOT RECEIVED** within one hour, the tourniquet **MUST BE LOOSENED** with great care, to check if bleeding has stopped.

- If there is still bleeding, tighten the tourniquet immediately and check again in one hour and every hour thereafter

- If bleeding has stopped, leave the loosened tourniquet in place so it can be tightened quickly if bleeding starts again

- Keep the casualty at rest

ALL CASUALTIES ON WHOM A TOURNIQUET HAS BEEN APPLIED MUST BE TAKEN TO MEDICAL AID

Mark each statement true (T) or false (F).

A. You untie a tourniquet. Bleeding seems to have stopped. Remove the tourniquet from the limb to prevent tissue damage.

B. After a tourniquet has been in place for one hour, it should be released and every 15 minutes following.

C. An ambulance is on its way. The tourniquet has been on for half an hour. It should be unfastened immediately.

D. You have released a tourniquet after one hour. Bleeding has stopped. After ten minutes it starts again. You should reapply pressure with the tourniquet.

E. Even if the tourniquet has been on for a very short time, the casualty should be seen by a physician.

A. F   B. F   C. F   D. T   E. T

4

4-38

A **COLD COMPRESS, ICE BAG** or **COLD PACK** may be used to relieve pain and control swelling caused by an injury.

A cold compress and an ice bag can be **IMPROVISED.**

A cold pack is **COMMERCIALLY** prepared and should be used following the manufacturer's directions.

To improvise a COLD COMPRESS:

- Soak a towel or a dressing in cold water
- Wring out excess water
- Wrap the towel around affected area
- Repeat as towel becomes warm

To improvise an ICE BAG:

- Fill plastic bag 2/3 full of crushed ice
- Expell excess air
- Seal the bag
- Wrap the bag in a towel
- Apply to affected area
- Replace ice as necessary

DO NOT APPLY AN ICE BAG OR COLD PACK DIRECTLY TO THE SKIN BECAUSE THE COLD CAN CAUSE INJURY

4-39

Mark each statement true **(T)** or false **(F).**

A. ☐ A cold face cloth should never be placed on the skin.

B. ☐ A cold pack can be used alone as direct pressure to stop bleeding.

C. ☐ An ice bag should always be wrapped in soft but thick material.

D. ☐ The use of cold helps to keep swelling to a minimum and to reduce discomfort.

E. ☐ When ice is placed directly on a wound, it may result in soft tissue damage.

4-39

A. F   B. F   C. T   D. T   E. T

4

4-40

Mark each statement true (T) or false (F).

A. [T] A triangular bandage can be used as a sling or folded and used as a broad or narrow bandage.

B. [T] A ring pad, bandaged in place over dressings, applies pressure around an object embedded in a wound.

C. [F] Blood-soaked dressings should be removed and replaced with clean, dry dressings.

D. [T] Cold fingers may indicate that a bandage on the injured arm is too tight.

E. [T] The blood trickling from the nose following a head injury should be gently absorbed with dressings.

F. [F] To control bleeding from an ear, pack the ear with cotton.

G. [F] Small amounts of blood in the body's waste products are a normal occurrence.

H. [T] A conscious casualty with suspected internal bleeding should be kept at rest with feet elevated and receive medical aid.

I. [F] An ice bag should be placed directly on a bruise to control swelling.

J. [T] An amputated part should be kept dry and cool and sent to the hospital with the casualty.

4-40

A. T B. T C. F D. T E. T F. F G. F H. T I. F J. T

For more information on this topic, refer to: *First Aid Safety Oriented*, Second Edition, Chapters 12, 13

END OF EXERCISE 4

NOTES

4

SHOCK

5-1

SHOCK occurs when there is inadequate circulation to the body tissues.

SHOCK may develop immediately following an incident **OR** much later.

SHOCK may result from -

- Bleeding (external and internal)
- Breathing problems
- Burns
- Serious fractures
- Heart failure
- Crush injuries
- Spinal cord or nerve injuries
- Severe allergic reactions

Some degree of shock is present with any injury or illness.

**GIVE THE APPROPRIATE FIRST AID QUICKLY TO
PREVENT SHOCK FROM BECOMING MORE SEVERE**

A person **CAN DIE** from shock even though the injury causing shock might **NOT** by itself be fatal.

5-2

Mark each statement true **(T)** or false **(F).**

A. ☐   Shock occurs when parts of the body do not receive enough blood.

B. ☐   Shock is often caused by blood loss from a wound.

C. ☐   First aid should be started only when marked signs of shock appear.

D. ☐   Shock is a serious condition.

E. ☐   Shock is caused only by life-threatening injuries.

5-2

A. T   B. T   C. F   D. T   E. F

5

The **SIGNS** and **SYMPTOMS** of shock may **NOT** appear immediately but many or all of the following may appear as shock progresses.

SIGNS

You may observe:

- Restlessness and anxiety

- Cold, sweaty and pale skin, becoming bluish-grey at the lips and fingertips

- Weak and rapid pulse

- Shallow, rapid breathing

- Gasping for air (in later stages of shock)

- Vomiting

- Changes in the level of consciousness

SYMPTOMS

The casualty may complain of:

- Faintness   • Thirst   • Nausea

When you recognize any of these signs and symptoms, **OBTAIN MEDICAL AID IMMEDIATELY**.

5-4

Choose the correct completions for the following statement.

When a casualty is in shock, usually the -

		Choice 1				Choice 2
A.	Skin is	☑ whitish.	OR	A.	☐	flushed.
B.	Skin is	☐ dry.	OR	B.	☑	moist.
C.	Skin is	☐ warm.	OR	C.	☑	cold.
D.	Breathing is	☑ fast.	OR	D.	☐	slow.
E.	Pulse is	☑ fast.	OR	E.	☐	slow.
F.	Casualty feels	☐ calm.	OR	F.	☑	uneasy.
G.	Casualty feels	☐ hungry.	OR	G.	☑	thirsty.

5-4

A.	1	B.	2	C.	2	D.	1	E.	1	F.	2	G.	2

5

To prevent shock from becoming more severe -

GIVE PROMPT AND EFFECTIVE FIRST AID

- **ATTEND TO** the cause or causes of shock (e.g. injuries, illnesses)

- **REASSURE** the casualty

- Handle the casualty **GENTLY**

- **LOOSEN** tight clothing

- Give **NOTHING BY MOUTH** if shock is severe

- Moisten lips only if casualty complains of thirst

- Keep the casualty **WARM** but **DO NOT** overheat

- Position the **CONSCIOUS** casualty **LYING DOWN** with feet and legs **ELEVATED** 15-30 cm (6-12 inches) - **SHOCK POSITION**, if injuries permit

- Place the **UNCONSCIOUS** casualty in the **RECOVERY POSITION**, if injuries permit

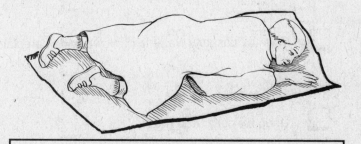

OBTAIN MEDICAL AID AS QUICKLY AS POSSIBLE

A casualty is showing signs and symptoms of severe shock. Which of the following should you do to prevent his condition from worsening?

Yes　　**No**

A. ☑　　☐　　Place blankets over and under the casualty to retain body heat.

B. ☑　　☐　　Give first aid for any obvious injury or illness.

C. ☑　　☐　　Avoid causing the casualty more discomfort.

D. ☐　　☑　　Rub the conscious casualty's limbs vigorously to improve his circulation.

E. ☐　　☑　　Place an unconscious casualty flat on his back.

F. ☑　　☐　　Position a conscious casualty on his back and place a support under his legs and ankles.

G. ☐　　☑　　Give the casualty water to drink when he complains of thirst.

H. ☑　　☐　　Undo his collar and belt.

5-7

When a **CONSCIOUS** casualty is showing signs of shock, the following positions are preferred for certain conditions or injuries:

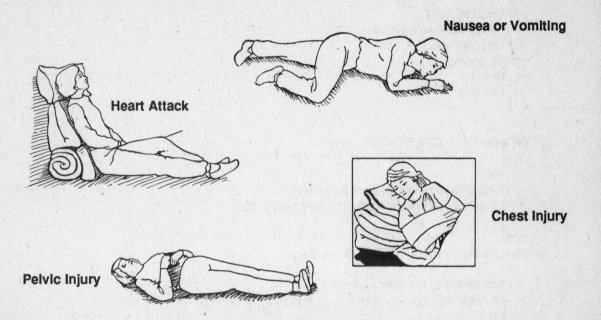

Nausea or Vomiting

Heart Attack

Chest Injury

Pelvic Injury

5-8

Match each condition or injury with the position of choice for a conscious casualty by placing the appropriate number in the boxes provided.

Condition or Injury

A.   Chest injury

B.   Vomiting

C.   Heart attack

D.   Nausea

E.   Pelvic Injury

Position of Choice

1. Recovery position

2. On the back with legs elevated 15-30 cm (6-12 inches)

3. Semisitting

4. Flat on the back

5-8

A. 3   B. 1   C. 3   D. 1   E. 4

5

5-9

Many injuries and illnesses are complicated by the **LOSS OF CONSCIOUSNESS,** e.g. -

- Head injuries
- Respiratory emergencies
- Heart attack
- Poisoning
- Shock
- Fainting

When a person is **CONSCIOUS,** he is -

- Alert
- Responsive to verbal or other stimuli
- Oriented (knows his name, the day, place, etc.)

When a person is **UNCONSCIOUS,** he is -

- Not aware of his surroundings
- Unresponsive to any stimuli (e.g. pinching, shouting)

5-10

Mark each statement true **(T)** or false **(F).**

A. [ ] If a conscious person is fully awake, he reacts to speech or pain and is aware of his environment.

B. [ ] A person may become unconscious following a sharp blow to the skull.

C. [ ] An unconscious person will try to move his hand if the fingers are squeezed.

D. [ ] A person may become unconscious as a result of an accident or sickness.

E. [ ] An unconscious person will answer faintly when spoken to.

5-10   A. [T]   B. [T]   C. [F]   D. [T]   E. [F]

5

A casualty's **level of consciousness** can be assessed by rating **3 of his responses** - EYE OPENING RESPONSE, BEST VERBAL RESPONSE and BEST MOTOR RESPONSE.

LEVELS OF CONSCIOUSNESS (Modified Glasgow Coma Scale)			
RESPONSE	**CONSCIOUS**	**SEMI-CONSCIOUS**	**UNCONSCIOUS**
EYE OPENING RESPONSE	Eyes open spontaneously	Eyes open to speech or pain	Eyes do not open
BEST VERBAL RESPONSE	Oriented and alert	Confused, can't understand	No response
Response to stimulus **BEST MOTOR RESPONSE**	*"Can you move your arm?"* *"Yes, I can move my arm."* Obeys commands	*Muscles flex slightly when inside of the forearm is pinched* Responds to pain	No response

Match each casualty's description with a level of consciousness by writing the appropriate number in the squares.

1. **Conscious**
2. **Semi-conscious**
3. **Unconscious**

A. [2] A woman is lying on the street. She opens her eyes only when you talk to her but she is unable to tell you her name or where she lives.

B. [3] A fellow worker is found lying on the floor and when you call out to him he neither opens his eyes nor answers.

C. [1] A child has fallen off his bicycle and is lying on the ground. As you near him, he opens his eyes and starts to cry and reaches for his bicycle.

CHANGES IN LEVEL OF CONSCIOUSNESS should be observed and noted. These are helpful in monitoring the casualty's condition and should be described to medical personnel when the casualty is handed over.

PROGRESSIVE LOSS OF CONSCIOUSNESS INDICATES A DETERIORATION OF THE PERSON'S CONDITION.

A casualty opens his eyes when you speak to him, knows where he is and what has happened and can move his arms when asked to do so.

Fifteen minutes later, his eyes remain closed when you speak to him, he is muttering senselessly and moves only when you pinch his earlobe.

The casualty's condition is -

A. [ ] Improving.

B. [ ] Unchanged.

C. [✓] Getting worse.

5-12 A. [2] B. [3] C. [1]

5-14 C. [✓]

5-15

When an **UNCONSCIOUS** person is lying on his back, the airway may become **BLOCKED** if -

- The **TONGUE** falls to the back of the throat

    OR

- **FLUIDS** drain into the airway

> **YOUR FIRST PRIORITY IS TO PREVENT A BREATHING EMERGENCY**

5-16

Which of the following conditions would endanger an unconscious casualty when he is lying face-up?

A. ☑ The throat is clogged with vomit.

B. ☑ The mouth is filled with blood.

C. ☑ The throat is obstructed by the tongue.

D. ☑ Respiration is difficult.

5-17

When caring for an **UNCONSCIOUS** casualty, you should perform the following sequence of actions -

- **ENSURE ADEQUATE BREATHING** (If necessary, open the airway and give artificial respiration.)

- **DO A SECONDARY EXAMINATION** (vital signs and head-to-toe examination)

- **GIVE FIRST AID** for injuries and conditions found

- **LOOSEN** constrictive clothing

- Place the casualty in the **RECOVERY POSITION**, if injuries permit

- Keep the casualty **WARM**

- Give **NOTHING** by mouth

- Obtain **MEDICAL AID**

5-16   A. ☑   B. ☑   C. ☑   D. ☑

5

An unconscious casualty is lying on his back and has a concealed fracture of the forearm. There is no indication of a neck injury.

Number, in the correct order, the first aid steps that you should follow for this casualty.

A. [3] Immobilize the fracture.

B. [2] Examine the casualty systematically and thoroughly.

C. [7] Get medical aid.

D. [5] Place the casualty in the recovery position.

E. [1] Make sure that the casualty is breathing.

F. [6] Cover the casualty with a blanket.

G. [4] Open the buttons on the person's clothes at the neck and waist.

| 5-18 | A. 3 | B. 2 | C. 7 | D. 5 | E. 1 | F. 6 | G. 4 |

5

5-19

FAINTING is temporary unconsciousness, caused by a shortage of oxygen to the **BRAIN**. Recovery usually takes place within minutes.

FAINTING may be caused by -

- Fear or anxiety
- Severe pain, injury or illness
- Fatigue, hunger or lack of fresh air
- Long periods of standing or sitting

The following signs and symptoms may warn you that a person is **ABOUT TO FAINT**.

SIGNS	SYMPTOMS
You may observe: • Paleness • Sweating	The casualty may complain of: • Feeling unsteady

5-20

Mark each statement true **(T)** or false **(F)**.

A. ☑ Fainting results from a lack of blood flow to the limbs.

B. ☑ When a person faints, he loses consciousness for a short time.

C. ☑ A person may faint when he is scared suddenly or when he is sick or hurt.

D. ☑ A person in a hot, stuffy room may report that he feels dizzy just before he faints.

E. ☑ When a person's face becomes flushed and dry, he may be in danger of fainting.

F. ☑ Lack of food and sleep may cause fainting.

G. ☑ Soldiers standing at attention for an extended time faint frequently.

5-20

A.	F	B.	T	C.	T	D.	T	E.	F	F.	T	G.	T

5

5-21

When a person **FEELS FAINT**, you may be able to prevent him from fainting.

You should -

- Ensure a supply of fresh air

- Loosen tight clothing, especially at the neck

- Place him in either of the following positions

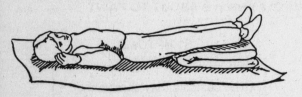 OR

**Lying with feet and legs raised
15-30 cm (6-12 inches)**

**Sitting with head
and shoulders lowered**

5-22

When a person turns pale and says that he feels unsteady, what should you do?

Yes   No

A. ☑   ☐   Open the window.

B. ☐   ☑   Tilt his head back and place a cold towel on his forehead.

C. ☑   ☐   Seat him and bend his upper body forward to his knees.

D. ☑   ☐   Unbutton his shirt at the collar.

E. ☑   ☐   Position him at rest on his back and place a support under his ankles.

5-22   A. Yes   B. No   C. Yes   D. Yes   E. Yes

5

When a person **HAS FAINTED**, you should –

- Ensure adequate breathing

- Loosen tight clothing at neck, chest and waist

- Place him in the recovery position

- Ensure a supply of fresh air

When he returns to consciousness, make him comfortable and keep him **LYING DOWN** for 10-15 minutes.

Obtain medical aid if the person does **NOT** recover quickly and completely.

A person in a hot stuffy room passes out and slumps to the floor. What should you do?

	Choice 1			**Choice 2**
A. ☑	Open the windows to ventilate the room.	OR	A. ☐	Carry him outside to refresh him.
B. ☑	Unbutton his collar.	OR	B. ☐	Remove his clothing.
C. ☐	Position him on his back.	OR	C. ☑	Place him in the recovery position.
D. ☐	Have him walk around as soon as he becomes conscious.	OR	D. ☑	Keep him at rest for a short time when he becomes conscious.
E. ☑	Call for medical help if he does not regain consciousness soon.	OR	E. ☐	Call for medical help as soon as he has fainted.

5-24

A.	1	B.	1	C.	2	D.	2	E.	1

5

5-25

Mark each statement true **(T)** or false **(F)**.

A. ☑ Shock may be a fatal condition.

B. ☑ A casualty who has fainted should be seated with head and shoulders lowered.

C. ☑ Pale, cold, clammy skin and vomiting are signs of shock.

D. ☑ When an unconscious person is lying on his back, the tongue may fall back and block the airway.

E. ☑ The most effective action to prevent shock from becoming more severe is prompt and effective first aid.

F. ☑ Fainting occurs when there is a lack of muscle strength in the legs.

G. ☑ The most important consideration for an unconscious person is to ensure adequate breathing.

H. ☑ A casualty in shock with nausea should be placed in a semisitting position.

I. ☑ The levels of consciousness are determined by assessing the vital signs.

5-25

A. T B. F C. T D. T E. T F. F G. T H. F I. F

5

For more information on this topic, refer to: *First Aid Safety Oriented*, Second Edition, Chapters 10, 11

END OF EXERCISE 5

5

NOTES

THE UPPER LIMB

6-1

BONES OF THE UPPER LIMB

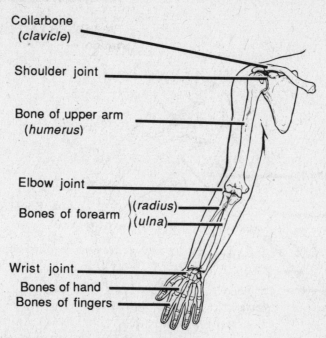

Collarbone (*clavicle*)

Shoulder joint

Bone of upper arm (*humerus*)

Elbow joint

Bones of forearm { (*radius*) (*ulna*)

Wrist joint
Bones of hand
Bones of fingers

The upper limb is divided by the elbow into 2 parts -

- The **UPPER ARM**

- The **FOREARM**

6-2

Mark each statement true (**T**) or false (**F**).

A. ☐ The forearm contains one long bone.

B. ☐ There is one long bone between the shoulder and the elbow.

C. ☐ There are two separate long bones between the elbow and the wrist.

D. ☐ There are three major joints in the upper limb.

6-2

A. F   B. T   C. T   D. T

6-3

BONES OF THE LOWER LIMB

The lower limb (leg) is divided by the knee joint into 2 parts -

- The **UPPER LEG** (thigh-bone)

- The **LOWER LEG** (shin-bone and calf-bone)

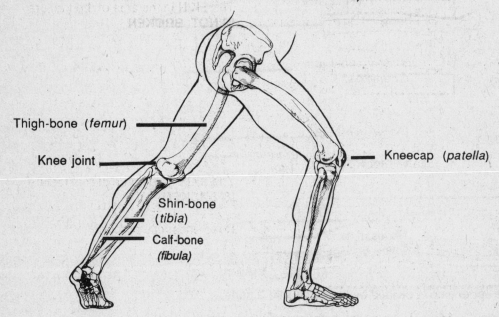

Thigh-bone (*femur*)

Knee joint

Kneecap (*patella*)

Shin-bone (*tibia*)

Calf-bone (*fibula*)

6-4

Match each bone with the best description.

A. Thigh-bone (femur)

B. Kneecap (patella)

C. Shin-bone (tibia)

D. Calf-bone (fibula)

1. A small flat bone protecting the middle joint of the lower limb.

2. The smaller bone between the knee and the ankle.

3. The long, thick bone in the upper leg.

4. The larger bone from knee to ankle.

6-4

A. 3   B. 1   C. 4   D. 2

6

6-5

A **FRACTURE** is any break or crack in a bone.

A fracture may be **CLOSED** or **OPEN**.

Closed Fracture

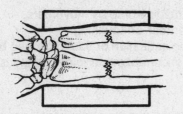

- The **SKIN** in the area of the fracture **IS NOT BROKEN**

Open Fracture

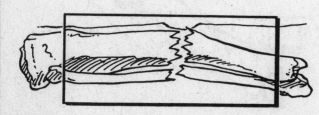

- The **SKIN** in the area of the fracture **IS BROKEN**

- Bone ends may protrude

6-6

Indicate with a **(C)** which of the following fractures would be closed and with an **(O)** the fractures which would be open.

A. ☐ A fractured rib caused by a gunshot wound.

B. ☐ A cracked thigh-bone over which the skin is bruised and swollen.

C. ☐ A broken kneecap caused by a bad fall from a bicycle. The skin is badly discoloured.

D. ☐ A fractured shin-bone over which heavy bleeding is seen.

6-6

A. ☐ O   B. ☐ C   C. ☐ C   D. ☐ O

Suspect a fracture if one or more of the following signs and symptoms are present -

| **SIGNS** | **SYMPTOMS** |

You may observe:

- Swelling and discolouration
- Deformity
- Protruding bone ends
- Inability to move
- Shock, increasing with severity of injury

The casualty may complain of:

- Pain, made worse by movement
- Tenderness on touching
- Grating sensation or sound caused by bone ends rubbing together (crepitus)

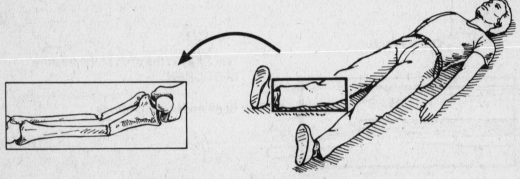

Severe Bending (Angulation) of the Lower Leg

6-8

Which of the following could indicate that a leg injury is a fracture?

A. ☐ A deep wound on the lower leg is gaping and bleeding profusely.

B. ☑ The end of a bone is sticking through the skin. There is a moderate amount of bleeding.

C. ☑ The casualty is pale and sweating, his skin feels cold, he says he may vomit and his lower leg is lying at right angles to the thigh.

D. ☑ The casualty screams when you touch his leg and he says he felt a sharp thrust when he fell.

6-8

B. ☑   C. ☑   D. ☑

FIRST AID FOR FRACTURES

The aim - **PREVENT FURTHER INJURY AND MINIMIZE PAIN**

FOREARM
(Closed Fracture)

LOWER LEG
(Open Fracture)

1. Treat the injury at the accident site

2. Steady and support the limb

NO WOUND TO DRESS   **3. Dress wound (if necessary)**

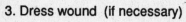

4. Immobilize the fracture

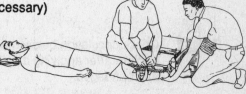

5. Gently raise and support the limb

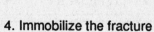

6. Check circulation

7. Get medical aid

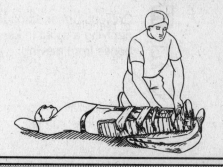

Listed below are pairs of actions that you could take when giving first aid for a fracture. From each pair, check off the action that is appropriate.

Choice 1   **Choice 2**

A. ☐ Dress the open wound; then steady and support the injured limb.   **OR**   A. ☑ Steady and support the injured limb; then dress the open wound.

B. ☐ Dress an open wound after immobilization.   **OR**   B. ☑ Dress an open wound before immobilization.

C. ☐ Move the casualty to make it easier to give first aid.   **OR**   C. ☑ Do not move the casualty for the purpose of giving first aid.

D. ☑ Check circulation below the fracture after applying a splint and bandages.   **OR**   D. ☐ Check circulation above the fracture after applying a splint and bandages.

E. ☑ Place the splinted limb in the most comfortable position to ease the hurt.   **OR**   E. ☐ Elevate the splinted limb even if the casualty complains of more discomfort.

F. ☑ Prevent further damage by applying a splint to keep bones from moving.   **OR**   F. ☐ Prevent further damage by putting bone ends together before splinting.

6-10

A.	2	B.	2	C.	2	D.	1	E.	1	F.	1

6

6-11

A **SPLINT** is used to prevent movement of fractured bone ends. Properly applied, a splint can -

- Reduce tissue damage

- Lessen pain

Splints may be **COMMERCIALLY PREPARED** or **IMPROVISED**.

Improvised splints could be made of, e.g. a ski, a walking stick, a piece of cardboard.

Even uninjured parts of the body can be used as splints, e.g. a leg, sides of the body.

The characteristics of a good splint are -

- **RIGID**

- **LONG ENOUGH** to prevent movement in the joints above and below the fracture

- **WIDE ENOUGH** to be comfortable

THERE MUST BE PADDING BETWEEN THE INJURED PART AND THE SPLINT

6-12

Mark each statement true (**T**) or false (**F**).

A. ☐ If a leg is fractured, the unbroken leg can be used as a splint.

B. ☐ A splint for a broken thigh must be long enough to go from the fracture site to below the knee.

C. ☐ A folded magazine or a hockey stick could be used as splints.

D. ☐ A splint for a fractured forearm must extend from the base of the fingers to beyond the elbow.

E. ☐ The limb must be protected from the hard splint.

6-12   A. ☐T   B. ☐F   C. ☐T   D. ☐T   E. ☐T

6-13

Mark each statement true (T) or false (F).

A. ☑ A fracture site is usually painful, swollen and deformed.

B. ☑ When a fracture is suspected, you should steady and support the limb to prevent further damage.

C. ☑ It is unwise to use the uninjured parts of the body as improvised splints.

D. ☑ A splint must be long enough to immobilize the joint above and the joint below the fracture.

E. ☑ To control bleeding from an open fracture, bandage a ring pad in place over tented dressings.

F. ☑ When you are securing a splint to a limb, the bandages should be tied over the fracture site.

G. ☑ A closed fracture is a bone injury without a surface wound.

H. ☑ A casualty with a fracture must be transported to medical aid before a splint is applied.

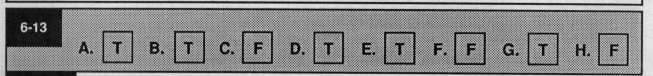

6-13   A. T   B. T   C. F   D. T   E. T   F. F   G. T   H. F

For more information on this topic, refer to: *First Aid Safety Oriented*, Second Edition, Chapters 2, 14

END OF EXERCISE 6

NOTES

FRACTURE OF THE THIGH (FEMUR)

7-1

The **THIGH-BONE** (femur) may be broken anywhere along its length.

Fractures of the thigh are always **SERIOUS** because of **INTERNAL BLEEDING** and the possibility of severe **SHOCK**.

When a fracture of the thigh is suspected, you should -

- Lay the casualty down

- If an open fracture, give first aid for the wound first

- Steady and support the limb and apply gentle but firm **TRACTION**

- **MAINTAIN TRACTION** until the leg has been **IMMOBILIZED** with splints and bandages

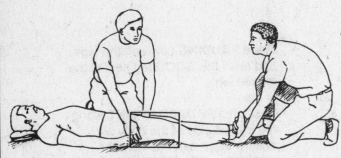

EVERY TIME TRACTION HAS BEEN APPLIED, MEDICAL AID MUST BE INFORMED

7-2

Mark each statement true (T) or false (F).

A. ☐   A fracture of the upper leg is considered to be an unimportant injury.

B. ☐   Shock seldom develops with a closed fracture of the thigh-bone (femur).

C. ☐   A broken upper leg should be kept aligned and still until the injury has been splinted.

D. ☐   Whenever a long bone has been aligned, the treating physician must be informed.

7-2

A. F   B. F   C. T   D. T

To immobilize a **CLOSED FRACTURE OF THE THIGH** for a long and rough journey to medical aid, use the following techniques -

- While traction is maintained, slide **SEVEN BANDAGES** into place under the body and legs

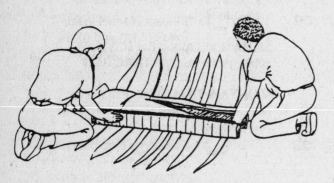

- Place **PADDING** between the legs and draw the **GOOD** leg next to the injured leg

- Position a **PADDED SPLINT** along the injured side of the body and ensure that it extends from the **ARMPIT** to **BELOW THE FOOT**

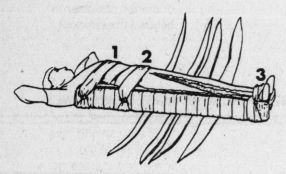

- **KNOT BANDAGES ON THE SPLINT** in the following order -

  1. Chest
  2. Hips
  3. Ankles and feet (figure-8)
  4. Above the fracture
  5. Below the fracture
  6. Knees
  7. Lower legs

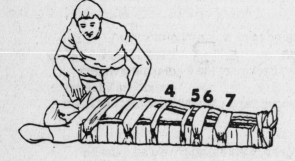

- **MONITOR** the condition of the casualty

Which of the following are the correct first aid techniques to immobilize a fracture of the left thigh when the casualty has to be moved?

Choice 1

Choice 2

A. ☐ Put 7 bandages in correct positions under left leg.

OR

A. ☑ Put 7 bandages in correct positions under chest, hips and both legs.

B. ☑ Place a blanket inside the left leg and move the right leg next to it.

OR

B. ☐ Place a blanket inside the right leg and move the left leg next to it.

C. ☐ Position 2 padded splints one on either side of the left leg, to extend from the thigh to beyond the heel.

OR

C. ☑ Position a long padded splint along the body to extend from the armpit of the left shoulder to beyond the left heel.

D. ☑ Tie the bandages at the chest and hips first, then at the ankles and finally at the upper and lower legs.

OR

D. ☐ Tie the bandages at the ankles first, then at the chest and hips and finally at the lower and upper legs.

E. ☑ If the fracture is open, dress the wound before applying the splint.

OR

E. ☐ If the fracture is open, dress the wound immediately following immobilization.

A. 2   B. 1   C. 2   D. 1   E. 1

To give first aid for a fracture of the upper arm **WHEN THE ELBOW CAN BE BENT -**

1. Place forearm across chest

2. Apply an arm sling

3. Place padding between chest and upper arm

4. Apply bandages above and below the fracture

5. Check circulation (colour, temperature)

7-6

Mark each statement true **(T)** or false **(F)**.

A.   The elbow should never be bent if the upper arm is broken.

B.   Padding should be placed around the upper arm.

C.   A sling should be used to support the upper arm following splinting.

D.   The bandages securing the arm to the chest should not apply pressure to the injury.

E.   The fingernails appearing blue and the hand feeling cold are signs that circulation has been impaired.

7-6

A. F   B. F   C. F   D. T   E. T

A **FRACTURE OF THE COLLARBONE** may be caused by a fall on the outstretched arm.

To relieve pain, the casualty may -

- Support his arm at the elbow

- Bend his head to the injured side

To give first aid, you should -

1. Apply a St. John tubular sling

2. Apply a narrow bandage to secure the arm to the body

7-8

Check (✔) the correct statements below.

A. ☐ The collarbone is a thick bone which can be fractured only by direct force.

B. ☑ A casualty with a broken collarbone on his left side will usually incline his head to the left.

C. ☐ A fractured collarbone should be bandaged tightly above and below the fracture.

D. ☑ When a collarbone is broken, the arm on the injured side must be immobilized.

7-8

B.   D. ☑

7-9

Mark each statement true (T) or false (F).

A. ☑ In an open fracture of the thigh, the limb should be immobilized before the wound is treated.

B. ☑ A fracture of the thigh can be a life-threatening injury.

C. ☑ Only enough traction should be applied to a fractured long bone to align the limb and relieve pressure on nerves and muscles.

D. ☑ Bandages used to immobilize a fracture should be tied loosely to allow movement of the splints.

E. ☑ Circulation in a splinted limb should be monitored to make sure that the bandages are not too tight.

F. ☑ The recommended first aid for a broken collarbone is to apply an arm sling and two bandages.

G. ☑ When traction is applied, it must be maintained until the limb is completely immobilized.

7-9

A.	F	B.	T	C.	T	D.	F	E.	T	F.	F	G.	T

7

For more information on this topic, refer to: *First Aid Safety Oriented*, Second Edition, Chapter 14

END OF EXERCISE 7

NOTES

INTRODUCTION TO HEAD AND SPINAL INJURIES

8-1

INJURIES TO THE HEAD AND SPINE ARE ALWAYS SERIOUS BECAUSE OF THE DANGER OF INJURY TO THE NERVOUS SYSTEM.

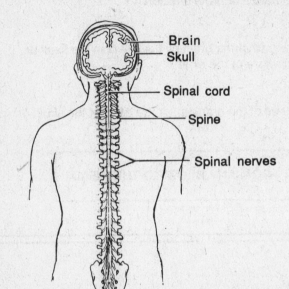

Brain
Skull
Spinal cord
Spine
Spinal nerves

The Nervous System is made up of the -

*   Brain
*   Spinal Cord and
*   Spinal Nerves

These delicate tissues are protected by the -

*   Skull (cranium) and the
*   Spine (backbone)

ALL BODILY FUNCTIONS (e.g. respiration, circulation, digestion, taste, touch, etc.) **ARE CONTROLLED BY THE NERVOUS SYSTEM.**

8-2

Mark each statement true **(T)** or false **(F)**.

A. ☐ Injury to the brain could affect the casualty's breathing.

B. ☐ The bony structure of the head protects the soft parts beneath.

C. ☐ A blow to the head may cause brain damage.

D. ☐ Although the parts of the nervous system are vulnerable, the body provides no covering for them.

8-2

A. ☐T   B. ☐T   C. ☐T   D. ☐F

8-3

HEAD INJURIES are always serious because of the possibility of injury to the brain and spine.

Three types of head injuries are -

• **CONCUSSION** - a temporary disturbance of brain function

• **COMPRESSION** - pressure on some part of the brain by fluids within the skull or by a depressed fracture of the skull

• **SKULL FRACTURE** - a break to the bones of the cranium, or the base of the skull, or the face

SPINAL INJURIES CAN RESULT FROM ANY BLOW TO THE HEAD

8-4

Mark each statement true (**T**) or false (**F**).

A. ☑ A broken bone in the skull may press on the brain.

B. ☑ Skull fractures only occur to the back of the head.

C. ☑ The effects of a concussion are permanent.

D. ☑ A broken jaw bone is considered a skull fracture.

E. ☑ An injury to the head may involve damage to the neck.

8-4

A. T   B. F   C. F   D. T   E. T

8

Some or all of the following signs and symptoms may be present with head injuries -

CONCUSSION

SIGNS

You may observe:

- Loss of consciousness for short time (partial or complete)
- Shallow breathing
- Cold, clammy, pale skin
- Rapid, weak pulse
- Vomiting upon recovery

SYMPTOMS

The casualty may complain of:

- Nausea
- Loss of memory of accident

COMPRESSION

SIGNS

You may observe:

- Unconsciousness
- Twitching of limbs
- Convulsions
- Paralysis
- Irregular, noisy breathing
- Unequal size of pupils
- Slow pulse
- Raised temperature
- Flushed face

SYMPTOMS

The casualty may complain of:

- Weakness

SKULL FRACTURE

SIGNS

You may observe:

- Unconsciousness
- Scalp, face or jaw are swollen, bruised or lacerated
- Depression in the bone
- Blood or straw-coloured liquid coming from ears or nose
- Discolouration below the eyes and behind ears
- Excessive bloody saliva
- Vomiting
- Difficulty in breathing and speaking

SYMPTOMS

The casualty may complain of:

- Pain
- Nausea

Match each injury with the correct signs and symptoms.

A. [2]   Concussion

1. A yellow fluid is coming from the ears. The casualty is unconscious and there is bruising beneath his eyes.

B. [3]   Compression

2. The casualty was knocked out for a few minutes. He appears pale. He says he doesn't know what happened and wants to throw up.

C. [1]   Skull fracture

3. The casualty is unconscious. His legs are jumpy. His face is red, feels hot to the touch and the pupils of his eyes do not react to light.

8-7

When a casualty has received a head injury, you should -

- Suspect a **SPINAL INJURY** and immobilize the neck

- Ensure an **OPEN AIRWAY** (use the jaw thrust without head tilt to open the airway)

- Ensure **ADEQUATE BREATHING** (give artificial respiration, if necessary)

- Obtain **MEDICAL AID**

8-8

Which of the following first aid actions should you perform when a casualty suddenly stops breathing following a severe blow to the head?

A. ☐ Begin artificial respiration, using the head tilt-neck lift method to open the airway.

B. ☑ Prevent movement of the neck.

C. ☑ Begin artificial respiration, using the jaw thrust without head tilt method to open the airway.

D. ☐ Place him in the recovery position.

E. ☑ Send someone for qualified help.

8-8

B. ☑   C. ☑   E. ☑

When a skull fracture is complicated by a scalp wound, you should -

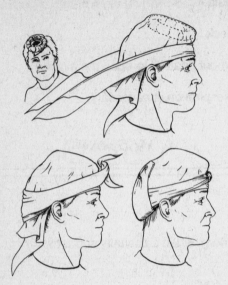

- Clean away loose dirt. **DO NOT PRESS OR PROBE** into the wound

- Apply **TENTED DRESSINGS** to extend well beyond the edges of the wound

- Apply a ring pad large enough to **AVOID PRESSURE ON THE FRACTURE SITE**

- Apply a bandage

TAKE THE CASUALTY TO MEDICAL AID

A child has had a bad fall in the playground. In addition to a cut on his head, he also shows signs of a skull fracture. Check (✓) the correct first aid procedures from the lists below.

Choice 1

A. ☐ Clean the bleeding area thoroughly.

B. ☑ Cover the hurt area with an adhesive dressing.

C. ☑ Place a large ring pad over the dressings to avoid pressure on any broken bones.

D. ☐ Use a broad bandage to secure the dressings and ring pad.

OR

Choice 2

A. ☑ Gently brush the sand away.

B. ☑ Apply loose dressings to cover the hurt area.

C. ☐ Place a large ring pad under the dressing to avoid pressure on the cut.

D. ☑ Use a triangular bandage as a whole cloth to secure the dressings and ring pad.

A. 2   B. 2   C. 1   D. 2

8-11

Spinal injuries are always serious because of the possibility of injury to the **SPINAL CORD** and **NERVES**.

The history of an accident is vital in helping you to recognize a **SPINAL INJURY**.

What happened?

8-12

Mark each statement true **(T)** or false **(F)**.

A. ☑ A man has fallen from a scaffold and has landed on his back. You should suspect a spinal injury.

B. ☐ The spinal cord is not likely to be injured when a person falls from a kitchen chair and hits his back on the cupboard below.

C. ☑ If an unconscious casualty is lying on the ground, you should ask witnesses and look at the circumstances that caused the accident.

D. ☑ When a person twists his back falling off his bicycle, just help him back onto the bicycle and tell him to see a doctor.

8-12   A. [T]   B. [F]   C. [T]   D. [F]

8

8-13

You should assume that a casualty has a **SPINAL INJURY** when he has -

- Received a **SEVERE BLOW** to his head, neck or back

- Experienced a sudden or violent **TWISTING** or **BENDING** of his neck or back

- Fallen and landed heavily on his **FEET** or **BACK**

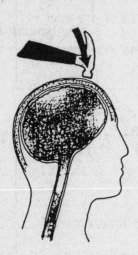 

8-14

In which of the following cases should you suspect a spinal injury?

A. ☑ A boy hits his head when he dives into a shallow swimming pool.

B. ☑ A woman injures her forehead on the windshield during a car accident.

C. ☐ A child becomes unconscious after swallowing sleeping pills.

D. ☑ A painter falls 5 m from a window and lands on his buttocks.

E. ☑ A heavy wooden crate falls from a hoist and hits a worker between the shoulder blades.

8-14

A. ✓   B. ✓   D. ✓   E. ✓

8

8-15

A spinal injury may cause some or all of the following signs and symptoms -

SIGNS

You may observe:

- Swelling along the backbone
- Paralysis or inability to move the limbs on one side or both sides of the body
- Paralysis of muscles that control chest movement in breathing

SYMPTOMS

The casualty may complain of:

- Severe pain
- Tenderness
- Numbness, tingling or loss of feeling in the limbs on one side or both sides of the body

8-16

Which of the following signs and symptoms may indicate a spinal injury? Check (✓) the correct completions.

The casualty -

A. ☑ Has a lump on the bony area at the back of the neck.

B. ☑ Cannot feel his hand being touched.

C. ☐ Is able to make a fist and wiggle his toes.

D. ☑ Tells you that he has a prickling sensation in his hands and feet.

E. ☑ Cries out in pain when the back of his neck is touched.

F. ☑ Cannot move his fingers or toes when asked to do so.

8-16

| A. ✓ | B. ✓ | D. ✓ | E. ✓ | F. ✓ |

8

8-17

Moving a casualty with a spinal injury may seriously damage the spinal cord or nerves and lead to **PERMANENT PARALYSIS** or even **DEATH**.

When the **history** of the accident leads you to suspect a spinal injury, **TREAT THE CASUALTY AS IF HE HAS A SPINAL INJURY** and follow this rule -

> **DO NOT MOVE THE CASUALTY**
>
> **EXCEPT FOR REASONS OF SAFETY**

8-18

Mark each statement true (T) or false (F).

A. You must obtain medical advice before you can assume a casualty has a spinal injury.

B. You should not move an injured person if you think there may be damage to his back unless there is danger.

C. Careless turning of a casualty with an injury to his spine may cause him to lose his ability to walk.

D. A casualty may be disabled for life as a result of damage to the spinal cord and nerves.

8-18

A. F   B. T   C. T   D. T

8

When a casualty with a suspected **SPINAL INJURY** is **NOT** in immediate danger, **DO NOT MOVE HIM**. Give first aid in the **POSITION FOUND**.

You should -

- **STEADY AND SUPPORT** the casualty to prevent bending or twisting of the head and spine

 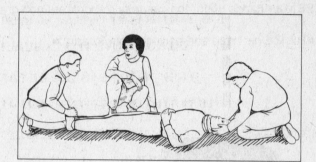

- **APPLY** a cervical collar

- Send for **MEDICAL AID**

- Keep the casualty **WARM** and **QUIET** until medical aid is available

- If breathing stops, begin artificial respiration using the **JAW THRUST WITHOUT HEAD TILT** method to open the airway

Check off (✔) the first aid actions which you should take when you suspect that a casualty has a spinal injury.

A. ☑ Immobilize the casualty's head, neck and back and make sure his body heat is maintained.

B. ☐ If artificial respiration is needed, open the airway by pressing backward on the casualty's head.

C. ☐ Place the casualty in the recovery position and keep him calm.

D. ☑ If artificial respiration is needed, open the airway by lifting the jaw forward and keeping the neck immobilized.

8-20

A. D. ✔

8

In some situations, a casualty with a suspected spinal injury may be in **IMMEDIATE DANGER**.

If you are alone, move the casualty to safety using the following **DRAG CARRY** method.

- **EASE** your hands under the casualty's shoulders and grasp his clothing on each side

- **STABILIZE** his head and neck on your forearms

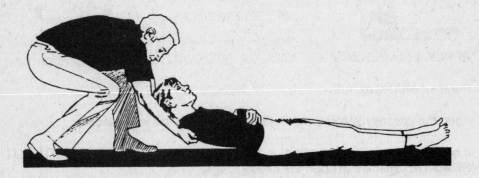

- Drag the casualty **LENGTHWISE**

**MOVE THE CASUALTY OUT OF DANGER
BUT NO FURTHER**

When the casualty is no longer in danger, **STEADY** and **SUPPORT** him to prevent bending or twisting of the spine. If you have to leave the casualty to get help, apply a cervical collar and place him in the recovery position.

To drag a casualty with a suspected spinal injury to safety, you should -

Choice 1		**Choice 2**
A. ☐ Grasp his feet and drag him feet first.	**OR**	A. ☑ Grasp his clothing under the shoulders and drag him head first.
B. ☐ Steady and support his arms and legs while you are dragging him.	**OR**	B. ☑ Steady and support his head and neck while you are dragging him.
C. ☑ Pull him in a straight line.	**OR**	C. ☐ Pull him sideways.
D. ☑ Move him only as far as necessary.	**OR**	D. ☐ Move him as far as possible.

When the casualty is safe and you have to go to call medical aid -

E. ☐ Roll him into the recovery position and provide a neck support.	**OR**	E. ☑ Immobilize his neck and roll him gently into the recovery position.

To remove a sitting casualty with a suspected neck injury from a life-threatening situation -

- Free the feet and legs

- Support the head and neck

- Encircle the casualty's chest and grasp the near wrist

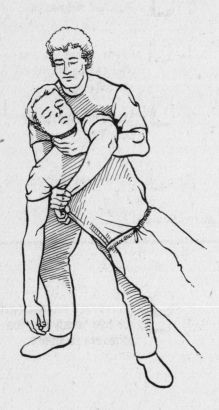

- Maintain position until you and the casualty are a safe distance from the accident

DO NOT MOVE HIM UNLESS IT IS ABSOLUTELY NECESSARY

A casualty has been found in a sitting position in a fuel truck. He must be moved out of danger because the truck is perched on the edge of a ravine. Choose the correct procedures from the lists below.

Choice 1

A. ☐ Pull the legs out of the truck before supporting the head and neck.

OR

Choice 2

A. ☑ Untangle lower limbs, if necessary and support the head and neck.

B. ☑ Support the head and neck with your hand and shoulder.

OR

B. ☐ Support the head and neck with a folded jacket while maintaining hand support.

C. ☑ Slide your other arm and hand behind the casualty's back.

OR

C. ☐ Slide a board behind the casualty's head and neck.

D. ☐ Secure head and upper body to a board with bandages at forehead, chin and chest.

OR

D. ☑ Grasp the wrist of the casualty's hand nearest you to form a tight grip.

E. ☐ Quickly roll the casualty from the truck.

OR

E. ☑ Quickly drag the casualty from the truck.

A. 2   B. 1   C. 1   D. 2   E. 2

8-25

Mark each statement true (T) or false (F).

A. ☐ Injuries to the skull or spine may cause damage to the brain, spinal cord or nerves.

B. ☐ Bleeding from the ears, the nose and the unequal size of the pupils of the eyes may be signs of a head injury.

C. ☐ When placing a casualty with a suspected back injury on a spine board, his head and spine must be kept in alignment and prevented from twisting.

D. ☐ The history of an accident is not important for the assessment of a spinal injury.

E. ☐ You should always assume there is a spinal injury when a casualty has received a sharp blow to the head.

F. ☐ A casualty with a spinal injury may have no feeling in his limbs and may be unable to move them.

G. ☐ When you suspect that a casualty has a spinal injury, your first aid priority is to transport him immediately to medical aid.

H. ☐ The aims of first aid for a spinal injury are to prevent damage to the spinal cord and to care for life-threatening conditions.

I. ☐ When you must move a sitting casualty with a suspected neck injury, the neck and upper body must be immobilized as a unit.

8-25

A. T B. T C. T D. F E. T F. T G. F H. T I. T

For more information on these topics, refer to:
First Aid Safety Oriented, Second Edition, Chapters 3, 16, 28

END OF EXERCISE 8

NOTES

INTRODUCTION TO JOINT INJURIES

9-1

A **JOINT** is formed where two or more bones come together.

The bones of a joint are held in place by **SUPPORTING TISSUE.**

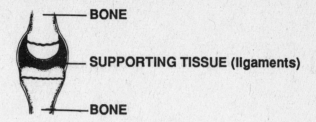

— BONE

— SUPPORTING TISSUE (ligaments)

— BONE

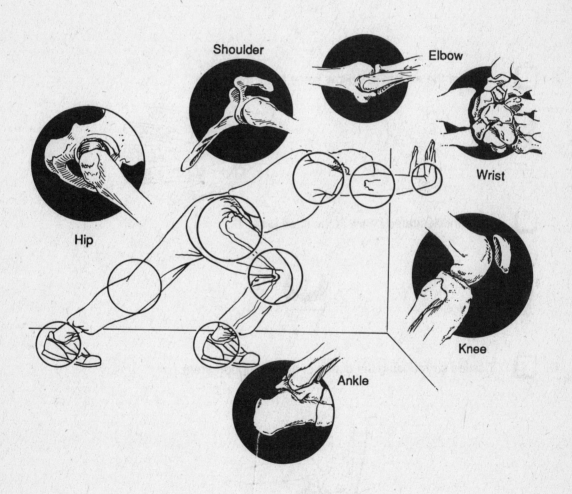

Shoulder

Elbow

Wrist

Hip

Knee

Ankle

Major Joints of the Body

Which of the following statements agree with the accompanying diagrams?

A. ☑ A joint is where two or more bones meet.

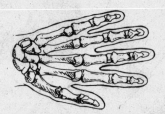

B. ☑ Joints of the extremities allow some body movement.

C. ☐ The joint illustrated below is the knee joint.

D. ☑ Tissues surrounding the bones of a joint support them.

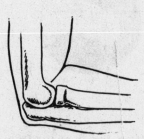

A. ✓   B. ✓   D. ✓

9

JOINT INJURIES

JOINT INJURIES result when the bones and surrounding tissues are forced to move **BEYOND** their normal range.

Two common joint injuries are -

- **SPRAINS**

- **DISLOCATIONS**

A **SPRAIN** occurs when the supporting tissue (ligaments) around the bones of a joint are **STRETCHED** or **TORN**.

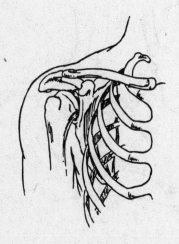
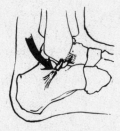
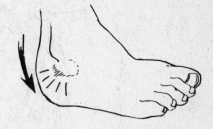

Normal Ankle   **Sprained Ankle**   **What You Will See**

A **DISLOCATION** occurs when the tissues around the joint are stretched or torn and the bones of the joint **REMAIN OUT OF POSITION.**

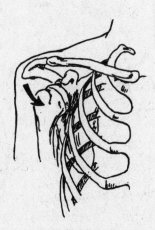
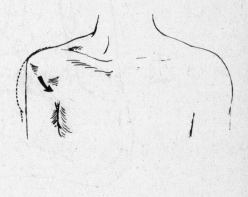

Normal Shoulder   **Dislocated Shoulder**   **What You Will See**

Identify each of the illustrations below as one of the following -

1	Normal joint
2	Sprain
3	Dislocation

A. 1

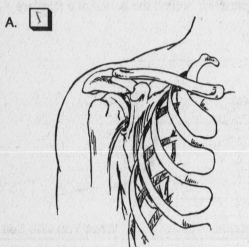

B. 3

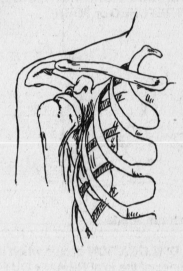

C. 1

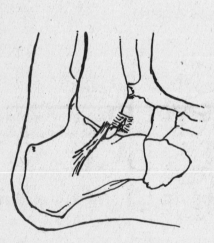

D. 2

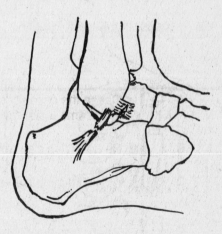

9-5

A **SPRAIN** may be recognized by some or all of the following signs and symptoms -

SIGNS

You may observe:

- Swelling
- Discolouration (bruise may not appear immediately)
- Inability to use the limb

SYMPTOMS

The casualty may complain of:

- Pain, increasing with movement

9-6

Choose the correct completions for the following statement.

A sprained ankle will usually -

Choice 1		Choice 2	
A. ☑ Cause the casualty's discomfort to become worse by walking.	**OR**	A. ☐ Cause the casualty's discomfort to be relieved by walking.	
B. ☐ Be normal in size and shape.	**OR**	B. ☐ Be enlarged.	
C. ☐ Allow the casualty to walk freely.	**OR**	C. ☐ Prevent the casualty from walking.	
D. ☐ Change colour some time after the injury.	**OR**	D. ☐ Keep the same colour after the injury.	

9-6

A. 1   B. 2   C. 2   D. 1

9

9-7

When you suspect a joint has been sprained, you should -

- **IMMOBILIZE** the injured part in the **POSITION OF MOST COMFORT**
- **APPLY GENTLE PRESSURE** with a bandage or padding to decrease swelling
- **APPLY ICE PACKS** to reduce pain and control swelling

 OR  OR

Figure-8 bandage   **Roller Bandage**   **Pillow Splint**

- **ELEVATE** the limb, if possible
- **MONITOR CIRCULATION** below the point of injury frequently; swelling may cause the bandages to restrict circulation
- Obtain **MEDICAL AID** to ensure that the joint is not fractured

---

9-8

Check (✓) the first aid procedures you should use when caring for a casualty with a sprain.

A. ☐ Apply a heating pad to a sprained elbow to ease the casualty's discomfort.

B. ☐ Bandage a folded cushion around a sprained ankle.

C. ☑ Apply cold to a sprained wrist to ease the casualty's discomfort.

D. ☑ Support a sprained ankle with a narrow bandage tied around the foot and ankle.

E. ☑ Stabilize and raise the injured part.

F. ☐ Assess blood flow to the hands and feet before bandaging.

9-8   B. ☑   C. ☑   D. ☑   E. ☑

9

A **DISLOCATION** of a joint may be recognized by some or all of the following signs and symptoms -

SIGNS

You may observe:

- Deformity or abnormal appearance (where bones are out of position)

- Swelling
- Discolouration (bruise may appear later)
- Inability to move the joint
- Casualty supports arm on the injured side away from the body when a shoulder is dislocated

SYMPTOMS

The casualty may complain of:

- Very severe pain (made worse by movement)

Which of the following signs and symptoms would help you to assess the casualty's injury as a dislocated right shoulder?

A. ☑ He is holding his right arm slightly outward from the body.

B. ☐ The right shoulder is normal in size and shape when compared to the left shoulder.

C. ☑ He complains violently when you try to lift his right arm.

D. ☐ He is able to rotate the right arm freely from the shoulder.

E. ☑ The right shoulder has an abnormal shape when compared to the left shoulder.

9-10   A. ☑   C. ☑   E. ☑

9

9-11

When you suspect a dislocation of a joint, you should -

- **NEVER** attempt to return bones to their normal position
- **STEADY** and **SUPPORT** the injured part in the **POSITION OF MOST COMFORT**
- **IMMOBILIZE THE JOINT** by applying suitable padding and a sling
- **APPLY ICE PACKS** to the joint to reduce pain and swelling
- **MONITOR CIRCULATION** to the limb by checking the colour and temperature of the hand or foot
- If circulation is impaired, obtain medical aid **AT ONCE**
- Obtain **MEDICAL AID**

9-12

To give first aid for a dislocation you should -

Choice 1

A. ☐ Apply heat to the injured part.

B. ☐ Place the dislocated bone back in position.

C. ☑ Stabilize the limb in the position that causes the least pain.

D. ☑ Check blood flow to the limb below the site of injury.

E. ☐ If signs and symptoms show decrease of blood flow to the limb, rotate the joint backward.

OR

Choice 2

A. ☑ Apply cold to the injured part.

B. ☑ Leave the dislocated bone in the position found.

C. ☐ Secure the limb tightly to the body.

D. ☐ Check blood flow to the limb above the site of injury.

E. ☑ If signs and symptoms show decrease of blood flow to the limb, seek medical help urgently.

9-12

A. 2	B. 2	C. 1	D. 1	E. 2

9

Bones at a joint may also be **FRACTURED**.

A FRACTURED WRIST will look like this -

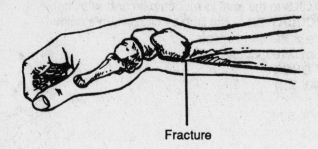

Fracture

To give **FIRST AID** for a fractured wrist -

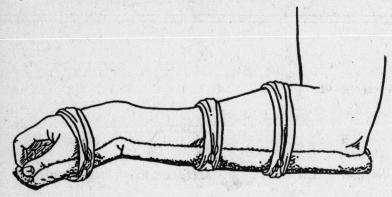

- **STEADY** and **SUPPORT**

- **APPLY** a padded splint

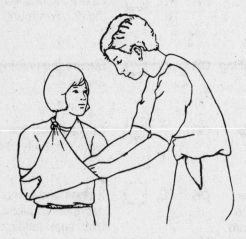

- **SUPPORT** the forearm in an arm sling

- **CHECK** for circulation to the fingers

9

Choose the correct completion of the following first aid procedures for a fractured wrist.

1. The splint used to immobilize a fractured wrist should be applied to the -

A. ☐ Top of the arm.

B. ☑ Palm side of the arm.

C. ☐ Side of the arm.

2. The splint must be long enough to extend from the -

A. ☑ Elbow to the base of the fingers.

B. ☐ Top of the wrist to the top of the thumb.

C. ☐ Wrist to the elbow.

3. The arm should be supported by -

A. ☐ Pillows.

B. ☐ The other arm.

C. ☑ A sling.

1. B   2. A   3. C

9

A **FRACTURE OF THE KNEE** may involve any of 3 bones.

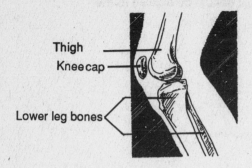
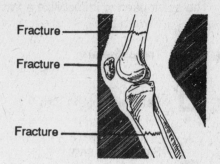

It may look like this and will result in severe pain.

To give **FIRST AID** for a fractured knee -

GENTLY STRAIGHTEN THE LIMB AND APPLY A SPLINT

SECURE THE SPLINT WITH BANDAGES

SUPPORT THE SPLINTED LEG

If the casualty will not allow the leg to be straightened, support with padding in the most comfortable position and transport.

> **NEVER APPLY TRACTION TO AN INJURED JOINT**

Check (✓) the correct completions of the following statements concerning a fracture of the knee.

1. There may be fractures to as many as -

A. ☐ Two bones.

B. ☑ Three bones.

C. ☐ Four bones.

2. A splint to immobilize a fracture about the knee should extend -

A. ☐ Over the whole knee.

B. ☐ From ankle to knee.

C. ☑ From heel to buttocks.

3. Place padding -

A. ☐ Around the entire leg.

B. ☐ Under the entire leg.

C. ☑ Under knee and ankle.

4. Secure the splint with -

A. ☐ 3 narrow bandages around ankle, thigh and lower leg.

B. ☑ One figure-8 bandage around ankle and foot, and with broad bandages above and below the fracture.

C. ☐ 3 figure-8 bandages around ankle, thigh and lower leg.

5. Support the leg -

A. ☑ In an elevated position.

B. ☐ In a flat position.

C. ☐ Bent at the knee.

1. **B**   2. **C**   3. **C**   4. **B**   5. **A**

9

9-17

A **STRAIN** is an injury that occurs when a muscle is stretched beyond its normal limits.

A strain is caused by -

- Sudden pulling or twisting of a muscle
- Poor body mechanics during lifting
- Failure to condition muscles before physical activity

A strain can be recognized by some or all of the following -

SIGNS	SYMPTOMS
You may observe: • Swelling of muscle • Discolouration	The casualty may complain of: • Sudden sharp pain • Severe cramps • Stiffness

Signs and symptoms of a strain may not appear immediately.

To give **FIRST AID** for a strain -

- **PLACE** the casualty in the **POSITION OF GREATEST COMFORT**
- **APPLY COLD** for 10 to 15 minutes and repeat every 20 or 25 minutes to help relax muscle spasm and prevent further tissue swelling

---

9-18

Check (✓) the correct statements below -

A. ☐ A strain is damage to any of the body's joints.

B. ☑ Back strain could be caused by improper raising and carrying techniques.

C. ☐ Athletes seldom warm up their muscles before competing.

D. ☑ A strained leg muscle may cause pain several hours later.

E. ☑ Use of an ice pack and rest is effective treatment for a strain.

9-18

B. ✓   D. ✓   E. ✓

9

9-19

In most emergency situations, **DO NOT MOVE THE CASUALTY**.

You should give first aid where the casualty is found and arrange for medical aid to come to the scene.

However, there are times when **YOU MUST MOVE** the casualty **IMMEDIATELY**. This is when -

- His life is threatened by a **HAZARDOUS SITUATION** such as fire, explosion, flood or poisonous gas.

- First aid for life-threatening conditions **CANNOT BE GIVEN** where he lies.

9-20

In which of the following situations should you move the casualty before you give first aid?

	Move	Do Not Move
A. A mechanic is lying inside a burning car.	☑	☐
B. An elderly man is lying unconscious on a sidewalk.	☐	☑
C. A woman is lying in a ditch of water with her face submerged.	☑	☐
D. A teenager is lying at the foot of a long stairway.	☐	☑
E. A child is floating in a lake under an overturned boat.	☑	☐

9-20 A. Move B. Do Not Move C. Move D. Do Not Move E. Move

If medical aid is **NOT READILY AVAILABLE** or is **TOO FAR AWAY**, you will be required to transport the casualty after giving first aid.

If you must **TRANSPORT** the casualty, you should -

• Ensure that his injuries are protected

• Select the method of transportation that poses the **LEAST RISK** to yourself and the casualty

• Use a **STRETCHER** whenever possible to move a casualty with serious injuries

• Use as many bystanders as needed to minimize risks

SPECIAL PRECAUTIONS

If the casualty has a suspected **SPINAL INJURY**	If the casualty is **UNCONSCIOUS**
• Apply a cervical collar • Immobilize the casualty • Use a firm, flat spine board • Place a support on each side of the head	• Transport him on a stretcher in the recovery position • Ensure his airway is open • Monitor his breathing

When you must carry a casualty for a long distance, which of the following should you do?

A. ☐ Move the casualty by yourself to avoid injury to bystanders.

B. ☑ Ensure that the airway does not become obstructed when the casualty is unconscious.

C. ☑ Take measures to prevent his injuries from becoming worse.

D. ☑ Use a rigid carrying device with head supports when you assume that the casualty has a neck injury.

E. ☐ Use a carrying device only if the casualty is unconscious.

9-22   B. ☑   C. ☑   D. ☑

9

When lifting and transporting a heavy object, such as a casualty, rescuers should protect themselves from injuries.

They should use **PROPER BODY MECHANICS** -

- Stand **CLOSE** to the casualty

- Bend the **KNEES**; do not stoop

- Get a **GOOD GRIP** on the casualty or equipment

- Use the thigh, leg and abdominal muscles to lift, and keep the back **STRAIGHT**

Ensure that rescuers lift together on a signal.

If the rescuers are unskilled, **PRACTISE** the proper techniques before moving the casualty.

LIFTING TECHNIQUES

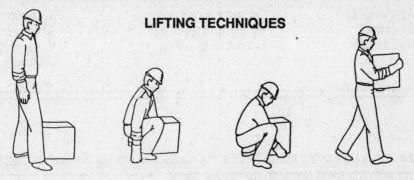

Which of the following are safety practices that would protect persons attempting to rescue a casualty?

A. ☐ Keep the legs straight as you bend from the waist to lift the casualty with your arms.

B. ☑ Position yourself next to the casualty and hold him firmly as you lift.

C. ☑ Use the power of your legs to lift the casualty.

D. ☐ Always lift the casualty by yourself and keep bystanders away.

E. ☑ Make sure that all rescuers can perform the correct procedures before attempting the rescue.

B. ✓   C. ✓   D. ✓

9-25

When **YOU ARE ALONE** and you must move a casualty, use one of the following rescue carries -

• PICK-A-BACK	• CRADLE CARRY	• HUMAN CRUTCH

To carry a lightweight casualty who cannot walk but who can use his upper limbs.	To carry a child or lightweight adult who is unable to walk.	To support a casualty who has one injured lower limb but can walk when helped.

9-26

There are three rescue carries listed. Place the number in the square which matches each casualty with the most appropriate rescue carry.

Casualties

Rescue Carries

A. ☐ Four-year-old who has sprained a wrist and ankle.

1. Pick-a-back

B. ☐ Heavy-set man who has a slightly sprained ankle.

2. Cradle carry

C. ☐ Young girl who has sprained both ankles.

3. Human crutch

D. ☐ Six-year-old who has dislocated an elbow.

9-26

A. 2   B. 3   C. 1   D. 2

9

When you must move a casualty and **YOU HAVE A HELPER**, use one of the following rescue carries -

• **CHAIR CARRY**

To transport either a **CONSCIOUS** casualty who **CANNOT WALK** or an **UNCONSCIOUS CASUALTY** through hallways or up and down stairways. (A third rescuer should assist when transporting on stairs.)

• **TWO-HAND SEAT**

To transport a **CONSCIOUS** casualty who **CANNOT SUPPORT HIS UPPER BODY.**

• **FOUR-HAND SEAT**

To transport a **CONSCIOUS** casualty who **HAS THE USE OF HIS ARMS.**

Mark each statement true (T) or false (F).

A. An unconscious man can be carried down a spiral staircase most easily with a chair when three rescuers are available.

B. It is best for two rescuers to use the four-hand seat to transport a girl who has a dislocated shoulder and a sprained ankle.

C. A boy who has a large nail embedded in his foot can be carried most comfortably by two people using the four-hand seat.

D. A casualty who has severe burns to his hands and feet can be carried by two rescuers using the two-hand seat.

9-29

The **BLANKET LIFT** is used by a team of rescuers (at least four) to carry a helpless or unconscious casualty.

Before attempting this lift, be sure to **TEST THE BLANKET** to ensure that it will carry the casualty's weight.

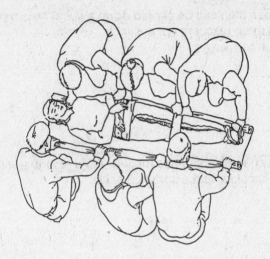

DO NOT USE THIS LIFT IF YOU SUSPECT THE CASUALTY HAS A SPINAL INJURY

9-30

In which situation would you use the blanket lift to move the casualty?

A. ☐ You must move a conscious casualty with an arm injury from the floor to a chair.

B. ☐ An unconscious casualty with an assumed neck injury must be carried for a short distance.

C. ☑ An unconscious casualty without assumed neck injuries must be carried for a short distance.

D. ☐ You must move an unconscious man down two steep flights of stairs.

9-30

C. ☑

9-31

If a stretcher is **NOT** available to transport a casualty, you can **IMPROVISE** a stretcher by using one of the following methods:

- **TWO POLES AND A BLANKET**

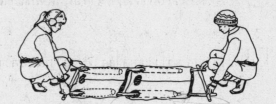

- **TWO POLES AND TWO JACKETS**

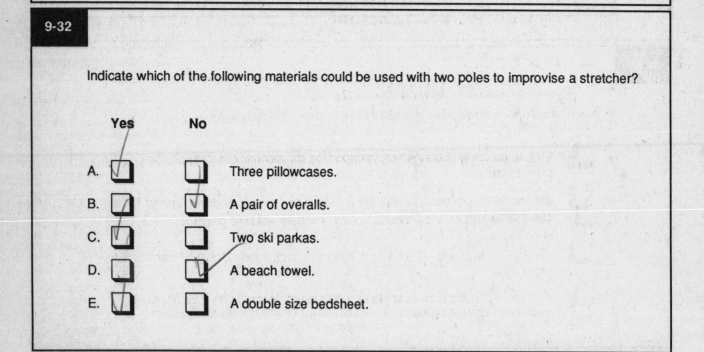

- **TWO POLES AND SACKS**

9-32

Indicate which of the following materials could be used with two poles to improvise a stretcher?

	Yes	No	
A.	☐	☐	Three pillowcases.
B.	☐	☑	A pair of overalls.
C.	☐	☐	Two ski parkas.
D.	☐	☐	A beach towel.
E.	☐	☐	A double size bedsheet.

9-32   A. `Yes`   B. `No`   C. `Yes`   D. `No`   E. `Yes`

9

9-33

Mark each statement true (**T**) or false (**F**).

A. ☑ A sprain may result in torn tissues around the bones of a joint.

B. ☑ A dislocation is a joint injury in which a bone pops out of position.

C. ☒ Before splinting a leg with a knee fracture, it should be realigned with firm traction.

D. ☑ A fractured wrist should be immobilized from the elbow to the base of the fingers.

E. ☑ You should apply cold to an injured joint to lessen pain and swelling.

F. ☑ When you give first aid for a dislocated right shoulder, support the right arm in the position that causes the least pain.

G. ☑ You should only move a casualty when his life is in danger or when life-saving first aid cannot be given where he lies.

H. ☑ Ensure an open airway when transporting an unconscious casualty on a stretcher.

I. ☒ The use of proper body mechanics by rescuers will help prevent further injury to the casualty.

J. ☑ To help immobilization of ankle or foot injuries, footwear may be left on if there is no open wound.

9-33

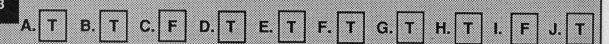

A. T | B. T | C. F | D. T | E. T | F. T | G. T | H. T | I. F | J. T

9

For more information on these topics, refer to:
First Aid Safety Oriented, Second Edition, Chapters 2, 14, 17, 28

END OF EXERCISE 9

INTRODUCTION TO CHEST INJURIES

10-1

The **CHEST CAVITY** is formed by the **BREASTBONE** (sternum), **RIBS** and **SPINE**.

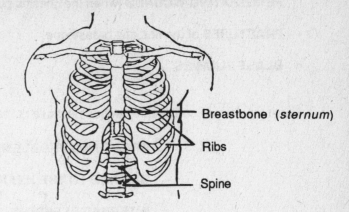

Breastbone (*sternum*)

Ribs

Spine

These bones form a cage which protects the **LUNGS, HEART** and **MAJOR BLOOD VESSELS** (aorta, superior vena cava, inferior vena cava).

Note: The above anatomical terms appearing in brackets will not be tested.

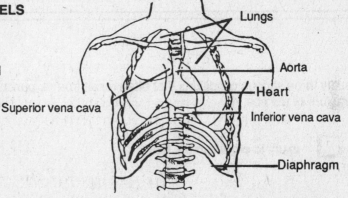

Lungs

Aorta

Heart

Superior vena cava

Inferior vena cava

Diaphragm

The chest cavity is separated from the abdominal cavity by the **DIAPHRAGM**.

10-2

Mark each statement true (**T**) or false (**F**).

A. The diaphragm forms the floor of the chest cavity.

B. ☒ The lungs and the heart are located in the abdominal cavity.

C. The breastbone, ribs and spine create the shape of the chest.

D. ☑ The bones forming the chest cavity help to prevent damage to important organs in the chest.

10-2

A. T   B. F   C. T   D. T

Three types of chest injuries are -

- **PENETRATING WOUNDS** (when the chest is punctured)

- **FRACTURES** of the ribs and breastbone

- **BLAST INJURIES**

Chest injuries are considered serious because of the possibility of -

- **BREATHING PROBLEMS**

- **DAMAGE TO THE HEART AND LUNGS**

- **INTERNAL BLEEDING**

10-4

Identify three serious conditions that often result from a puncture wound of the chest or a fracture of the ribs.

A. ☐ Injury to organs in the head.

B. ☑ Blood escaping into the chest cavity.

C. ☐ Severe bleeding coming from the ears.

D. ☑ Injury to the organs in the chest.

E. ☑ Laboured breathing.

10-4   B. ☑   D. ☑   E. ☑

10

10-5

A **PENETRATING CHEST WOUND** results when an object punctures the chest.

The penetrating object creates an **OPEN WOUND** in the chest wall.

The open wound allows air to enter **DIRECTLY INTO** the chest cavity and results in serious breathing problems.

Some puncture injuries, such as gunshot wounds, may have both an **ENTRY** and an **EXIT** wound.

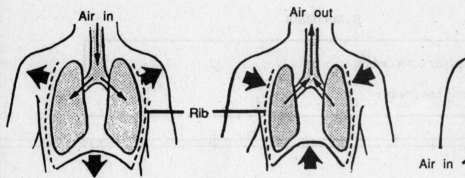

Normal Chest Action

Penetrating Chest Wound

10-6

Which of these conditions may be present following a puncture wound of the chest?

A. ☐ The casualty's breathing is unchanged.

B. ☑ Air flows into the chest cavity through the hole in the chest.

C. ☐ There is a possibility of two wound sites when a puncture wound is inflicted.

D. ☐ The chest cavity is open to the outside air.

10-6

B. ✓   C. ☑   D. ☑

10

Some or all of the following signs and symptoms may indicate a penetrating chest wound -

SIGNS

You may observe:

- Sound of air being sucked into the chest when the casualty breathes in
- Bloodstained bubbles at the wound site when the casualty breathes out
- Coughing up of frothy blood
- Laboured breathing

SYMPTOMS

The casualty may complain of:

- Pain during breathing

10-8

Which of the following are signs and symptoms of a penetrating chest wound?

Choice 1			**Choice 2**	
A. ☐ The casualty breathes normally.	**OR**	A. ☑	The casualty breathes with difficulty.
B. ☑ Foamy blood appears around the wound.	**OR**	B. ☐	Blood is not seen around the wound.
C. ☑ Sucking noises are heard when the casualty breathes.	**OR**	C. ☐	Breathing is very shallow and quiet.
D. ☐ The casualty coughs up a clear fluid.	**OR**	D. ☑	The casualty coughs up foamy blood.

10-8   A. 2   B. 1   C. 1   D. 2

10

10-9

A severe blow or crushing force to the chest may produce a **FLAIL CHEST**.

FLAIL CHEST is a term used to describe a condition in which several ribs are fractured in **MORE THAN ONE PLACE**, loosening a segment of the chest wall.

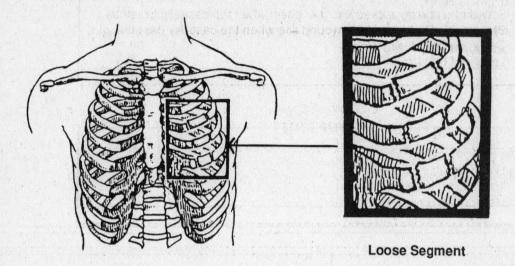

Loose Segment

The loose segment will move independently and not with the bony chest wall during breathing.

Breathing difficulties result.

10-10

Mark each statement true **(T)** or false **(F)**.

A. ☑ When many ribs are broken in several places, a part of the rib cage may become separated.

B. ☒ A flail chest does not affect the casualty's breathing.

C. ☒ A flail chest results when an object punctures the chest from outside.

D. ☑ A flail chest could result from a person being thrown against the steering wheel during a car collision.

10-10

A. T   B. F   C. F   D. T

10

The following are signs and symptoms of a flail chest -

SIGNS

You may observe:

- Abnormal movement of a segment of the chest wall during breathing
- Laboured, ineffective breathing

SYMPTOMS

The casualty may complain of:

- Pain during breathing

10-12

Which of the following signs and symptoms may indicate a flail chest?

A. ☐ Breathing is normal and regular.

B. ☑ The casualty complains that his chest hurts when he breathes.

C. ☐ The casualty has a large open chest wound.

D. ☑ Part of the chest wall does not rise and fall with the rest of the rib cage.

10-12

B. ☑   D. ☑

10

The aim of first aid for a flail chest is to **STABILIZE THE LOOSE SEGMENT** in order to ease breathing.

To stabilize the loose segment, you should -

- Bend the casualty's arm across the chest on the **INJURED** side

- Apply **TWO BROAD BANDAGES** over the arm, tying them on the **UNINJURED** side

OR

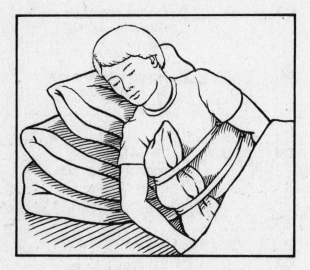

- Bandage a **FIRM PAD** or **PILLOW** over the injured area

10-14

Check (✓) the appropriate first aid procedures for a casualty with a flail chest.

A. ☐ To relieve pain, allow the injured segment to move freely.

B. ☑ Continually monitor breathing.

C. ☑ To relieve pain, ensure that the separated portion of the chest wall is supported.

D. ☐ Leave the chest uncovered.

10-15

Choose the correct techniques for stabilizing a flail chest on the casualty's right side.

Choice 1		Choice 2
A. ☐ Lay the casualty's left arm over his chest.	OR	A. ☑ Lay the casualty's right arm over his chest.
B. ☑ Secure the arm to the chest with two broad bandages.	OR	B. ☐ Support the arm in a St. John tubular sling.
C. ☐ Tie off bandages against the right side of the chest.	OR	C. ☑ Tie off bandages against the left side of the chest.

An alternative technique is to -

D. ☑ Bandage a large, folded towel over the right side of the chest.	OR	D. ☐ Bandage a large, folded towel over the left side of the chest.

10-14 B. ✓ C. ✓

10-15 A. 2 B. 1 C. 2 D. 1

10

Once you have applied bandages to support a flail chest, you should -

- Place the casualty in a **SEMISITTING** position, inclined to the **INJURED SIDE** to assist breathing

- Obtain **MEDICAL AID**

In what position should you place a conscious casualty with a suspected flail segment on the left side of his chest?

A. ☐ In the recovery position, with his head turned to the left.

B. ☐ Flat on his back, with his head turned to the right.

C. ☐ Lying on his right side, with his head and shoulders raised and supported.

D. ☑ Lying on his left side, with his head and shoulders raised and supported.

10-17   D. ☑

CLOSED FRACTURES of one or more ribs may show no external signs of injury.

They can usually be recognized by these signs and symptoms -

SIGNS

You may observe:

- Short, shallow breaths

SYMPTOMS

The casualty may complain of:

- Sharp chest pain on breathing
- Localized pain at site of injury

FIRST AID should reduce movement of broken ribs and ease pain.

IF THE CHEST BANDAGE CAUSES DISCOMFORT, REMOVE it but continue to provide **SUPPORT** to the arm on the injured side by applying a St. John tubular sling.

Mark each statement true **(T)** or false **(F)**.

A.   To relieve the distress caused by a broken rib, tie a broad bandage around the chest with the widest part over the injury.

B.   After the broad bandage has been applied, it should only be removed by a doctor.

C. ☑ A sling should be used to support the arm on the injured side whether the chest is bandaged or not.

A. | T | B. | F | C. | T |

10

10-20

A FRACTURE OF THE BREASTBONE is usually caused by CRUSH INJURIES.

In addition to the fracture, the casualty will often suffer damage to the ORGANS and BLOOD VESSELS under the breastbone.

FIRST AID FOR A FRACTURED BREASTBONE -

- Keep the casualty QUIET and monitor his BREATHING

- Place the casualty in a SEMISITTING POSITION to assist breathing

- LOOSEN tight clothing around neck, chest and waist

- Prevent SHOCK from worsening

- Obtain MEDICAL AID

- USE A STRETCHER if casualty must be moved

10-21

A construction worker has been pinned under a heavy piece of machinery which has fallen on his chest. After he has been removed from beneath the machinery, which of these first aid procedures should you follow?

A. ☒ Assist the casualty to walk around so you can assess how seriously he is hurt.

B. ☑ Help his breathing by raising the upper part of his body.

C. ☑ Undo his belt, trousers and shirt.

D. ☑ Cover him with a blanket while he is sitting and leaning against the machine.

E. ☒ Apply a broad bandage loosely around his chest.

F. ☑ Call an ambulance.

10-21

| B. ✓ | C. ✓ | D. ✓ | F. ✓ |

10

10-22

The shock wave of an explosion can damage the lungs and internal organs.

HISTORY, SIGNS AND SYMPTOMS are important in identifying blast injuries.

HISTORY	SIGNS	SYMPTOMS
You may find out: • Type of explosion • Extent of explosion • Location of explosion • Casualty's position relative to explosion	You may observe: • Frothy blood being coughed up • Laboured breathing	The casualty may complain of: • Chest pain.

To give first aid for a blast injury -

• Assist the conscious casualty to a **SEMISITTING POSITION**

• **CHECK BREATHING** and continue to monitor

• Give **ARTIFICIAL RESPIRATION**, if required

• Prevent **SHOCK** from worsening

• Transport to **MEDICAL AID** immediately

10-23

Mark each statement true (**T**) or false (**F**).

A. ☑ It is important to know exactly what happened in an explosion to recognize the type of injuries.

B. ☑ If a casualty who has been injured in a natural gas explosion has bubbly blood coming from his mouth, he requires immediate medical help.

C. ☑ Blast injuries may cause difficulty in breathing and shock.

D. ☒ A conscious casualty with blast injuries should be put in the recovery position.

10-23

A. [T]   B. [T]   C. [T]   D. [F]

10

10-24

Mark each statement true (**T**) or false (**F**).

A. ☑ The ribs, breastbone and backbone protect the lungs, heart and major blood vessels.

B. ☑ The aim of first aid for chest injuries is to relieve pain and ensure adequate breathing.

C. ☒ Two stab wounds of the chest are referred to as a flail chest.

D. ☑ An open puncture wound of the chest allows air to flow directly into the chest cavity.

E. ☒ A flail chest allows air to escape from the chest cavity.

F. ☑ A sign of a penetrating chest wound is the sound of air being sucked into the chest cavity.

G. ☑ When a number of ribs are fractured in several places, a segment of the chest wall may be loosened.

H. ☑ Frothy blood is likely to be seen around a penetrating chest wound.

I. ☑ When you have sealed a penetrating chest wound and the casualty develops severe breathing distress, you should loosen the tape on one side of the airtight covering.

10-24   A. T   B. T   C. F   D. T   E. F   F. T   G. T   H. T   I. T

For more information on these topics, refer to: *First Aid Safety Oriented*, Second Edition, Chapters 2, 15

END OF EXERCISE 10

THE HUMAN HAND

11-1

The hand is made up of many bones and joints which connect them.

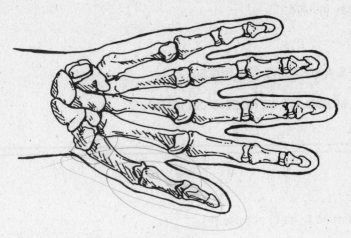

Add to these the complex systems of: **NERVES**
                                              TENDONS
                                              MUSCLES
                                              BLOOD VESSELS

The hand is a complicated structure. Each part depends on many others to allow for the wide range of **MOVEMENT** and to give it **STRENGTH** and **DEXTERITY**.

11-2

Mark each statement true **(T)** or false **(F)**.

A. ☑   Each part of the hand functions on its own.

B. ☑   The palm of the hand contains one flat bone.

C. ☑   An injury to one part of the hand may involve many other parts.

D. ☑   The hand contains many bony structures and different soft tissues.

11-2

A. ☐ F   B. ☐ F   C. ☐ T   D. ☐ T

11

11-3

Even minor injuries to the hand must be considered serious.

Most hand injuries result in temporary or permanent **LOSS OF MOVEMENT** and **FUNCTION** of the fingers.

A hand injury may involve -

- **WOUNDS**

- **FRACTURES AND JOINT INJURIES**

- **DAMAGED MUSCLES, TENDONS OR NERVES**

11-4

Mark each statement true **(T)** or false **(F)**.

A. A wound to a hand may heal, but the hand may not be able to move normally.

B. A serious accident to the hand could result in several broken bones.

C. Hand movement may be impaired if the soft parts of the hand are damaged.

D. Hand injuries without heavy bleeding require little attention.

11-4

A. T   B. T   C. T   D. F

11

The frequency of hand injuries is very high. **SAFETY PRACTICES** can help to prevent hand injuries.

You should -

- **WEAR HAND PROTECTION** for dangerous work or sports activities

- **OBTAIN PROPER CARE** for minor hand injuries

- Know and follow the **RULES FOR SAFE OPERATION OF MACHINERY**

- **NOT WEAR JEWELLERY** when working with machinery

- **TURN OFF MOTORS** and **SHUT DOWN MACHINES** before attempting repairs

- Handle **SHARP OBJECTS** with care

Which of the following actions should you take to protect your hands from injury?

	Yes	No	
A.	☐	☑	Leave hands uncovered to have a better feeling for the equipment you work with.
B.	☐	☑	Store knives in drawers with sharp edges turned up.
C.	☑	☐	Switch off the power before you clean the blades of a lawn-mower.
D.	☑	☐	Read the operating directions before you use a power saw.
E.	☑	☐	Put on safety gloves when you work with dangerous chemicals or equipment.
F.	☑	☐	Avoid wearing rings or bangles when using mechanical equipment.

11-6

A. No   B. No   C. Yes   D. Yes   E. Yes   F. Yes

An injured hand should be placed **PALM DOWN** in a relaxed position, with the fingers slightly curled over a pad of dressings.

This position is called the **POSITION OF FUNCTION.**

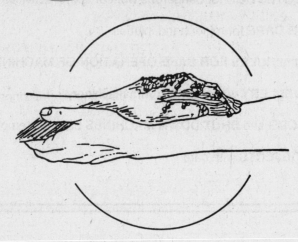

Position of Function

This is usually the most comfortable position for a badly injured hand.

11-8

Which position would ease the pain for a hand that has been caught in the door of a car?

A. ☐   Resting with the palm upwards and the fingers relaxed.

B. ☐   The fingers closed tightly in a fist.

C. ☐   Resting with the fingers turned downwards and supported on a wad of tissues.

D. ☐   Stretched out, with the palm lying on a flat, hard surface.

11-8

C. ☑

11

11-9

A **CRUSHED HAND** is caused by a severe blow to or large force on the hand.

The first aid given for a **CRUSHED HAND** depends on whether or not medical aid is readily available.

When medical aid is **READILY AVAILABLE** you should -

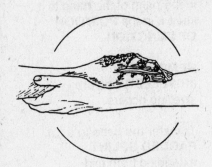

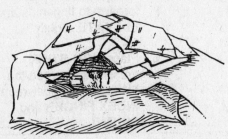

- **STEADY AND SUPPORT** the injured hand while you seat the casualty

- Place a pad of dressings in the **PALM OF THE HAND**

- **REMOVE** any jewellery before swelling occurs

- Place the hand on a firm, soft pad or pillow in the **POSITION OF FUNCTION**

- Cover the injured hand with **CLEAN DRESSINGS**

- Transport the casualty to medical aid **IMMEDIATELY**

11-10

One of your co-workers has crushed his hand in a machine. Medical aid is within walking distance.

What first aid should you give before getting him to medical aid?

A. ☒ Soak the hand in cool water to ease the pain.

B. ☑ Rest the hand on a padded surface with fingers supported and cover the hand with several gauze squares.

C. ☒ Leave the hand uncovered and have the casualty support his arm.

D. ☑ Take off all rings before the fingers become puffy.

11-10

B. ✓   D. ✓

When medical aid is **NOT READILY AVAILABLE**, you should -

1.

2.

3.

4.

5.

1. **STEADY AND SUPPORT** the injured hand

2. Place a pad of dressings in the palm of the hand to keep it in the **POSITION OF FUNCTION**

3. **REMOVE** any **JEWELLERY** before swelling occurs

4. Transfer the hand to a **PADDED SPLINT** extending from mid-forearm to fingertips and **ELEVATE** slightly

5. Place **NON-STICK** dressings between the **FINGERS** and between **INDEX FINGER** and **THUMB**

6. Cover the injured hand with **STERILE DRESSINGS** or a **CLEAN CLOTH**

7. Starting at the fingertips, apply a **ROLLER BANDAGE** to secure the hand to the splint

8. Apply an **ARM SLING**

6.

7.

8.

Transport the casualty to medical aid.

When giving first aid to a casualty with a crushed hand and medical aid is not readily available, you should -

	Choice 1			Choice 2
A. ☐	Grasp the injured hand at the wrist and take off any rings.	OR	A. ☑	Rest the injured hand on your hand and take off any rings.
B. ☑	Support the palm of the hand and fingers with a clean pad of tissues.	OR	B. ☐	Support the hand in a flat position and place dressings between the fingers.
C. ☑	Rest the injured hand on a padded splint before bandaging.	OR	C. ☐	Place the injured hand on a padded splint after bandaging.
D. ☐	Place gauze dressings that will stop the bleeding between the fingers and between index finger and thumb.	OR	D. ☑	Place dressings that will not stick to the wound between the fingers and between index finger and thumb.
E. ☑	Cover the hand with sterile gauze squares.	OR	E. ☐	Cover the wound with many open triangular bandages.
F. ☑	Use a roller bandage to keep the covered hand on the padded splint.	OR	F. ☐	Use a narrow bandage to tie the hand to the padded splint.
G. ☐	Begin applying the roller bandage at the wrist.	OR	G. ☑	Begin applying the roller bandage at the fingers.
H. ☐	Support the splinted hand in a St. John tubular sling.	OR	H. ☑	Support the splinted hand in an arm sling.

A.	2	B.	1	C.	1	D.	2	E.	1	F.	1	G.	2	H.	2

11

A deep **WOUND IN THE PALM OF THE HAND** usually results in severe bleeding.

You should control bleeding from a wound across the palm of the hand (transverse wound) with **DIRECT PRESSURE, ELEVATION** and **REST**.

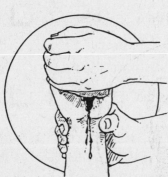

- **MAKE A FIST** and apply pressure to the wound; at the same time, **ELEVATE** the hand

- **SEAT** the casualty

- **PLACE A WAD** of gauze dressings over the wound and close the fingers around the wad to maintain pressure

- **ELEVATE** the hand again to a higher position

11-14

Which two of the following procedures should you use to control bleeding from a deep cut across the palm of a hand?

A. ☑ Close the hand tightly and elevate it while you place the casualty at rest.

B. ☐ Position the hand palm up on a flat surface and cover it with facial tissues.

C. ☐ Cover the hand with a clean dressing and support it in an arm sling.

D. ☐ Fold the fingers to hold a thick pad tightly in the palm as you raise the hand to shoulder level.

11-14

A. ✓   D. ✓

11

When you have controlled the severe bleeding from a wound across the palm of the hand, **APPLY A BANDAGE** to maintain pressure over the dressings -

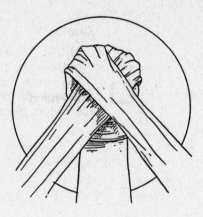

- Bandage the hand in the **CLOSED POSITION**

- Place the mid-point of a **NARROW** bandage on the **INSIDE** of the wrist

- Bring the ends around the **BACK** of the hand

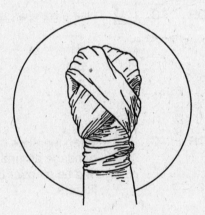

- **CROSS** the ends over the fingers

- Tie off the bandage at the **WRIST**

- Support the bandaged hand and arm in a **ST. JOHN TUBULAR SLING**

11

Which of the following bandaging techniques should you use for a transverse wound in the palm of the hand?

Choice 1   **Choice 2**

A. ☐ Bandage the hand with the fingers straight.   OR   A. ☑ Bandage the hand with the fingers clenched.

B. ☐ Use a roller bandage.   OR   B. ☑ Use a narrow bandage.

C. ☑ Cross the ends of the bandage over the fingers and tie off at the wrist.   OR   C. ☐ Wrap the ends of the bandage around the hand and tie off over the fingers.

D. ☑ Apply a sling that elevates the hand as high as possible.   OR   D. ☐ Apply a sling that elevates the hand slightly.

A. [2]   B. [2]   C. [1]   D. [1]

11

When a wound is **LENGTHWISE** (longitudinal) in the palm of the hand -

- Place dressings **ALONG THE WOUND**
- Fold the **SIDES** of the hand around the wound
- **ELEVATE** the hand and **SEAT** the casualty

When bleeding is under control, **MAINTAIN PRESSURE** by applying a bandage -

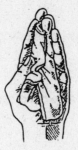 

- Wrap a roller bandage around the folded hand

- Start at the fingers, work to the wrist and back again

- Apply a St. John tubular sling

11-18

How would you bandage a longitudinal wound in the palm of the hand?

A. ☐ Wrap a gauze roller bandage loosely around the flat hand.

B. ☐ Wrap a broad bandage tightly around the hand so that the sides remain folded. Use a sling to maintain elevation.

C. ☐ Wrap a gauze roller bandage around the palm of the hand so that the sides remain folded. Place in the position of function.

D. ☐ Wrap a gauze roller bandage over the entire hand so that the sides remain folded. Use a sling to maintain elevation.

11-18

D. ☑

11-19

Mark each statement true **(T)** or false **(F)**.

A. ☐ Hand injuries may involve wounds, fractures and damage to other tissues.

B. ☐ A hand with a deep wound can still function easily.

C. ☐ Many hand injuries can be prevented by adopting safe practices at work and at home.

D. ☐ The most comfortable position for an injured hand is resting with the fingers curled tightly.

E. ☐ A wound in the palm of the hand does not usually bleed heavily.

F. ☐ A hand can be crushed by a severe blow or a smashing force.

G. ☐ When medical aid is nearby, a casualty with a crushed hand does not require an arm sling.

H. ☐ Because of the complicated structure of the hand, even minor injuries must be considered serious and receive medical attention.

I. ☐ Rings should be left on the fingers of a crushed hand to avoid causing further injury.

11-19

A. T   B. F   C. T   D. F   E. F   F. T   G. T   H. T   I. F

11

For more information on this topic, refer to:
First Aid Safety Oriented, Second Edition, Chapters 2, 13, 14

END OF EXERCISE 11

NOTES

STRUCTURE OF THE EYE

12-1

The **EYE** is the very delicate organ of sight.

To give safe and appropriate care, the First Aider should know the basic structure of the eye.

- **EYEBALL** - Fluid filled globe which is the main part of the eye.

- **CORNEA** - Thin, transparent covering of the front part of the eyeball.

- **EYELIDS** - Movable lids of skin and muscle (upper and lower) which provide protection for the eye.

MOVEMENT OF ONE EYE CAUSES MOVEMENT OF THE OTHER EYE

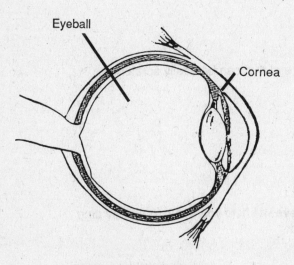

Cross-sectional View

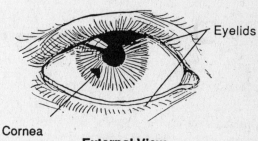

External View

Mark each statement true **(T)** or false **(F)**.

A. ☑ Movement of the eyelids protects the eyeball from the entry of foreign material.

B. ☒ The eyeball is a hard, solid structure resistant to injury.

C. ☒ Each eye moves independently from the other.

D. ☑ The cornea is the outer layer of the eye that can be easily scratched.

E. ☑ Knowing the basic structure of the eye will help you to avoid aggravating existing injuries when giving first aid.

A. **T**   B. **F**   C. **F**   D. **T**   E. **T**

12

12-3

Any injury to the eye may result in **IMPAIRED VISION** or **BLINDNESS**.

When an eye is injured, a person closes his eyes to reduce pain.

This person needs your help **IMMEDIATELY**.

> **YOUR QUICK RESPONSE AND CORRECT
> FIRST AID CAN PREVENT AN EYE INJURY
> FROM CAUSING PERMANENT DAMAGE**

12-4

Mark each statement true **(T)** or false **(F)**.

A. ☒ A person with an eye injury tries to relieve the discomfort by holding the eye open.

B. ☐ Any eye injury may cause complete loss of sight.

C. ☑ A First Aider's fast action following an eye injury may save a casualty many hours of suffering.

D. ☑ Loss of vision caused by an injury can often be avoided by prompt first aid.

12-4

A. | F | B. | T | C. | T | D. | T |

12-5

EYE PROTECTION helps to prevent eye injuries.

You should -

- Wear safety glasses or a face shield when you work with tools or dangerous chemicals

- Wear eye protection when you take part in sports such as squash, racquetball or hockey

- Wear dark glasses in sunlight or when the sun reflects from snow or water

- Avoid looking into bright lights such as an arc welding flash or an eclipse of the sun

12-6

Which of the following illustrations show practices that would help to prevent eye injuries?

A.

B.

C.

D.

E.

12-6

A. ✓   D. ✓   E. ✓

12-7

Particles may enter the eye causing pain, redness and watering of the eye.

TELL THE PERSON TO AVOID RUBBING THE EYE

If tears do not wash away a small loose particle and it **CAN BE SEEN**, you should try to remove it with the **MOIST CORNER** of a clean facial tissue or cloth.

If the particle is causing pain **UNDER THE UPPER LID,** instruct the person to **PULL THE UPPER LID DOWN OVER THE LOWER LID.**

The eyelashes on the lower lid may brush away the particle.

12-8

Which of the following techniques can be used to remove a small piece of loose dirt floating in the eye?

A. ☐   Tell the person to pull the top eyelid over the bottom one, if the speck of dirt is under the top lid.

B. ☐   Use the damp end of a clean handkerchief to lift off the dirt, if it is visible.

C. ☐   Tell the person to close his eye and slide the upper lid back and forth.

D. ☑   Allow the free flowing natural fluids in the eye to wash it away.

12-8

A. ☑   B. ☑   D. ☑

12

12-9

If a particle in the eye cannot be seen or removed immediately, it may be necessary to **EXAMINE** the eye.

You should -

- Have the casualty sit **FACING A GOOD LIGHT**

- **WASH YOUR HANDS**

- Spread the eyelids apart with your thumb and index finger

- Look for the particle

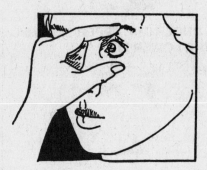

12-10

A small grain of sand has entered a person's eye. The tears have not washed it away and it is not immediately visible on the eyeball.

Which of the following should you do?

Yes	No	
A. ☒	☐	Seat the casualty and shine a bright light at the eye.
B. ☐	☑	Seat the casualty with his back to a bright lamp to keep the light out of his eyes.
C. ☑	☐	Ensure that your hands are clean.
D. ☒	☐	Hold the eyelids away from the eyeball and examine the eye.

12-10   A. Yes   B. No   C. Yes   D. Yes

12

If your first examination does not locate the particle in the eye, you should **EXAMINE UNDER THE EYELIDS.**

To examine **UNDER THE UPPER EYELID**, you should -

- Position yourself beside the seated casualty and ask him to **LOOK DOWN**

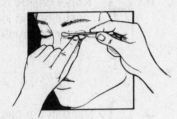

- Place a cotton-tipped applicator stick **ACROSS THE CLOSED UPPER EYELID**

- **GRASP** the upper eyelashes between thumb and index finger

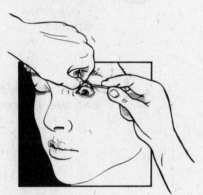

- **DRAW** the lid out and then up and **OVER** the applicator stick and roll the applicator back

If the particle is **VISIBLE** -

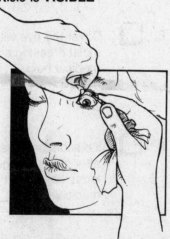

- **REMOVE** it with the moist corner of a clean facial tissue or cloth

- **IF PAIN LASTS** after removal, obtain medical aid

Select the correct techniques for examining under the upper eyelid.

	Choice 1			**Choice 2**
A. ☐	Lay the casualty down.	OR	A. ☑	Ask the casualty to sit down.
B. ☑	Stand near the casualty's shoulder on the injured side.	OR	B. ☐	Kneel beside the casualty and look up under the eyelid.
C. ☐	Instruct the casualty to roll his eyeball upward.	OR	C. ☑	Instruct the casualty to roll his eyeball downward.
D. ☑	Roll the upper eyelid back to expose the underside of the lid.	OR	D. ☐	Pull the upper eyelid down over the lower lid.

If you can see the loose object -

E. ☑	Try to lift it out with the moistened edge of a clean tissue.	OR	E. ☐	Cover the eye with a moist dressing and get medical help.
F. ☐	If discomfort persists after lifting out the loose object, place cool compresses over the eye.	OR	F. ☑	If discomfort persists after lifting out the loose object, get medical help.

To examine under the **LOWER EYELID**, you should -

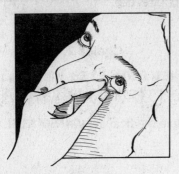

- Position yourself facing the seated person

- Draw the lower eyelid **DOWNWARDS** and **AWAY** from the eyeball

- Ask the person to **LOOK UP**

If the particle is **VISIBLE** -

- **REMOVE** it with the moist corner of a clean facial tissue or cloth

- **IF PAIN PERSISTS** after removal, obtain medical aid

12-14

Select the correct techniques for examining under the lower eyelid.

	Choice 1			**Choice 2**
A. ☑	Tell the person to sit down.	**OR**	A. ☐	Tell the person to lie down.
B. ☐	Stand behind the person.	**OR**	B. ☑	Stand in front of the person.
C. ☑	Pull the lower eyelid down and out.	**OR**	C. ☐	Pull the lower eyelid over the upper eyelid.
D. ☑	Tell the person to roll the eyeball up.	**OR**	D. ☐	Tell the person to roll the eyeball down.

12-14

A. [1]   B. [2]   C. [1]   D. [1]

12

If a particle does **NOT** become visible during your examination and the irritation persists, **DO NOT CONTINUE YOUR ATTEMPTS**.

You should -

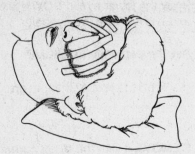

- **COVER BOTH EYES** with soft pads of cotton wool and tape them in place

- Obtain medical aid **IMMEDIATELY**

You have been unsuccessful in locating a particle under either the upper or lower eyelid of the left eye.

What should you do next?

A. ☐ Repeat the examination.

B. ☑ Secure soft dressings over both eyes and take the casualty to the nearest medical centre.

C. ☐ Tell the casualty to pull his left upper lid down over the lower lid.

D. ☐ Cover only the left eye and take the casualty to the nearest medical facility.

12-16

B. ☑

12

When a foreign object is **STUCK** to the **CORNEA, EMBEDDED** in the eyeball or in the soft tissue near the eye -

> **DO NOT ATTEMPT TO REMOVE IT**

You should keep the casualty **LYING DOWN** and instruct him **NOT** to touch or rub the eye.

Use one of the following bandaging techniques depending on the size of the foreign object -

PARTICLE		LARGE FOREIGN OBJECT

PARTICLE

- Lay the casualty down

- **COVER** the **INJURED EYE** with a soft pad of cotton wool

- Tape it **LIGHTLY** in place (Do not put pressure on the eyeball.)

- **COVER** the **UNINJURED EYE** to reduce movement of both eyes

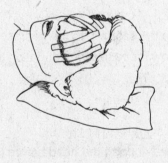

OR

LARGE FOREIGN OBJECT

- Lay the casualty down

- Place the **DRESSING** around the object

- Tape a **PAPER CUP** or **CONE** over the object to prevent movement

- Place a dressing over the **UNINJURED EYE** and apply a **NARROW BANDAGE**

In both cases, immobilize the head and transport the casualty on a stretcher to medical aid.

Classify each of the following actions as a **Do** or **Do Not** when giving first aid for an embedded object in the eye.

	Do	Do Not	
A.	☐	☑	Use a cotton applicator to lift out a particle embedded in the eyeball.
B.	☐	☑	Place the casualty in a sitting position before you begin bandaging.
C.	☑	☐	Secure a soft dressing loosely over the eye when there is a tiny piece of metal embedded in the eyeball.
D.	☑	☐	Cut a hole in a dressing before applying it over a 3 cm splinter protruding from an eyeball.
E.	☑	☐	Secure a cuplike covering over an embedded object when it is protruding from an eyeball.
F.	☐	☑	Keep the uninjured eye open to allow for easier transportation to medical aid.
G.	☑	☐	Place the casualty on a stretcher and support the head before taking him to medical aid.

A. Do Not   B. Do Not   C. Do   D. Do   E. Do   F. Do Not   G. Do

12

12-19

A **CONTUSION** (bruise) to the soft tissue around an eye is usually the result of a blow from a blunt object.

The bruise may not appear immediately but there may be underlying damage.

You should -

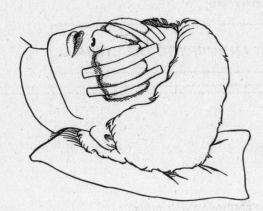

- Lay the casualty down

- Cover the **INJURED EYE** with a soft pad of cotton wool to avoid pressure on the eyeball

- Cover the **UNINJURED EYE** to prevent movement

- Transport the casualty on a stretcher with his head immobilized to **MEDICAL AID**

12-20

Mark each statement true **(T)** or false **(F)**.

A. ☑ Hitting the area around the eye with the end of a hockey stick may cause a bruise.

B. ☑ A bruise around the eye involves bleeding into the tissues under the skin and requires medical attention.

C. ☒ A bruised eye should be bandaged tightly to stop internal bleeding.

D. ☒ When one eye is bruised, the other eye should be left uncovered to give the casualty a feeling of security.

12-20

A. T   B. T   C. F   D. F

An **OPEN WOUND** in the eyelids or the soft tissue around the eye may bleed profusely. To give first aid -

- Close the eyelid

- Use a soft pad of cotton wool to control bleeding. **NEVER** apply pressure to the eyeball

- Secure lightly in place, treat as for a contusion (bruise)

> **IF THE EYELID IS INJURED, SUSPECT AN INJURY TO THE EYEBALL**

Check (✓) the correct statements.

A. ☑ Heavy bleeding beside the eye can be controlled with pressure.

B. ☒ A cut eyelid should be pinched strongly between the thumb and index finger to control bleeding.

C. ☒ When an eyelid is torn, little blood appears.

D. ☑ If an eyelid is bleeding, the eyeball may also be damaged.

E. ☑ When heavy bleeding from a wound on the eyelid is stopped, leave the dressings in place and bandage both eyes.

A. ✓   D. ✓   E. ✓

12

12-23

A **WOUND TO THE EYEBALL** is very serious.

DO NOT APPLY PRESSURE

You should -

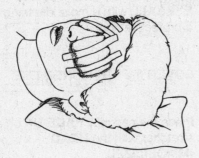

- Lay the casualty down

- Cover the **INJURED** eye lightly with a **SOFT PAD** of cotton wool and tape it in place

- Cover the **UNINJURED** eye to reduce eye movement

- Place the casualty on a stretcher with a **SUPPORT** on each side of the head

- Transport quickly to **MEDICAL AID**

12-24

A boy has fallen on a sharp object resulting in a cut to the left eyeball.

An ambulance has been called.

What should you do while awaiting medical aid?

A. ☐ Hold clean dressings tightly over the left eye.

B. ☐ Place the boy at rest and hold the eyelids of the left eye open.

C. ☑ Lay the boy down and secure soft dressings loosely over both eyes.

D. ☐ Sit the boy down and tape soft dressings tightly across both eyes.

12-24

C. ☑

12-25

Severe injury may force the eyeball out of the socket (extruded eyeball).

DO NOT PLACE THE EYEBALL BACK INTO THE SOCKET

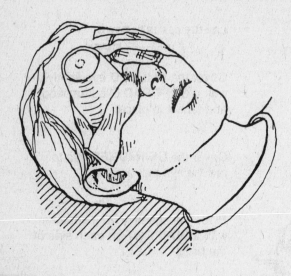

- Gently **COVER THE INJURED EYEBALL** with a moist dressing and a protective cone

- **COVER** the **UNINJURED EYE**

- Place the casualty **FACE-UP** on a stretcher with the **HEAD IMMOBILIZED**

- Transport with care to **MEDICAL AID**

12-26

A football player has an extruded eyeball. Before placing the casualty on a stretcher, which first aid procedures should you follow?

A. ☐ Support the eyeball with a firmly applied dressing and bandage.

B. ☑ Apply a damp dressing loosely over the extruded eyeball and cover with a paper cup.

C. ☑ Secure a gauze square over the other eye.

D. ☐ Place the casualty on a stretcher with the face turned toward the injured eye.

12-26

B. ☑   C. ☑

12

CHEMICALS in the eyes cause **SERIOUS BURNS** in a very short time.

YOU MUST ACT QUICKLY

When a **LIQUID CHEMICAL** enters both eyes, you should -

- **FLUSH** the eyes **IMMEDIATELY** with running water, keeping the eyes **OPEN**

When only one eye is affected -

- **COVER** the **UNINJURED EYE**

- **FLUSH AWAY** from the uninjured eye to avoid contamination

 OR  OR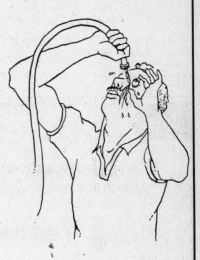

Emergency Eye Washes

- **CONTINUE** flushing for **AT LEAST 10 MINUTES**

- **COVER BOTH EYES** with dressings

- Obtain **MEDICAL AID** as soon as possible

One of your co-workers has spilled corrosive acid into his eyes. He is in pain and holding both eyes closed.

Select from the four choices the correct answer for questions A and B and write the numbers in the space provided.

A. Which of the following actions should you take immediately?

1. Cover his eyes with dressings and take him to medical aid.

2. Lead the casualty to a fountain, hold his eyes open and flush with water for 15 minutes.

3. Keep his eyes open and let the tears flush out the chemicals.

4. Place him on his back and pour water into his eyes for 5 minutes.

B. What should you do following your initial actions?

1. Apply moist pads to the eyes and change them as they become warm.

2. Keep both eyes uncovered and take the casualty to medical aid quickly.

3. Lay the casualty down in a darkened room for at least one hour.

4. Apply gauze squares to the eyes and take the casualty to medical aid.

If the chemical that enters the eye is a **DRY POWDER**, you should -

- **BRUSH** the chemical from around the eye with a clean, dry cloth

- **FLUSH** with water for **AT LEAST 10 MINUTES**

- **COVER BOTH EYES** with dressings

- Obtain **MEDICAL AID**

12-30

Corrosive lime powder has blown into a person's eyes.

Number the following first aid steps in the correct order of performance.

A. ☐ 2 Guide the person to an eyewash fountain and wash his eyes for approximately 12 minutes.

B. ☐ 4 Get the casualty to qualified help.

C. ☐ 1 Quickly remove any loose powder from the face.

D. ☐ 3 Tape gauze squares over both eyes.

| 12-30 | A. 2 | B. 4 | C. 1 | D. 3 |

12-31

BURNS to the eye may be caused by INTENSE LIGHT such as direct or reflected sunlight, an arc welder's flash, infrared rays or laser beams.

When a casualty complains of burning in the eyes after exposure to bright, intense light, you should -

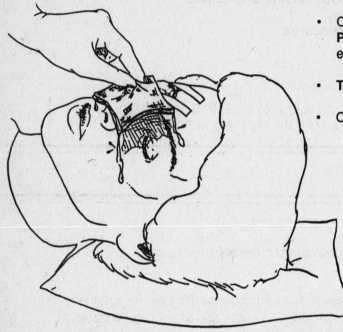

- Cover the eyes with THICK MOIST PADS to keep out light and cool the eyes

- TAPE the pads in place

- Obtain MEDICAL AID

PAIN MAY NOT OCCUR IMMEDIATELY

12-32

A welder suffers light burns to his eyes when his face shield is damaged.

What first aid should you give?

A. ☐ Apply dry sterile dressings and take the casualty to medical aid.

B. ☐ Place the casualty at rest in a cool darkened room until the pain lessens.

C. ☐ Keep the eyes uncovered and allow the tears to cool them.

D. ☑ Secure cold compresses to the eyes and take the casualty to medical aid.

12-32

D. ☑

12

12-33

Extreme high temperatures cause the eyes to close. This protects the eyeballs. In cases of fire, the eyelids may be burned.

To give first aid for **BURNED EYELIDS** -

- **COVER** the eyelids with **THICK, COOL, MOIST DRESSINGS**

- **TRANSPORT IMMEDIATELY** to medical aid

> **REMEMBER - WHEN THERE IS AN INJURY TO AN EYELID,
> THE EYEBALL MAY BE INJURED ALSO**

12-34

Which statements are correct?

A. ☐ Burns to the eyelids are not considered serious and do not require medical treatment.

B. ☑ First aid for burned eyelids is limited to the application of many layered dressings which have been soaked in cold water.

C. ☐ Nature protects the eyeballs from heat by cooling them with tears.

D. ☑ The application of many layered, cool, damp dressings to burned eyelids reduces the skin temperature and relieves pain.

12-34

B. D. ✓

12

12-35

Mark each statement true (T) or false (F).

A. ☑ The eye is delicate and any injury can result in permanent damage.

B. ☑ Eye injuries are less frequent when eye protection is worn.

C. ☑ Floating particles visible in the eye can be removed with the moist corner of a clean facial tissue.

D. ☑ Ensure that your hands are clean before you examine an eye.

E. ☑ You should make no attempt to remove an object that is embedded in or around the eye.

F. ☒ If a particle in the eye cannot be found by examining the eye, the examination should be repeated until successful.

G. ☐ A casualty with an object embedded in the soft tissues around the eye should be transported to medical aid on a stretcher with both eyes bandaged and the head supported.

H. ☑ You should make no attempt to remove a particle that is stuck to the eyeball.

I. ☒ Burned eyelids should be covered with dry dressings, cones and bandages.

12-35

A. T   B. T   C. T   D. T   E. T   F. F   G. T   H. T   I. F

12

For further information on this topic, refer to: *First Aid Safety Oriented*, Second Edition, Chapter 18

END OF EXERCISE 12

12

The content of this Module is based on the **PRINCIPLES OF EMERGENCY SCENE MANAGEMENT** covered in Exercise 1 and applied to a multiple injury situation.

PRIORITY ACTION APPROACH

13-1

PROMPT ACTION is vital at the scene of a multiple injury emergency.

As a First Aider you must **act quickly** and **systematically** to perform **Priority Action Approach (PAA)** -

- **TAKE CHARGE**

- **CALL FOR HELP TO ATTRACT BYSTANDERS**

- **ASSESS THE HAZARDS**

- **MAKE THE AREA SAFE FOR YOURSELF AND OTHERS**

- **IDENTIFY YOURSELF AS A FIRST AIDER AND OFFER HELP**

- **ASSESS THE CASUALTY FOR LIFE-THREATENING CONDITIONS**

- **GIVE FIRST AID FOR LIFE-THREATENING CONDITIONS**

- **SEND FOR HELP**

Organize bystanders to   - help in making the area safe
                                    - ensure that all casualties have been found
                                    - call ambulance, police, hydro personnel
                                    - assist with first aid

Following Priority Action Approach -

- Perform secondary examinations and give required first aid

- Monitor the conditions of the casualties

You are the first to arrive at the scene of a serious one-vehicle bus accident. The driver seems to be unhurt but the passengers need help. The bus is perched precariously on the edge of a sharp incline. What would you do?

Choice 1		**Choice 2**
A. ☐ Tell the driver you have first aid training and will take charge.	OR	A. ☐ Tell the driver to take charge as he is responsible for his passengers.
B. ☐ Deal with any life-threatening conditions on the bus and instruct the driver to do the same.	OR	B. ☐ Enlist the driver's help in removing the passengers from the bus and deal with any life-threatening conditions.
C. ☐ Assume that all the casualties are lying in the bus.	OR	C. ☐ Check outside the bus to account for all casualties.
D. ☐ Do a secondary assessment of each casualty when all passengers are out of the bus.	OR	D. ☐ Do a secondary assessment only of the casualties with life-threatening conditions when all passengers are out of the bus.

13-3

When there is more than one injury or casualty, **FOCUS YOUR ATTENTION QUICKLY ON SIGNS** of the three conditions which are a **THREAT TO LIFE** and give first aid **IMMEDIATELY** in this order -

1. STOPPED BREATHING

2. SEVERE BLEEDING

3. UNCONSCIOUSNESS

> **EACH CASUALTY SHOULD BE EXAMINED AND GIVEN FIRST AID FOR THE THREE LIFE-THREATENING CONDITIONS BEFORE ANY OTHER INJURIES ARE CARED FOR**

13-4

An industrial explosion has caused serious injuries to four workers. All are conscious. One worker is bleeding profusely. Another worker has painful burns. The third is pale, sweating and showing signs of shock and the fourth is walking around aimlessly.

Which casualty would you attend to first?

A. ☐   The worker who is burnt.

B. ☐   The worker who is bleeding.

C. ☐   The worker who may go into shock.

D. ☐   The worker who is confused.

13-4

B. ☑

13

13-5

When you are caring for one or more casualties, remember that -

- **ASSIGNED PRIORITIES FOR GIVING FIRST AID SHOULD BE REVIEWED FREQUENTLY AND CHANGED IF ANY OF THE CASUALTIES' CONDITIONS REQUIRE MORE URGENT CARE**

For example:

You are giving first aid to a conscious casualty with a severely bleeding wound on the leg. Suddenly another casualty starts gasping for air and stops breathing.

You would show the bleeding casualty how to maintain pressure on his wound and immediately begin artificial respiration on the casualty who stopped breathing.

13-6

The priority in which to give first aid to several casualties at the scene of an accident or illness, should be:

A. ☐ Established during the primary examination and remain unchanged.

B. ☐ Reassessed during the secondary examination and based on minor injuries.

C. ☐ Reassessed often and based on the most immediate need for help.

D. ☐ Established by medical aid and followed accordingly.

13-6

C. ☑

13

After immediate first aid is given, the casualties must be **MAINTAINED** in the best possible condition until hand-over to medical aid.

- **CALL MEDICAL AID** if someone else has not already done so

- **MONITOR** the casualties' conditions for changes and give first aid as required

- **DO NOT MOVE** the casualties, except for reasons of safety

- **PROTECT** and **SHELTER** the casualties to the best of your ability

- **ASSIST** in the evacuation by ambulance if requested

- **ENSURE** that the casualties not requiring medical aid are placed in the care of friends or relatives

When handing over casualties to more qualified persons, you should be prepared to **GIVE A FULL REPORT** on the condition of each one and what first aid has been given while waiting for medical aid.

To keep the casualties in the best possible condition until medical aid arrives, which of the actions listed below should you take?

A. ☐ Make certain that medical assistance is not delayed.

B. ☐ Line the casualties up to facilitate removal by medical personnel.

C. ☐ Keep the casualties safe, warm and as comfortable as possible.

D. ☐ Observe the casualties' conditions for any changes and give appropriate first aid.

E. ☐ Move all casualties closely together to facilitate monitoring of their conditions.

F. ☐ Encourage casualties who seem recovered to leave on their own to seek medical aid.

G. ☐ Give to medical personnel a detailed account of each casualty's injury or illness and the care provided.

13-9

Mark each statement true **(T)** or false **(F)**.

A. ☐   When dealing with multiple casualties, examine one casualty completely and give first aid for all injuries before moving on to the next casualty.

B. ☐   In an emergency situation, one person should take charge to avoid confusion.

C. ☐   An unconscious, breathing casualty should be given first aid before one who is bleeding heavily but is still conscious.

D. ☐   Assigned priorities for giving first aid should be reassessed often and changed if any of the casualties' conditions requires more urgent care.

E. ☐   Part of first aid is to stay with the casualty and keep him in the best possible condition until medical help arrives.

F. ☐   The order of the steps of Priority Action Approach should be changed according to the circumstances of the emergency situation.

G. ☐   A head-to-toe examination should be performed before any first aid is given.

13-9

| A. F | B. T | C. F | D. T | E. T | F. T | G. F |

13

For more information on this topic, refer to: *First Aid Safety Oriented*, Second Edition, Chapter 1

END OF EXERCISE 13

THERE IS NO WORKBOOK EXERCISE 14

For information on this topic, refer to: *First Aid Safety Oriented*, Second Edition, Chapter 8

NOTES

INTRODUCTION TO ABDOMINAL INJURIES

15-1

The **ABDOMEN** is the body area below the chest.

The **ABDOMINAL CAVITY** is the space between the **DIAPHRAGM** and the lower part of the **PELVIS**. It contains the major organs of digestion and excretion -

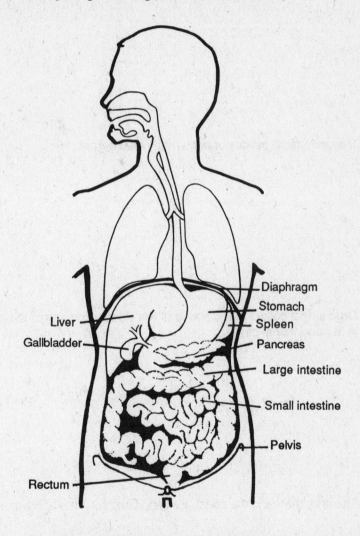

Abdominal Cavity and its Contents

The individual organs of the abdominal cavity are indicated for general information and will not be questioned.

15

Mark each statement true **(T)** or false **(F)**.

A. ☐ All organs of digestion and excretion are found in the upper abdominal cavity.

B. ☐ The abdominal cavity contains many vital organs.

C. ☐ Organs that collect and dispose of the waste products of the body are located in the abdominal cavity.

D. ☐ The abdomen and the chest are separated by the diaphragm.

15-3

An injury to the **ABDOMEN** may be **CLOSED** or **OPEN**.

CLOSED INJURIES are those in which the abdomen is damaged by a severe blow but the skin remains intact.

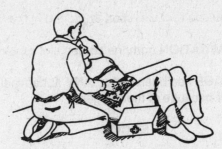

OPEN INJURIES are those in which a foreign body has entered the abdomen through the abdominal wall and the skin has been broken.

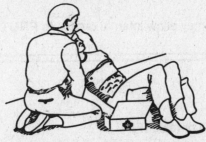

Closed and open injuries to the abdomen may result in injuries to the internal organs.

15-4

Mark each statement true **(T)** or false **(F)**.

A. ☐ An abdominal injury without obvious bleeding is of little concern to the First Aider.

B. ☐ A gunshot wound of the abdomen is an open wound.

C. ☐ An open or closed wound to the abdomen may cause damage to the underlying tissues.

D. ☐ A deep open wound to the abdomen will usually cause external as well as internal bleeding.

15-4

A. F   B. T   C. T   D. T

15

It is difficult to determine the **EXTENT OF DAMAGE** caused by an abdominal injury.

There may be -

- **SEVERE INTERNAL BLEEDING** from damaged organs

and

- **CONTAMINATION** from the contents of ruptured organs

Assume that **MAJOR DAMAGE** has been done. **ANY** abdominal wound should be treated as a **SERIOUS CONDITION** because of the danger of -

- **SHOCK**

and

- **INFECTION**

A gaping abdominal wound may allow internal organs to **PROTRUDE** outside the body.

Mark each statement true **(T)** or false **(F)**.

A. ☐ Following a heavy blow to the abdomen, serious injury to underlying organs may not be obvious.

B. ☐ Any wound to the abdomen must be considered as life-threatening.

C. ☐ Bleeding from a closed abdominal wound can be seen immediately.

D. ☐ Spillage of the ingredients of abdominal organs may result in a serious infection.

E. ☐ When the abdominal wall is opened by an injury, internal tissues may come out of the body cavity.

15-6   A. T   B. T   C. F   D. T   E. T

15

To give first aid for an **OPEN** abdominal wound -

- **OBTAIN MEDICAL AID IMMEDIATELY**

- **PREVENT THE WOUND FROM OPENING WIDER;** usually by positioning the casualty with head and shoulders slightly raised and supported; and knees bent and supported

- **DO NOT** give anything by mouth

ORGANS NOT PROTRUDING	ORGANS PROTRUDING

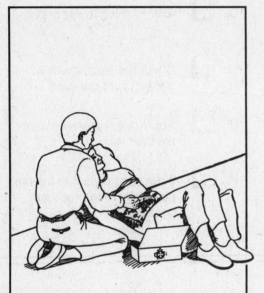 OR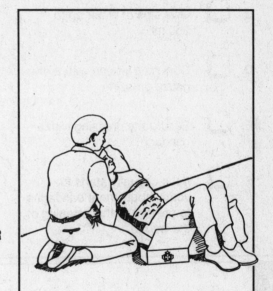

ORGANS NOT PROTRUDING

- Apply a **DRY DRESSING**

- Bandage **FIRMLY** over the dressing

ORGANS PROTRUDING

- Do **NOT REPLACE ORGANS**

- Apply a **LARGE, MOIST DRESSING**

- Bandage **LOOSELY** over the dressing

If the casualty begins to cough **FORCEFULLY** or to **VOMIT**, apply **TWO BROAD BANDAGES** to support the abdomen. Bandages may have to be adjusted, for the casualty's comfort. Be alert and ready to act.

Choose the correct first aid procedures from the choices below for a casualty with an open abdominal wound when organs are **NOT PROTRUDING**.

	Choice 1			Choice 2
A. ☐	Send immediately for medical help.	**OR**	A. ☐	Give first aid and then send for medical aid.
B. ☐	Place the casualty in the recovery position with a support under his abdomen.	**OR**	B. ☐	Position the casualty so that the wound remains closed.
C. ☐	Give sips of water up to 250 ml.	**OR**	C. ☐	Give nothing to eat or drink.
D. ☐	Cover the wound with a dry gauze dressing.	**OR**	D. ☐	Cover the wound with a damp gauze dressing.
E. ☐	Secure the dressing with a bandage.	**OR**	E. ☐	Apply direct pressure over the dressing.
F. ☐	If the casualty starts to vomit, apply more bandages to prevent further opening of the wound.	**OR**	F. ☐	If the casualty starts to vomit, place him in the recovery position.

When organs are **PROTRUDING** through a wound in the abdomen, you should -

	Choice 1			Choice 2
A. ☐	Gently push the organs back.	**OR**	A. ☐	Make no attempt to push the organs back.
B. ☐	Cover the wound with a clean, damp cloth and bandage lightly.	**OR**	B. ☐	Cover the wound with a clean, dry cloth and bandage tightly.

15-8 A. 1 B. 2 C. 2 D. 1 E. 1 F. 1

15-9 A. 2 B. 1

15

15-10

The Pelvis

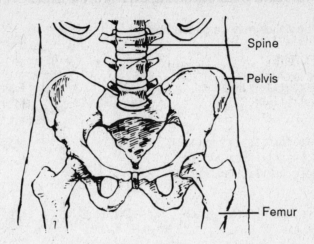

Spine

Pelvis

Femur

The **PELVIS** is a large, thick ring of bones which is attached to the lower part of the spine.

The upper end of the thigh bones joins the pelvis at the hip joints.

Important functions of the **PELVIS** are -

- To **SUPPORT** the organs of the lower abdomen

  and

- To **PROTECT** these organs

15-11

Mark each statement true (**T**) or false (**F**).

A. ☐ The pelvis is the bony structure adjoining the tail of the backbone.

B. ☐ The pelvis is made up of two long, flat bones which are fused together.

C. ☐ The pelvic bones help to prevent injury to the soft tissues that they enclose.

D. ☐ The legs are connected to the pelvis at the hips.

15-11

A. T   B. F   C. T   D. T

15

15-12

A **PELVIC FRACTURE** is a break or crack in any of the bones of the pelvis.

A fracture of the pelvis may be caused by -

• **DIRECT FORCE**
- the pelvis is crushed
  by heavy impact

OR

• **INDIRECT FORCE**
- force is applied to the pelvis
  through the leg and hip joint

Even a simple fall on the pelvic area can result in a fracture, especially in the elderly.

15-13

Mark each statement true (**T**) or false (**F**).

A. ☐   To suffer a broken pelvis, a person must receive a blow right on one of the pelvic bones.

B. ☐   The pelvis may be broken in a car accident when the knees strike the dashboard with great force.

C. ☐   The pelvis is a strong, thick structure which is rarely injured in people over 60 years of age.

D. ☐   A construction worker who has fallen from a scaffold and landed on his feet may have injured his pelvis.

15-13

A. F   B. T   C. F   D. T

15

Fracture of the pelvis often results in damage to the **BLADDER** leading to serious infection.

If the pelvis has been fractured, the following signs and symptoms may be present -

SIGNS

You may observe:

- Signs of shock
- Inability to stand or walk
- Inability to urinate
  or
- Bloody urine
- Bruising in the pelvic area

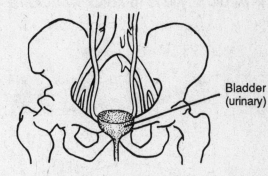

Bladder (urinary)

The Pelvis

SYMPTOMS

The casualty may complain of:

- Sharp pain in the pelvic area
- Pain in the lower back
- Increased pain on movement

15-15

Check (✓) the conditions which may indicate a pelvic fracture.

A. ☐ Discomfort around the hips.

B. ☐ The passing of pinkish urine.

C. ☐ Pallor, sweating and a rapid pulse.

D. ☐ Fracture of the thighs.

E. ☐ Unable to move around.

15-15

A. ☑   B. ☑   C. ☑   E. ☑

A pelvic fracture should be treated as a **SERIOUS CONDITION**.

The first aid to be given depends on whether -

- Medical aid is **READILY AVAILABLE**

OR

- Medical aid will be **DELAYED**

IF MEDICAL AID IS READILY AVAILABLE -

- **POSITION THE CASUALTY COMFORTABLY** (usually flat on his back)

- If the casualty wishes to bend his knees, place a support under them

- **PLACE PADDING BETWEEN THE ANKLES**

- **IMMOBILIZE THE FEET** with a figure-8 bandage

- **SUPPORT** each side of the pelvis with heavy objects

DO NOT GIVE ANYTHING BY MOUTH

The history, signs and symptoms indicate that a casualty has fractured his pelvis. Medical aid has been summoned and will arrive soon.

What should you do in the meantime?

Choice 1		**Choice 2**
A. ☐ Place him in the recovery position.	OR	A. ☐ Place him face-up on a level surface.
B. ☐ Place pillows under his knees if he wants to bend them.	OR	B. ☐ Insist that he keeps his legs straight.
C. ☐ Place a splint between his legs and immobilize with padding and bandages.	OR	C. ☐ Place soft material between the ankles and tie a narrow bandage around the ankles and feet.
D. ☐ Encourage him to drink water to help him urinate.	OR	D. ☐ Give him nothing to eat or drink.
E. ☐ Position a sandbag beside each hip.	OR	E. ☐ Position a sandbag beside each knee.

A. 2   B. 1   C. 2   D. 2   E. 1

15

A casualty with a suspected pelvic fracture will require **MORE SUPPORT** when -

- Medical aid will be **DELAYED**

- **A LONG OR ROUGH JOURNEY** to medical aid is necessary

To give first aid in this situation -

- Place **SOFT PADDING** between knees and ankles

- Tie a figure-8 bandage around **ANKLES AND FEET**

- Apply 2 **BROAD OVERLAPPING BANDAGES** around the pelvis with the wide parts on the injured side

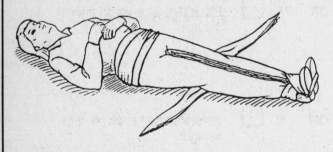

- Apply a **BROAD BANDAGE** around the knees

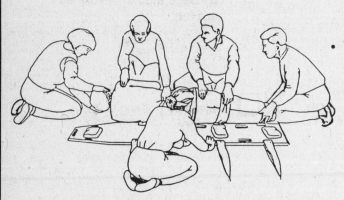

- **LOGROLL** the casualty onto a long spine board with a minimum of four rescuers; the casualty being rolled toward the First Aiders and the uninjured side

- **SUPPORT EACH SIDE** of the pelvis with a suitable heavy object and **COVER** the casualty

- **TRANSPORT** with a minimum of four bearers

If the casualty complains of discomfort, **LOOSEN** or **REMOVE** bandages around the pelvis **IMMEDIATELY**.

Choose the correct first aid procedures to be used for a casualty with a pelvic fracture who must be transported a long distance over rough terrain.

Choice 1		**Choice 2**
A. ☐ Place a splint between the legs before tying them together.	**OR**	A. ☐ Put towels between knees and ankles before tying the legs together.
B. ☐ Place bandages around the ankles, pelvis and knees.	**OR**	B. ☐ Place bandages around the chest, pelvis and knees.
C. ☐ Apply the widest part of the pelvic bandages to the injured side for extra support.	**OR**	C. ☐ Tie off the pelvic bandages on the injured side for extra support.
D. ☐ If bandages at the pelvis cause more pain, relieve the pain by tying them more tightly.	**OR**	D. ☐ If bandages at the pelvis cause more pain, relieve the pain by untying them immediately.
E. ☐ Logroll the casualty with five bearers onto a spine board.	**OR**	E. ☐ Lift the casualty with two bearers onto a spine board.
F ☐ Position a sandbag beside each hip.	**OR**	F. ☐ Position a sandbag beside each knee.
G. ☐ Transport using two rescuers for easier coordination of procedures.	**OR**	G. ☐ Transport using six rescuers to keep the board as level as possible.

15-19   A. 2   B. 1   C. 1   D. 2   E. 1   F. 1   G. 2

15

15-20

A **CRUSH INJURY** occurs when any part of the body is compressed by **EXTREME WEIGHT**, e.g. from machinery, sand.

CRUSH INJURIES may cause extensive damage to bones and soft tissues including -

- Wounds
- Fractures
- Internal bleeding (rupture of internal organs)

and may be complicated by -

- Infection (spillage of contents from abdominal organs)
- Severe shock

Because of the possible extent of internal injuries, **MEDICAL AID** must be obtained **IMMEDIATELY.**

In the meantime -

- Give nothing by mouth
- Combat shock
- Handle the casualty gently to avoid complicating injuries

AVOID MOVING THE CASUALTY IF AT ALL POSSIBLE

15-21

Check (✓) the correct answers.

A casualty who has been pinned under an automobile in the area of his abdomen may be suffering from -

A. ☐ Serious injuries to the pelvis and underlying organs.

B. ☐ Bleeding into the abdominal cavity and contamination leading to serious infection.

Before medical aid arrives -

C. ☐ Immediately free the casualty and place him in the most comfortable position.

D. ☐ Prevent movement and give first aid to minimize discomfort.

15-21

A. ✓   B. ✓   D. ✓

15

15-22

Mark each statement true (T) or false (F).

A. ☐ A blow to the abdomen may cause severe injuries without any visible signs of bleeding.

B. ☐ A heavy weight falling on the hips could fracture the pelvis and cause damage to internal organs.

C. ☐ A deep wound to the abdominal wall may allow organs to protrude through the opening.

D. ☐ Organs protruding from an abdominal wound should be replaced immediately before cooling occurs.

E. ☐ Rupture of the bladder can lead to contamination and serious infection.

F. ☐ For a casualty with severe crush injuries, first aid to combat shock must be started immediately to keep it from getting worse.

G. ☐ A casualty with a pelvic fracture seldom shows signs of shock.

H. ☐ A crush injury can result in massive internal injuries and severe shock.

15-22   A. T   B. T   C. T   D. F   E. T   F. T   G. F   H. T

15

For further information on this topic, refer to:
First Aid Safety Oriented, Second Edition, Chapters 2, 13, 14

END OF EXERCISE 15

INTRODUCTION TO RESPIRATORY EMERGENCIES

16-1

STOPPED BREATHING is the most common life-threatening situation in infancy and childhood.

Common causes of stopped breathing in the very young are -

- **AIRWAY OBSTRUCTION** (choking)
- **SMOKE INHALATION**
- **NEAR-DROWNING**
- **SUFFOCATION**
- **STRANGULATION**
- **POISONING**
- **SUDDEN INFANT DEATH SYNDROME** (crib death)

ANYONE, who at **ANYTIME** is entrusted with the care of a child should have the knowledge and skills to -

- **PREVENT** stopped breathing from occurring, when possible
- **RECOGNIZE** when breathing has stopped
- **ACT** immediately to restore breathing

16-2

Mark each statement true **(T)** or false **(F)**.

A. ☐   Parents, teachers and babysitters should be trained to handle respiratory emergencies.

B. ☐   Situations which result in interrupted breathing in babies and children are very rare.

C. ☐   A child who is not breathing must receive appropriate first aid immediately.

D. ☐   Many breathing emergencies are the result of an accident situation.

16-2

     A. **T**   B. **F**   C. **T**   D. **T**

16

When normal breathing is interrupted, a **RESPIRATORY EMERGENCY** exists.

BRAIN DAMAGE may result after **4 minutes** of stopped breathing.

Soon the heart will **CEASE TO FUNCTION.**

BREATHING MUST BE RESTORED AS QUICKLY AS POSSIBLE

Check (✓) the correct statements.

A. ☐   A breathing emergency occurs when an infant or child is unable to breathe for more than 4 minutes.

B. ☐   If an infant's brain is deprived of oxygen for a short time, its functioning may be permanently impaired.

C. ☐   A child who cannot breathe is in grave danger.

D. ☐   In a breathing emergency, an infant or child should be allowed several minutes to begin breathing on their own.

B. ✓   C. ✓

16

The **PRINCIPLES** of **FIRST AID** are the same for all **BREATHING EMERGENCIES** regardless of the casualty's age.

TECHNIQUES, however, may vary depending on whether the casualty is considered -

- **AN INFANT**- under one year of age

- **A CHILD** - from one to eight years of age

- **AN ADULT**- over eight years of age

These three age groups are to be used in first aid as a **GUIDELINE** only.

COMMON SENSE is vital in choosing the correct first aid techniques. You must consider the **SIZE** and **BUILD** of each child or infant in making your decision.

16-6

For each of the casualties below and based on the age groups given above, indicate whether you would use the first aid techniques for an infant (**I**), a child (**C**) or an adult (**A**).

A. ☐ A tiny, delicate nine-year-old girl.

B. ☐ A tall, husky seven-year-old boy.

C. ☐ An average sized eight-month-old boy.

D. ☐ A small five-year-old girl.

16-6   A. [C]   B. [A]   C. [I]   D. [C]

16

16-7

To assess if the heart is beating and pumping blood to vital tissues, you must check the pulse.

On a **CHILD**, check the **CAROTID PULSE** -

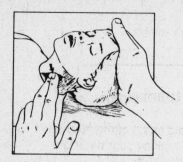

- **USE** the same method as for the adult

- **LOCATE** the Adam's apple with 2 fingers, then slide them into the groove on the neck and press lightly

On an **INFANT** - check the **BRACHIAL PULSE** -

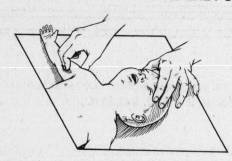

- **PLACE** the thumb on the outside of the upper arm

- **PLACE** two fingertips inside of the upper arm and press lightly between muscle and the bone

---

16-8

Mark each statement true **(T)** or false **(F)**.

A. ☐ When giving rescue breathing to an infant, you should take the brachial pulse.

B. ☐ The carotid pulse is the preferred pulse check for an infant.

C. ☐ The brachial pulse is found at the neck.

D. ☐ To feel the brachial pulse, place two fingertips in the armpit.

E. ☐ The pulse of a six-year-old child would be taken at the neck.

16-8

| A. | T | B. | F | C. | F | D. | F | E. | T |

16

PULSE RATES vary according to the **AGE** of the person.

AGE	NORMAL PULSE RATES
8 years and up	**50-100** beats per minute
1 to 8 years	**80-100** beats per minute
birth to 1 year	**80-140** beats per minute

Mark each statement true **(T)** or false **(F)**.

A. ☐ Pulse rates are the same in children and infants of different ages.

B. ☐ A pulse rate of 135 is normal for an 11-month-old girl.

C. ☐ Children will normally have a faster pulse rate than adults.

D. ☐ A pulse rate of 120 is fast for a 7-year-old.

E. ☐ Pulse rate increases as you grow older.

16-10

A. F   B. T   C. T   D. T   E. F

16

16-11

For a **CHILD** large enough to allow a seal between his mouth and the mouth of the First Aider, the **MOUTH-TO-MOUTH METHOD** is used. Use the same techniques as for an adult, with the following modifications -

- **DO NOT** overextend the neck when opening the airway

- Use **LIGHT BREATHS** of air

- Give one breath **EVERY 4 SECONDS**

16-12

Mark each statement true **(T)** or false **(F)**.

A. ☐ Beside age, the size of a child must be considered in choosing the method of artificial respiration that would be the most effective.

B. ☐ The rate of ventilations for a child should be about 15 breaths per minute.

C. ☐ When opening the airway, the head of a child should be tilted back slightly less than for an adult.

D. ☐ The volume of air for a child should be the same as for an adult.

16-12

| A. | T | B. | T | C. | T | D. | F |

16

16-13

A special method is used to give **ARTIFICIAL RESPIRATION** to -

- **INFANTS**
- **SMALL OR DELICATE YOUNG CHILDREN**

This is the **MOUTH-TO-MOUTH-AND-NOSE METHOD** of artificial respiration.

16-14

Mark each statement true **(T)** or false **(F)**.

A. To give artificial respiration to an 8-month-old girl, cover her mouth and nose with your mouth and ventilate.

B. Techniques for giving artificial respiration to small children under one year are the same as for older, larger children and adults.

C. A very tiny 14-month-old would be ventilated in the same way as an infant.

D. You must use common sense when deciding which method of artificial respiration is to be used when the casualty is an infant or a child.

16-14   A. T   B. F   C. T   D. T

16

To use the **MOUTH-TO-MOUTH-AND-NOSE METHOD,** follow the same procedures as for the mouth-to-mouth method, with the following modifications -

- **DO NOT** overextend the head back when opening the airway

- Make a tight seal with your mouth over **THE MOUTH AND NOSE**

- Use **GENTLE PUFFS** of air

- Give one breath **EVERY 3 SECONDS**

- Check the **BRACHIAL PULSE**

Which of the following techniques are used when giving artificial respiration to an infant?

Choice 1		**Choice 2**
A. ☐ Take the pulse at the neck.	OR	A. ☐ Take the pulse at the inside of the upper arm.
B. ☐ Cover the mouth tightly.	OR	B. ☐ Cover the mouth and nose tightly.
C. ☐ Blow into the mouth with lighter breaths than for a child.	OR	C. ☐ Blow into the mouth with stronger breaths than for a child.
D. ☐ Give ventilations at the same rate as for a child.	OR	D. ☐ Give ventilations at a faster rate than for a child.
E. ☐ When opening the airway, gently tilt the head back.	OR	E. ☐ When opening the airway, extend the neck as far as possible.

16-16

A. 2   B. 2   C. 1   D. 2   E. 1

16

CHOKING is a breathing emergency which occurs when the airway is blocked and air cannot enter the lungs.

CHOKING in **CHILDREN AND INFANTS** is usually caused by food or small objects.

Each year many children die as a result of choking.

16-18

Select the best completions for the following statement.

When a baby is choking -

Choice 1		**Choice 2**
A. ☐ The air passage is clogged.	OR	A. ☐ The air passage is clear.
B. ☐ It is usually caused by foreign matter.	OR	B. ☐ It is usually caused by strong crying.
C. ☐ His lungs lack oxygen because of poor air exchange.	OR	C. ☐ His lungs are receiving good air supply.
D. ☐ There is little danger to his life.	OR	D. ☐ It is a life-threatening condition.
E. ☐ It is a rare occurrence.	OR	E. ☐ It is a frequent occurrence.

16-18

A. 1	B. 2	C. 1	D. 2	E. 2

CHOKING may result when children and infants -

- **DO NOT CHEW** food well before swallowing
- **EAT UNSUITABLE FOODS** (e.g. hotdogs, nuts, popcorn, melted cheese, thickly spread peanut butter, hard candies)
- **PUT SMALL TOYS OR OTHER OBJECTS** into their mouths
- **RUN, PLAY AND LAUGH** while eating
- Are **NOT SUPERVISED** when eating and drinking
- Are **NOT SUPERVISED** when playing

Each of these items was responsible for a choking incident.

16-20

Which of the following situations could result in a choking incident?

A. ☐ A fifteen-month-old has removed the eyes from his teddy bear.

B. ☐ A two-year-old playing marbles with his seven-year-old sister.

C. ☐ A group of three-year-olds sitting at a table with their teacher listening to music as they eat a snack at nursery school.

D. ☐ An eighteen-month-old playing in his mother's sewing box while she talks on the telephone.

E. ☐ Two four-year-olds eating a bag of peanuts quickly before their mother finds out.

F. ☐ An infant left unattended and playing with a string of beads.

16-20

A. ✓   B. ✓   D. ✓   E. ✓   F. ✓

16

MOST CHOKING INCIDENTS INVOLVING CHILDREN AND INFANTS CAN BE PREVENTED

To prevent choking -

- **SUPERVISE** children when they are playing and eating

- **KEEP SMALL OBJECTS** out of a child's reach

- Do not allow small children to **EAT UNSUITABLE FOODS**

- **CHOOSE TOYS** that comply with federal and manufacturer's recommendations for use

- **CHECK** large objects and toys for small **DETACHABLE PARTS**

Mark each statement true **(T)** or false **(F)**.

A. ☐ Hot dogs make good party food for preschoolers because they are soft and easy to chew.

B. ☐ All toys on the market have been tested and are safe for infants and small children.

C. ☐ Floors should be kept clear of small objects if there is a baby in the house.

D. ☐ Items which dissolve in the mouth, such as ice cubes and hard candies, create a choking threat to children.

E. ☐ A baby should not be given a teething biscuit to eat while alone in his crib.

16-22 A. F   B. F   C. T   D. T   E. T

16-23

When a child or infant is choking, **YOU MAY OBSERVE** any of the signs seen in an adult depending on the **DEGREE OF OBSTRUCTION**. However, since a very young child or an infant cannot communicate like an adult,

INITIATE FIRST AID for choking **IMMEDIATELY** when you observe -

- The child/infant choking on an object
- Weak, ineffective coughing
- Acute breathing difficulty
- High-pitched crowing noises
- Bluish tinge to the skin
- Sudden inability to breathe, cough or speak
- Clutching the throat

> When a child or infant has breathing difficulties and has been ill with fever, has a barking cough or has an allergic reaction, **DO NOT ATTEMPT FIRST AID FOR CHOKING. GET MEDICAL AID URGENTLY**

16-24

Which of these conditions might indicate that a child or infant is choking?

A. ☐ A baby is pale and sweating.

B. ☐ A child is whimpering and gagging at the dinner table.

C. ☐ A child playing with small toys suddenly cannot make any sound.

D. ☐ A baby has a high temperature and respiratory problems.

E. ☐ A young child is staring wide-eyed with his hands on the front part of his neck.

16-24

B. ✓   C. ✓   E. ✓

16

FIRST AID FOR A CHOKING CHILD

FIRST AID for choking in a child involves the same manoeuvres as for an adult. **HOWEVER**, care must be taken to avoid injuries to smaller casualties. Use **LESS FORCE** than for an adult casualty.

For a **CONSCIOUS CHOKING CHILD**, give first aid as follows -

- **ASSESS** the degree of obstruction

- **ASK**: "Are you choking?"

As long as the cough is forceful and the child can breathe, he may be able to expel the object.

STAND BY AND ENCOURAGE COUGHING

If he CANNOT breathe, cough or speak, the airway is **COMPLETELY OBSTRUCTED**. Start the following procedures **IMMEDIATELY** -

- Stand behind the child

- Wrap your arms around the child's waist

- Locate the tip of the xiphoid process with one hand and the navel with the other

- Position your fist just above the navel, but well below the xiphoid process

- Grasp the fist with the other hand

- Give repeated, quick upward thrusts

CONTINUE UNTIL SUCCESSFUL OR UNTIL THE CHILD BECOMES UNCONSCIOUS

16

Choose the correct procedures for a conscious choking child.

Choice 1 | **Choice 2**

A. ☐ Determine if the child can inhale some air. **OR** A. ☐ Determine what the child may have swallowed.

B. ☐ If the airway is partially obstructed, begin back blows immediately. **OR** B. ☐ If the airway is partially obstructed, tell the child to cough up the object.

C. ☐ If the airway is completely clogged, landmark the same way as for an adult just above the navel. **OR** C. ☐ If the airway is completely clogged, landmark by placing your hand in the middle of the breastbone.

D. ☐ Administer repeated upward pushes in the abdominal area. **OR** D. ☐ Administer repeated hard blows on the back.

E. ☐ Continue your efforts until the object is expelled or the casualty loses consciousness. **OR** E. ☐ Give only ten upward pushes then call medical aid.

16-26

A. ☐ 1   B. ☐ 2   C. ☐ 1   D. ☐ 1   E. ☐ 1

16

If a choking child BECOMES UNCONSCIOUS -

- **EASE** the child to the floor, on his back
- Call out **"HELP"** or send for help

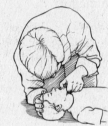

- **OPEN** the mouth using the tongue-jaw lift
- **CHECK** the mouth and remove any loose objects
- **DO NOT** make blind finger sweeps

- **OPEN** the airway with the head tilt-chin lift method
- Attempt to **VENTILATE**

If the lungs do not inflate -

- **KNEEL** astride the child at his feet so that you can reach the upper abdomen with your hands
- **LANDMARK.** Place the heel of one hand just above the navel and well below the xiphoid process and the other hand on top, with fingers raised or interlocked
- **GIVE 6 to 10** distinct upward **ABDOMINAL THRUSTS**

REPEAT FOREIGN BODY CHECKS/FINGER SWEEPS, ATTEMPTS TO VENTILATE AND ABDOMINAL THRUSTS UNTIL THE CHILD STARTS TO BREATHE AGAIN OR MEDICAL AID TAKES OVER

Mark each statement true **(T)** or false **(F)**.

A. ☐ A choking child who becomes unconscious should be placed face-up on a hard surface.

B. ☐ Look into the mouth before trying to dislodge any foreign matter.

C. ☐ Position yourself over the child's lower legs to keep your arms straight when giving upward pushes into the stomach area.

D. ☐ Abdominal thrusts when administered to a child are given with one hand.

E. ☐ An unconscious child should receive abdominal thrusts continuously until he regains consciousness.

F. ☐ Attempt to ventilate before you administer a series of forceful pushes in the abdominal area of an unconscious child.

When an infant is choking, the following precautions and differences in first aid procedures must be observed -

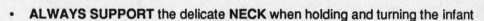

- Give **FOUR BACK BLOWS** using **LIGHT FORCE**

  - Follow with **FOUR RAPID CHEST THRUSTS**

- **ALWAYS SUPPORT** the delicate **NECK** when holding and turning the infant

- **NEVER USE ABDOMINAL THRUSTS** on an infant

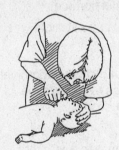

- **CHECK THE MOUTH** using the tongue-jaw lift and remove **ONLY** loose objects that can be seen. **NEVER MAKE BLIND FINGER SWEEPS**

- **VENTILATE** with **GENTLE PUFFS,** using the mouth-to-mouth-and-nose method

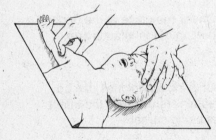

- Use the **BRACHIAL** artery for checking the pulse

Because of the size of the infant, you are able to continue all choking procedures while you transport the infant to medical aid or get help.

Choose the correct procedures to be used in giving first aid to a choking infant.

Choice 1		**Choice 2**
A. ☐ When handling the infant, protect his fragile spine.	**OR**	A. ☐ When handling the infant, protect his tender arms.
B. ☐ Attempt to blow with normal breaths through the mouth.	**OR**	B. ☐ Attempt to blow with light puffs through the mouth and nose.
C. ☐ Lay the baby lengthwise on your forearm with his head lower than his body.	**OR**	C. ☐ Roll the baby onto his side on a flat surface.
D. ☐ Give 4 distinct back blows to remove the obstruction.	**OR**	D. ☐ Give 4 distinct abdominal pushes to remove the obstruction.
E. ☐ Give 4 chest thrusts using two fingertips.	**OR**	E. ☐ Give 4 chest thrusts using the heel of one hand.
F. ☐ Clear the mouth when you assume that the object has been dislodged.	**OR**	F. ☐ Clear the mouth of any foreign material after you have visualized it.
G. ☐ Check the pulse at the neck of the infant.	**OR**	G. ☐ Check the pulse at the upper portion of the infant's arm.
H. ☐ Chest thrusts and back blows can only be given on a stationary hard surface.	**OR**	H. ☐ Choking techniques can be administered while the infant is being carried.

A. 1 B. 2 C. 1 D. 1 E. 1 F. 2 G. 2 H. 2

16

16-31

When the obstruction has been cleared from the airway of a child or an infant, you should **ASSESS BREATHING** and give **ARTIFICIAL RESPIRATION** if necessary until breathing is restored.

Then proceed to -

- Monitor breathing closely
- Place the unconscious child in the recovery position and obtain medical aid
- Take the conscious child or infant to a medical facility as quickly as possible

A child or an infant must always receive medical care following -

- Abdominal thrusts
- Chest thrusts
- Back blows

16-32

Check (✓) the correct completions.

Back blows and chest thrusts have been administered to a choking infant. The airway obstruction has been removed and breathing restored.

Following first aid the casualty should -

A. ☐ Require no medical care.

B. ☐ Be checked by a doctor.

C. ☐ Be placed lying down with feet elevated.

D. ☐ Be watched to ensure continued breathing.

E. ☐ Be positioned to keep the airway open.

F. ☐ Eat nothing solid for 2 days.

16-32

B. ✓   D. ✓   E. ✓

16

CPR is a combination of two basic life support techniques.

The two techniques consist of -

- **ARTIFICIAL RESPIRATION**
  and
- **ARTIFICIAL CIRCULATION**

CPR is used to maintain the life of a casualty when -

- **BREATHING HAS STOPPED**
  and the
- **HEART HAS STOPPED BEATING**

The **ABC's** of CPR are -

AIRWAY - open the airway

BREATHING - check for breathing; if absent begin artificial respiration

CIRCULATION - check the pulse; if absent start chest compressions

CPR should only be done by rescuers trained to recognized standards.

16-34

Mark each statement true **(T)** or false **(F)**.

A. ☐ The aim of CPR is to restore breathing and maintain the the heart beat.

B. ☐ If breathing has ceased and the pulse is absent, CPR should be started immediately.

C. ☐ The first step to restore breathing is to begin ventilations.

D. ☐ Rescue breathing is an essential part of CPR.

16-34 A. T   B. T   C. F   D. T

16

CPR for all age groups is based on the same principles. However, **CPR TECHNIQUES** vary by **AGE** and **BODY SIZE** -

	CHILD (1 to 8 years)	**INFANT** (under 1 year)
• VENTILATIONS -	 Mouth-to-Mouth Light Breaths	 Mouth-to-Mouth-and-Nose Puffs of Air
• PULSE -	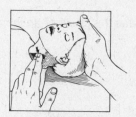 Carotid	 Brachial
• CHEST COMPRESSIONS -	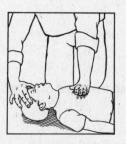 One Hand	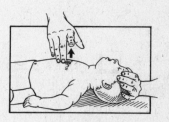 Two Fingers
Depth -	2.5 to 3.8 cm (1 to 1 1/2 ins.)	1.3 to 2.5 cm (1/2 to 1 in.)
Rate -	80 to 100 per min.	at least 100 per min.
Ratio -	5:1	5:1

Check (✓) the correct procedures below for giving CPR to a child and an infant.

A. ☐   Tilt the head slightly more in a child than in an infant to open the airway.

B. ☐   Check the pulse at the same place on a child and an infant.

C. ☐   Procedures for CPR vary by the age and build of the casualty.

D. ☐   Use two fingers to compress the chest of an infant.

E. ☐   Compress an infant's chest at a faster rate than for an older child.

F. ☐   Use two hands to compress the chest of a child.

G. ☐   Compress a child's chest more deeply than an infant's chest.

16-36

A. ✓   C. ✓   D. ✓   E. ✓   G. ✓

16

16-37

These questions are based on this workbook exercise, your practical session and the audio-visual.

Mark each statement true (T) or false (F).

A. ☐ Procedures for dealing with breathing emergencies are the same for casualties of all ages.

B. ☐ To give artificial respiration to a tiny 18 month-old, you may have to use the mouth-to-mouth-and-nose method.

C. ☐ On an infant, the brachial is easier to locate than the carotid pulse.

D. ☐ An infant's pulse rate is slower than an adult's.

E. ☐ Abdominal thrusts should never be given to a choking infant.

F. ☐ Abdominal thrusts should be used only when a child's airway is completely obstructed.

G. ☐ Two fingertips are used to deliver chest thrusts to a choking infant.

H. ☐ CPR should be started only when the lungs are not functioning and there is no pulse.

I. ☐ The rate of chest compressions is slower for an infant than for a child.

16-37   A. F   B. T   C. T   D. F   E. T   F. T   G. T   H. T   I. F

16

For further information on this topic, refer to:
First Aid Safety Oriented, Second Edition, Chapters 5, 7, 8, 9

END OF EXERCISE 16

16

THERE IS NO WORKBOOK EXERCISE 17

For information on this topic, refer to: *First Aid Safety Oriented*, Second Edition, Chapter 7

NOTES

THE SKIN

18-1

The skin is composed of two layers.

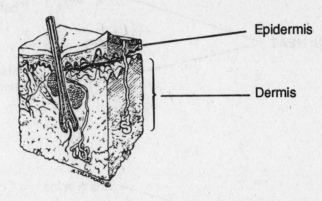

Epidermis

Dermis

THE SKIN IS ONE OF THE MOST IMPORTANT ORGANS OF THE BODY -

- It **PROTECTS** the body against bacteria, injury and extreme temperatures
- It **HELPS** to **CONTROL** body temperature
- It **GETS RID OF** waste products in the form of perspiration

18-2

Mark each statement true **(T)** or false **(F)**.

A. ☑   The outer part of the skin is a thin layer.

B. ☑   The second layer of the skin contains nerves and blood vessels.

C. ☒   The skin is not necessary for adequate body functioning.

D. ☑   The skin guards the body against infections.

E. ☑   The skin assists the body to adjust to environmental changes.

18-2

A. [T]   B. [T]   C. [F]   D. [T]   E. [T]

Burns damage the skin and other underlying tissues.

Burns may be caused by -

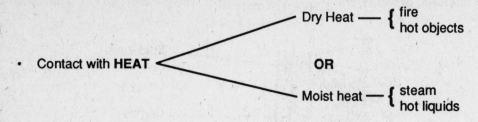

- Contact with **HEAT**
  - Dry Heat — { fire / hot objects
  - **OR**
  - Moist heat — { steam / hot liquids

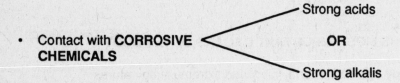

- Contact with **CORROSIVE CHEMICALS**
  - Strong acids
  - **OR**
  - Strong alkalis

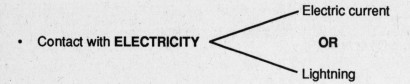

- Contact with **ELECTRICITY**
  - Electric current
  - **OR**
  - Lightning

- Exposure to **RADIATION**
  - Sun's radiation
  - **OR**
  - Radioactive materials

In each of the following situations, a person is burned. Match each burn with one of the five causes by writing the appropriate number in each square.

Causes of Burns

1	Dry heat
2	Moist heat
3	Corrosive chemicals
4	Electricity
5	Radiation

A. A girl receives a sunburn while sleeping on the beach.

B. A mechanic spills battery acid which burns his arms.

C. [4] A man receives burns when he is struck by lightning.

D. A child in the bath is burned by hot water.

E. While she is cooking, a woman is burned when a fire breaks out in a pan.

Most burns can be prevented by adopting **SAFETY PRACTICES**.

You should -

- Use **HAND PROTECTION** when you lift or touch hot objects or work with corrosive chemicals

- Keep electric equipment in **GOOD REPAIR**

- Ensure that flammable materials and liquids are **STORED IN A WELL-VENTILATED AREA**

- Ensure that corrosive chemicals or radioactive materials are **CLEARLY LABELLED** and stored in a safe place

- Take precautions to prevent injury from fire, for example, by installing **SMOKE ALARMS** and **FIRE EXTINGUISHERS,** and by **NOT SMOKING IN BED**

- Use **PROTECTIVE CLOTHING** and **SUNSCREEN LOTIONS** when you are out in the sun for a long time

- **SUPERVISE CHILDREN** and **ELDERLY PERSONS** around hot stoves or in the bath

- **IF YOUR CLOTHING CATCHES FIRE**

  STOP - don't run
  DROP - to the ground
  ROLL - to put flames out

Each picture illustrates a dangerous situation.

Match each illustration with the safety practice that would prevent a burn.

Dangerous Situations   **Safety Practices**

A.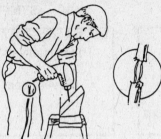

1. Supervise children in the bath.

B.

2. Wear hand and eye protection when you work with dangerous chemicals.

C.

3. Keep electric tools in good repair.

D.

4. Store flammable materials in a well-ventilated area.

18-7

Signs and symptoms of burns depend on whether the burn is superficial or deep.

SUPERFICIAL

SIGNS	SYMPTOMS
You may observe: • Reddened skin • Swelling • Blisters	The casualty may complain of: • Severe pain

OR

DEEP

SIGNS	SYMPTOMS
You may observe: • Charred skin	The casualty may complain of: • Slight pain

18-8

Mark each statement true (T) or false (F).

A. ☐ Blackened skin layers indicate a deep burn.

B. ☒ The hurt accompanying a deep burn is greater than that of a superficial burn.

C. ☒ An arm is not likely to swell when it has been burned.

D. ☑ Skin that is slightly burned may be deep pink with water bubbles.

18-8

A. T   B. F   C. F   D. T

18

18-9

The seriousness of a burn depends on the -

- **AMOUNT OF BODY SURFACE** burned

- **LOCATION** of the burn

- **DEPTH** of the burn

- **GENERAL HEALTH** of the casualty

- **AGE** of the casualty

MEDICAL AID is always required when a burn -

- Covers a large area
- Is deep
- Is located on the face, mouth or throat
- Is caused by chemicals or electricity
- Is received by an infant or an elderly person

18-10

Which of the following casualties would require medical aid?

A. ☑ A 10-month-old baby burned by hot water.

B. ☑ The skin on a casualty's legs is burned away.

C. ☑ A casualty's chest and both arms are burned.

D. ☑ An 80-year-old man burns his thigh on a wood stove.

E. ☑ A worker splashes acid on his arms.

F. ☑ A teenager has difficulty swallowing after drinking a cup of steaming hot tea.

18-10 A. ✓ B. ✓ C. ✓ D. ✓ E. ✓ F. ✓

18

18-11

A burn may be complicated by -

- **SHOCK**
- **INFECTION**
- **BREATHING PROBLEMS**
- **SWELLING**

18-12

Mark each statement relating to complications of burns as true **(T)** or false **(F)**.

A. ☒   Give first aid only for the burned area of skin.

B. ☑   Watch for respiratory difficulties.

C. ☑   Remove any jewellery before the tissue at the burned area starts to bulge.

D. ☑   Watch for signs such as a weak, rapid pulse and cold, clammy skin.

E. ☑   Cover deep burned areas with clean dressings to prevent contamination.

18-12

A. F   B. T   C. T   D. T   E. T

18

18-13

The lungs can be damaged seriously by inhaling smoke from a fire.

To reduce the risk of smoke inhalation -

- Stay close to the ground

- Cover your mouth with a wet cloth

- Get out of the area as quickly as possible

- In industrial fires, don't enter the fire area without the proper safety equipment

18-14

Check (✔) the diagrams which show how to avoid smoke inhalation during a fire.

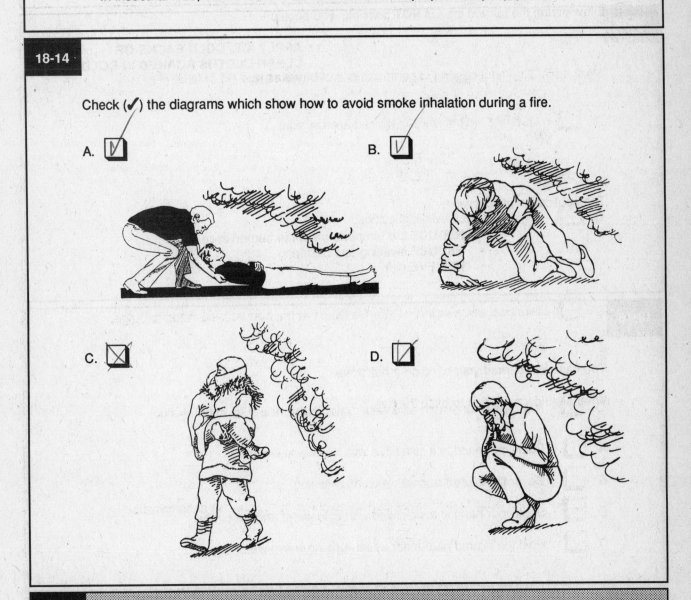

A. ☑   B. ☑

C. ☒   D. ☑

18-14

 A. ✔   B. ✔   D. ✔

18-15

When you receive a burn you should -

- **IMMEDIATELY IMMERSE THE BURNED PART IN ICE WATER**

If immersing the burned area is **NOT** possible, you should -

- **APPLY ICE, COLD PACKS OR CLEAN CLOTHS SOAKED IN COLD WATER**

The application of cold will -

- **REDUCE** the temperature of the burned area
- **REDUCE** swelling and blistering
- **RELIEVE** pain

18-16

You have just burned your hand on a hot stove.

What should you do first to ease the pain?

A. ☐ Soak your hand in a sink filled with lukewarm water.

B. ☐ Cover the injured part with a clean dressing.

C. ☑ Soak your hand in a sink filled with cold water and ice cubes.

D. ☐ Hold the injured part under a fast-running warm-water tap.

18-16

C. ☑

18

18-17

A man receives a burn to his chest and stomach area. How should you lessen the pain while he is being transported to medical aid?

A. ☐ Apply towels soaked in warm water to the burn.

B. ☑ Cover the burn with cold moist cloths.

C. ☐ Rinse the affected area with cold salted water.

D. ☐ Apply direct pressure to the burned area.

18-18

While you are immersing a burned part in cold water, you should -

- **REMOVE JEWELLERY AND LOOSEN TIGHT CLOTHING BEFORE SWELLING OCCURS**

18-19

Which two of the following actions should you perform while soaking your burned hand?

A. ☑ Remove any rings or bracelets from your hand and arm.

B. ☐ Gently rub the burned area to relieve pain.

C. ☐ Gradually raise the temperature of the water to body temperature.

D. ☑ Loosen the cuff or sleeve of your shirt.

18-17	
B. ☑	

18-19		
A. ☑	D. ☑	

18

When the pain from a burn has lessened, you should -

- **COVER THE BURNED AREA** loosely with a sterile dressing or a clean material

- **SECURE THE DRESSING**, ensuring that the tape does **NOT** touch the burned area

- **OBTAIN MEDICAL AID**

18-21

What should you do for a burn when the intense hurt has gone?

A. ☐ Leave the burn uncovered and obtain medical aid.

B. ☐ Apply a pressure dressing to control swelling.

C. ☑ Apply a clean dressing and obtain medical aid.

D. ☐ Cover the burn with a warm, moist dressing and bandage.

18-22

When giving first aid for a burn, avoid causing further injury and contamination.

DO NOT -

- **APPLY LOTIONS**, oils or butter

- **BREAK BLISTERS**

- **TOUCH THE BURN** with your fingers

- **BREATHE** or **COUGH** over the burn

- **REMOVE CLOTHING** that is sticking to the burn

- **COVER THE BURN** with cotton wool or sticky material such as tape

---

18-21

C. ☑

18

Classify each of the following actions as a **Do** or **Do Not** when giving first aid for a burn.

	Do	Do Not	
A.	☐	☑	Apply baby oil to the burn.
B.	☐	☑	Cut away a casualty's blouse when it is clinging to burned skin.
C.	☑	☐	Apply a clean dressing and secure it in place.
D.	☐	☑	Remove ashes around the burn by blowing on the skin.
E.	☐	☑	Use clean fingers to remove pieces of burned skin and clothing.
F.	☐	☑	Drain blisters before applying a dressing.
G.	☑	☐	Position adhesive tape so that it does not touch the burn.

A. | Do Not | B. | Do Not | C. | Do | D. | Do Not | E. | Do Not | F. | Do Not | G. | Do |

18-24

A **CORROSIVE CHEMICAL** will continue to burn as long as it is in contact with the skin.

To minimize the effects of a **LIQUID** corrosive chemical on the skin -

• **FLOOD** the area with water **IMMEDIATELY** as clothing is removed

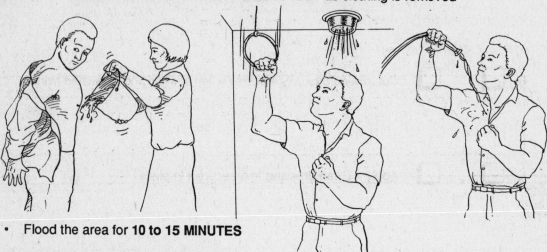

• Flood the area for **10 to 15 MINUTES**

• Cover with a **CLEAN DRESSING**

• Obtain **MEDICAL AID**

18-25

A workman has spilled strong liquid acid on his arms and chest.

What should he do?

A. ☐ Avoid touching the contaminated area and obtain medical aid.

B. ☑ Flush his upper body with water while he takes off his shirt and pants and continues flushing for approximately 12 minutes.

C. ☐ Cover the burn with a clean, moist dressing after removing the contaminated shirt and pants.

D. ☐ Remove his shirt and pants and then pour buckets of water over the body for 2 or 3 minutes.

18-25

B. ☑

18

If the spilled corrosive chemical is a **DRY POWDER** you should -

- **REMOVE** contaminated clothing

- **BRUSH OFF** any powder from the skin - **DO NOT USE YOUR BARE HANDS**

- **FLOOD THE AFFECTED AREA** with water for **10 to 15 MINUTES**

- Apply a **CLEAN DRESSING**

- Obtain **MEDICAL AID**

> First Aid for specific burns, e.g. from liquid sulfur, may vary from these general rules. You should know the chemicals in use in your work environment and learn the recommended first aid.

Listed below are the first aid steps to be followed when a dry chemical has been spilled on the skin.

Number the steps in the correct order of performance.

A. $\boxed{3}$ Cover the burned area with sterile gauze.

B. $\boxed{1}$ Take off clothing and use a dry cloth to knock away any loose chemical.

C. $\boxed{4}$ Obtain medical aid.

D. $\boxed{2}$ Flush the contaminated skin with water for about 12 minutes.

18-27   A. $\boxed{3}$ B. $\boxed{1}$ C. $\boxed{4}$ D. $\boxed{2}$

FIRST AID FOR ELECTRICAL BURNS

BURNS from an electrical current may be more serious than they appear. As well as **deep burns** at the point of **entry and exit**, an electrical shock can also cause -

- **ASPHYXIA**

- **CARDIAC ARREST**

- **FRACTURES AND DISLOCATIONS**

To give first aid for a casualty with electrical burns -

1.

Shut current off

2.

Check breathing and pulse
(Give AR or CPR if needed)

3.

Dress the burn

4.

Give first aid for fractures or dislocations if necessary

5.

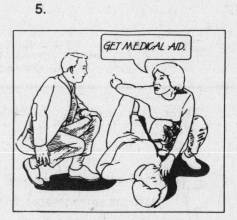

GET MEDICAL AID.

Get medical aid

Mark each statement true **(T)** or false **(F)**.

A. ☒ When treating burns from electricity, the burned areas are the top priority for first aid.

B. ☑ Breathing may stop after an electric shock.

C. ☒ There will usually be only one deep wound from an electrical burn.

D. ☒ In an electrical accident, you should first drag the casualty from the source of electricity.

E. ☑ When a casualty has received a violent electrical shock, you should suspect injuries to joints and bones.

F. ☑ A casualty's heart may stop following an electrical charge through his body.

18-29   A. F   B. T   C. F   D. F   E. T   F. T

18

18-30

There is no specific first aid for radiation burns caused by X-rays or radioactive material.

But first aid can be given for a minor **SUNBURN** -

- **COVER** the area with a cloth soaked in a solution of 10mL of salt to a litre of cool water (tablespoon to a quart)

- **APPLY** an ointment or a cream prepared for this purpose

- **PROTECT** burned areas from the sun

- **DO NOT** break blisters

18-31

Check (✓) the correct statements.

A. ☑ Towels drenched in a salt solution are soothing when applied to sunburned skin.

B. ☒ Unlike other burns, blisters caused by a sunburn should be drained before applying wet towels.

C. ☑ Get medical aid for people who have been exposed to radioactive materials.

D. ☑ Stay in the shade if you have a sunburn.

18-31   A. ✓   C. ✓   D. ✓

18

18-32

Mark each statement true **(T)** or false **(F)**.

A. ☑ Burned skin may be red and blistered.

B. ☑ Shock and infection may result from a burn.

C. ☑ Burns can be prevented by following safe practices at work, at home and at play.

D. ☒ To minimize the effects of a liquid corrosive chemical on the hand, soak the hand in a small bucket of cold water.

E. ☑ When a corrosive powder spills onto the skin, brush it off before flooding the area with water.

F. ☒ A burn to the arm of an infant does not require medical aid.

G. ☑ All casualties with burns caused by electricity or chemicals should obtain medical aid.

H. ☑ Electrical burns may be accompanied by stopped breathing and heart malfunction.

I. ☑ To avoid smoke inhalation in a fire stay near the floor.

18-32

A. T B. T C. T D. F E. T F. F G. T H. T I. T

18

For further information on this topic, refer to: *First Aid Safety Oriented,* Second Edition, Chapters 2, 21

END OF EXERCISE 18

POISONS

19-1

A **POISON** is any substance that can impair health or cause death if taken into the body.

Some substances are labelled as poisons.

| DANGER POISON | WARNING POISON | CAUTION POISON |

Many common poisons are not identified. Examples of these are -

- cigarettes
- alcohol
- unprescribed drugs
- household plants
- contaminated food
- prescribed medications

19-2

Which of the following substances could cause poisoning?

A. ☐ Children's cough syrup.

B. ☐ A spoiled cream pie.

C. ☐ Furniture polish.

D. ☐ Model airplane glue.

E. ☐ Aspirin.

19-2

A. ☑ B. ☑ C. ☑ D. ☑ E. ☑

19-4

Poisons enter the body in four ways.

A poison may be -

- **TAKEN BY MOUTH:** e.g. contaminated food, poisonous liquids

- **INHALED** through the airway: e.g. exhaust fumes, silo gas

- **ABSORBED** through the skin: e.g. agricultural chemicals

- **INJECTED** through the skin: e.g. drugs, insect stings

19-4

Write into the box beside each picture, the appropriate number from the list to identify how the poison enters the body.

1. Swallowed (ingested)
2. Inhaled
3. Absorbed
4. Injected

A. ☐

B. ☐

C. ☐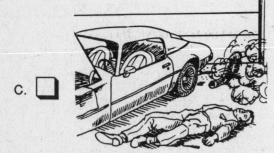

D. ☐

19-4

| A. | 4 | B. | 1 | C. | 2 | D. | 3 |

THE BEST WAY TO DEAL WITH POISONING
IS TO PREVENT IT FROM HAPPENING

To prevent accidental poisoning, you should take the following safety measures -

- Keep poisonous substances in original or special containers

- Read instructions on labels before using medicines, chemicals or insecticides

- Ventilate areas where engine or chemical fumes are present

- Keep poisonous products and plants out of the reach of children and teach children to avoid poisonous plants outdoors

- Use childproof caps on medicines and flush unused portions down the toilet

Each picture illustrates a dangerous situation that could lead to poisoning.

Match each situation with the appropriate safety measure.

Dangerous Situations

Safety Measures

A. ☐

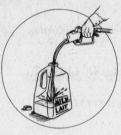

1. Ensure fresh air in rooms where gas fumes are present.

B. ☐

2. Keep medications in a locked cupboard.

C. ☐

3. Avoid storing harmful substances in drink bottles.

D. ☐

4. Dispose of unused medicines by flushing them down the toilet.

19-7

The **HISTORY** of a poisoning emergency is necessary to help you decide what first aid to give.

Try to find out -

- **WHAT** poison was taken?

- **HOW** did the poison enter the body?

- **HOW MUCH** poison was taken?

- **WHEN** was the poison taken?

19-8

You find a 3-year-old playing in the garden with an open bottle of liquid pesticide in his hands.

What information should you try to find out immediately?

A. ☐   Where did he find the pesticide?

B. ☐   Did he drink the pesticide?

C. ☐   Was the pesticide in a locked cupboard?

D. ☐   What quantity of pesticide, if any, did he drink?

E. ☐   If he drank the pesticide, how long has it been since he drank it?

19-8

B. ✓   D. ✓   E. ✓

19

Use **COMMON SENSE** and your other **SENSES** to find out all you can about a poisoning incident.

Which of the following would provide helpful information about the history of a poisoning emergency?

A. ☐   Smelling the casualty's breath.

B. ☐   Counting pills spilled on the floor and the ones remaining in the bottle and comparing the total to the prescribed quantity.

C. ☐   Noting noxious fumes in the area.

D. ☐   Reading the label on the suspected poison container.

E. ☐   Questioning the conscious casualty.

19-10

A. ✓   B. ✓   C. ✓   D. ✓   E. ✓

19

19-11

Whenever you suspect that a person has taken any poison, you should **IMMEDIATELY** -

- Try to determine the **HISTORY** of the incident

- Contact the **POISON INFORMATION CENTRE** or a physician and give the complete history and the present condition of the casualty

- **FOLLOW THE DIRECTIONS** you are given by the Poison Information Centre or physician

19-12

An elderly man tells you he has accidentally swallowed a poison.

You should -

	Yes	No	
A.	☐	☐	Ask him what he took, how much and when.
B.	☐	☐	Give him a glass of milk to drink.
C.	☐	☐	Telephone the Poison Information Centre and tell them what you know about the poisoning.
D.	☐	☐	Telephone a doctor if you cannot reach the Poison Information Centre.
E.	☐	☐	Give first aid for poisoning before attempting to contact a medical authority.

19-12   A. Yes   B. No   C. Yes   D. Yes   E. No

19

When a person has taken a poison by mouth and is **CONSCIOUS**, the Poison Information Centre will probably instruct you to give **IPECAC SYRUP** to **MAKE HIM VOMIT**.

However, if the poison taken is a **CORROSIVE** (such as a drain cleaner) or a **PETROLEUM-BASED PRODUCT** (such as kerosene), you will be told **NOT TO MAKE HIM VOMIT**. Corrosives will burn again when vomited and petroleum product fumes when vomited may also affect the lungs.

Ipecac syrup can be purchased in single-dose bottles (14mL) at any drug store without a prescription.

Two or more bottles should be kept in a locked medicine cabinet and should be given **ONLY** under the direction of the Poison Information Centre or a physician.

Mark the following statements true **(T)** or false **(F)**.

A. ☐   Ipecac syrup is used to induce vomiting in a conscious person who has swallowed a poison.

B. ☐   A doctor's prescription is necessary for the purchase of ipecac syrup.

C. ☐   More damage will be caused to the airway if the casualty is forced to vomit after he has swallowed a corrosive or petroleum based substance.

D. ☐   Give ipecac syrup for poisoning only when told to do so by a recognized authority.

E. ☐   A casualty who has swallowed a strong acid solution should be made to vomit immediately.

A. [T]   B. [F]   C. [T]   D. [T]   E. [F]

When a casualty is **UNCONSCIOUS** as a result of poisoning, you must **FIRST** -

- **CHECK** for **BREATHING** and give artificial respiration, if necessary

- **PLACE** the casualty in the recovery position, if she is breathing

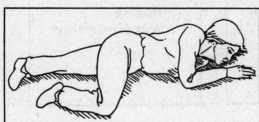

- Obtain medical aid **IMMEDIATELY**

NEVER INDUCE VOMITING IN AN UNCONSCIOUS CASUALTY

19-16

A casualty is unconscious as a result of taking an overdose of sleeping pills.

Which of the following should you do?

	Yes	No	
A.	☐	☐	Place him flat on his back with feet elevated.
B.	☐	☐	Maintain an open airway.
C.	☐	☐	Dilute the poison by moistening his lips with water.
D.	☐	☐	Provide mouth-to-mouth ventilations if he stops breathing.
E.	☐	☐	Get medical assistance as soon as possible.
F.	☐	☐	Give him ipecac syrup to induce vomiting.

19-16

A. No   B. Yes   C. No   D. Yes   E. Yes   F. No

19

19-17

The following signs and symptoms may indicate that a poison was **TAKEN BY MOUTH -**

SIGNS	SYMPTOMS
You may observe: • Discoloured lips • Burns in the mouth (corrosive) • Odour on the breath (petroleum based) • Vomiting	The casualty may complain of: • Nausea • Abdominal cramps

Signs and symptoms may appear **IMMEDIATELY** or they may be **DELAYED**.

19-18

Your toddler is found playing in the bathroom. Somehow she managed to open the cupboard containing cleaning supplies. Which of the following might indicate that she has swallowed some poison?

A. ☐ She has a deep cut on her cheek.

B. ☐ Her lips have a trace of white powder on them.

C. ☐ One of the containers is open and empty.

D. ☐ There are blisters on her tongue.

E. ☐ She seems to be in pain.

19-18

B. ✓   C. ✓   D. ✓   E. ✓

19

When the person who has swallowed a poison is **CONSCIOUS** and you **CANNOT** reach the **POISON INFORMATION CENTRE**, you should -

- First - **DILUTE THE POISON:** give the person several glasses of cool water to drink

- Second - **INDUCE VOMITING:** give the person several glasses of warm water to drink. If this does not cause vomiting, have the person place his fingers at the back of his throat and tickle to induce vomiting

> **DO NOT INDUCE VOMITING IF THE POISON IS A CORROSIVE OR A PETROLEUM BASED PRODUCT**

> **NEVER INDUCE VOMITING IN INFANTS** (less than 1 year old) **EXCEPT ON ADVICE OF THE POISON INFORMATION CENTRE**

- Third - **OBTAIN MEDICAL AID**

Mark each statement true (**T**) or false (**F**).

A. ☐   If a conscious person has swallowed a non-corrosive poison you should immediately induce vomiting by giving several glasses of warm water.

B. ☐   You must obtain medical attention for a casualty who has swallowed a poison, even if he has been made to vomit.

C. ☐   Cold liquids will induce vomiting.

D. ☐   You should give ipecac syrup to a conscious casualty who has swallowed a corrosive poison if you can't reach the Poison Information Centre.

E. ☐   Cool water will weaken the concentration of the poison in the stomach.

F. ☐   Vomiting in a 3-month old baby should only be initiated on the recommendation of a physician.

19-20	A. F	B. T	C. F	D. F	E. T	F. T

19-21

The following signs and symptoms may indicate that a poison was **INHALED** -

SIGNS	SYMPTOMS
You may observe:	The casualty may complain of:
• Breathing problems • Unconsciousness • Coughing	• Headache • Dizziness • Chest Pain

You should -

- **MOVE** the casualty into fresh air

- **GIVE** artificial respiration, if necessary

- **OBTAIN MEDICAL AID**

19-22

A casualty is found unconscious in a small room. Fumes suggest that he has inhaled poisonous gas. Which of the following would you do?

A. ☐   Take him outside.

B. ☐   Check for breathing.

C. ☐   Give liquids to dilute the poison.

D. ☐   Begin artificial respiration if breathing has stopped.

E. ☐   Apply ice packs to reduce head and chest pain.

F. ☐   Take him to the hospital.

19-22   A. ✓   B. ✓   D. ✓   F. ✓

19

19-23

The following signs and symptoms may indicate that a poison has been **ABSORBED** through the skin -

SIGNS	SYMPTOMS
You may observe: • Reddened skin, blisters, swelling • Breathing problems • Unconsciousness	The casualty may complain of: • Headache • Dizziness • Nausea

You should -

• **FLUSH** the affected skin with large amounts of water. (If the poisonous substance is a powder, brush off excessive amounts with a dry cloth before flushing.)

• **WASH THE SKIN** with soap and water, if possible

• **MONITOR BREATHING** and give artificial respiration, if necessary

• **OBTAIN MEDICAL AID**

19-24

Choose the correct completions for the following statement.

When a poison has been absorbed through the skin -

A. ☐   Artificial respiration may be required for the casualty.

B. ☐   You should give the casualty several glasses of cool water to drink.

C. ☐   The involved area may appear burned.

D. ☐   The contaminated area of the body should be flooded with water and then cleaned.

E. ☐   The casualty does not usually require medical attention.

19-24

A. ✓   C. ✓   D. ✓

19

19-25

When a poison has been **INJECTED** through the skin, the following signs and symptoms may appear -

SIGNS	**SYMPTOMS**
You may observe:	The casualty may complain of:
• Irritation at the site of injection • Breathing problems • Unconsciousness	• Headache • Dizziness • Nausea

To reduce the spread of the poison throughout the body, you should -

• **FLUSH OFF** any poison that remains on the skin

• Keep the casualty **AT REST**

• Keep the affected limb at **HEART LEVEL**

• **MONITOR BREATHING** and give artificial respiration, if required

• **OBTAIN MEDICAL AID**

19-26

Mark each statement true (T) or false (F).

A. ☐ A respiratory emergency can develop following a wasp sting.

B. ☐ When a poison has been injected, your first concern is to slow down the circulation of the poison.

C. ☐ A person who has been poisoned by an injected poison should be encouraged to move around to prevent unconsciousness.

D. ☐ When a poison has been injected into a casualty's lower arm, you should lay him down and maintain his arm at heart level.

19-26 A. T B. T C. F D. T

19

ANIMAL BITES cause puncture wounds or a laceration. Contaminated saliva entering the body can cause a serious infection.

If you **SUSPECT** that the bite was caused by an animal infected with **RABIES, ACT QUICKLY** and obtain medical aid **URGENTLY**. The infection can be prevented by **IMMEDIATE IMMUNIZATION.**

Take all necessary precautions against your own contamination -

- **SCRUB** your hands thoroughly after giving first aid

- **WEAR GLOVES** when the infected animal must be handled

To give first aid for an animal bite -

- **ALLOW MODERATE BLEEDING** to cleanse the wound

- **WASH** the wound with an antiseptic soap or detergent

- **RINSE** with running water as hot as the casualty can bear or apply a salt solution

- **APPLY** a dressing and bandage

EACH ANIMAL BITE SHOULD BE FOLLOWED BY MEDICAL CARE

Which of the following statements and first aid procedures are correct when dealing with an animal bite?

A. ☐ Assume that any domestic animal behaving in an unusually aggressive way may be infected with rabies.

B. ☐ Rabies is a potentially deadly disease caused by a virus carried in the body fluids of a rabid animal.

C. ☐ You can help avoid a serious infectious disease resulting from an animal bite by getting medical assistance without delay.

D. ☐ Use a mask, gloves and protective clothing when giving first aid.

E. ☐ Let heavy bleeding get rid of the virus.

F. ☐ A person who has been bitten by an animal should be advised to see a doctor.

G. ☐ Use cold water to kill germs in the wound.

H. ☐ Cleanse the bite area with a solution of dishwashing detergent and water.

I. ☐ Following cleansing, use salted water for flushing the wound.

19-28   A. ✓   B. ✓   C. ✓   F. ✓   H. ✓   I. ✓

Identify a **POISONOUS SNAKEBITE** by the following signs and symptoms -

SIGNS

You may observe:

- Two tiny holes in the skin
- Swelling
- Discolouration
- Vomiting
- Breathing may be affected
- Chills
- Sweating

SYMPTOMS

The casualty may complain of:

- Burning in area of bite
- Nausea
- Severe pain
- Weakness

FIRST AID IS REQUIRED URGENTLY

- **PLACE** the casualty at rest

- **CALM** and **REASSURE** the casualty

- **STEADY** and **SUPPORT** the affected limb

- **FLUSH** the bite area with soapy water

- **APPLY A SPLINT** to immobilize the limb

- **KEEP THE AFFECTED PART AT HEART LEVEL**

- **TRANSPORT TO MEDICAL AID IMMEDIATELY**

There are also several things that **MUST BE AVOIDED** in giving first aid for snakebite -

- **DO NOT** allow the casualty to walk
- **DO NOT** give alcoholic beverages
- **DO NOT** attempt to suck poison with your mouth

19

Check (✓) the procedures to be followed when giving first aid for a snakebite.

A. ☐ Lay the casualty down.

B. ☐ Make a cut at the puncture site and suck out the poison.

C. ☐ Use dishwashing detergent and water to clean the wound.

D ☐ Give the casualty a shot of brandy to calm him.

E. ☐ Keep the limb from moving by using a splint.

F. ☐ Elevate the limb as high as possible.

G. ☐ Obtain medical aid urgently.

A. ☑ C. ☑ E. ☑ G. ☑

19-31

An **INSECT BITE** or **STING** usually causes the following -

SIGNS	SYMPTOMS
You may observe: • Swelling • Redness	The casualty may complain of: • Mild pain • Itching

To give **FIRST AID** for a bite or a sting -

- **APPLY** rubbing alcohol
  or
  a weak ammonia solution
  or
  a paste of cooking soda and water

- **SCRAPE** the stinger and poison sac carefully from the skin. (Do not squeeze the stinger while removing it.)

- If the sting is in the mouth, give the casualty a **MOUTHWASH** of one teaspoonful of baking soda to a glass of water or **ICE TO SUCK**

19-32

Mark each statement true (T) or false (F).

A. ☐ Discomfort and a stinging sensation are normal reactions to an insect bite.

B. ☐ Baking soda mixed with water will soothe a sting.

C. ☐ The stinger should be left in the skin as any embedded object to prevent further contamination.

D. ☐ Cold application may help to reduce pain and swelling in the mouth.

19-32

A. T   B. T   C. F   D. T

Some people have severe **ALLERGIC REACTIONS** to bee and wasp stings. They are recognized by the following -

SIGNS	SYMPTOMS

You may observe:

- Breathing difficulty
- Vomiting
- Hives and swelling around eyes and mouth
- Unconsciousness

The casualty may complain of:

- Nausea

The **FIRST AID** for a person allergic to bee and wasp stings while awaiting medical aid is to -

- **ASSIST** in taking prescribed medication

- **MONITOR** breathing

- **BEGIN** artificial respiration if necessary

MEDICAL AID IS URGENTLY REQUIRED

Check (✔) the correct statements.

A. ☐ People who are allergic to bee stings often carry their own medicine.

B. ☐ Breathing may stop as a result of an allergic reaction to a bee or wasp sting.

C. ☐ To ensure adequate breathing and relieve local discomfort, first aid must be continued until medical personnel arrive.

D. ☐ A person having a severe allergic reaction may require artificial respiration.

A. ✔   B. ✔   C. ✔   D. ✔

19

19-35

LEECHES (blood suckers) attach themselves to the human body by making a tiny hole in the skin.

TICKS bite through the skin and anchor themselves with barbed mouth parts and then bury under the skin.

Forceful removal of leeches and ticks may cause infection.

The **FIRST AID** for these bites is to -

- **REMOVE** a leech or tick by applying -

    Salt
      or
    Extreme heat (heated pin or lighted match)
      or
    Kerosene, turpentine or oil

- **WASH** the area around the bite

- **APPLY** a solution of baking soda or ammonia

If a tick is buried under the skin, seek medical aid.

19-36

Mark each statement true (T) or false (F).

A. ☐ A lighted cigarette or match could be used to remove a tick or leech.

B. ☐ Leeches should always be pulled from the human body.

C. ☐ Cooking soda and water will relieve the itch of a tick bite.

D. ☐ Leeches and ticks attach themselves firmly to the human tissue.

19-36   A. T   B. F   C. T   D. T

19

19-37

Mark each statement true (T) or false (F).

A. ☐ Poisonous substances should be kept in original containers and out of the reach of children.

B. ☐ Unused medicines should be thrown into covered garbage cans.

C. ☐ The history of a poisoning is determined by knowing what and how much poison was taken, how it was taken and when.

D. ☐ The Poison Information Centre should be contacted after you give the immediate first aid for poisoning.

E. ☐ Ipecac syrup should be given to induce vomiting when a casualty has swallowed any poison and is conscious.

F. ☐ Medical aid is required for any casualty who has been poisoned.

G. ☐ Some people experience a severe allergic reaction when stung by a bee or wasp.

H. ☐ Poisoning may be caused by many common items found in and around the home.

I. ☐ The aim of first aid for a snakebite is to prevent absorption of the venom and to obtain medical aid as quickly as possible.

19-37

A. T   B. F   C. T   D. F   E. F   F. T   G. T   H. T   I. T

19

For further information on this topic, refer to: *First Aid Safety Oriented*, Second Edition, Chapter 22

END OF EXERCISE 19

19

NOTES

THE HEART

20-1

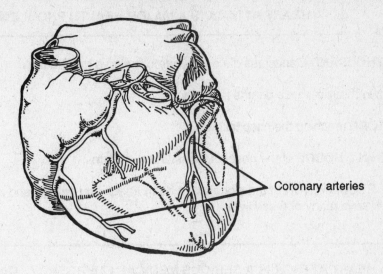

Healthy Heart

The **HEART** acts as a pump. It continuously circulates blood to the lungs and all parts of the body including its own muscle tissue.

The heart needs a constant supply of blood rich in oxygen and nutrients to continue to do its work. The heart receives this blood through its own system of arteries - the **CORONARY ARTERIES**.

20-2

Mark each statement true **(T)** or false **(F)**.

A. ☐   The heart muscle requires continuous oxygen and food to function.

B. ☐   Special arteries provide oxygenated blood to the heart muscle.

C. ☐   When the body is at rest, it does not require oxygen.

D. ☐   The blood is sent to all parts of the body by the heart.

20-2

A. ☐ T   B. ☐ T   C. ☐ F   D. ☐ T

20-3

A HEART ATTACK IS A MAJOR HEALTH PROBLEM

FIFTY THOUSAND Canadians die each year following a heart attack.

Nearly two thirds of these deaths take place -

- **BEFORE** reaching the hospital

- **WITHIN 2 HOURS** of the onset of signs and symptoms

EARLY RECOGNITION of the signals of a heart attack and prompt and appropriate first aid could save many of these lives.

A HEART ATTACK IS A SERIOUS MEDICAL EMERGENCY. CASUALTIES MUST BE TREATED AT THE HOSPITAL AS SOON AS POSSIBLE

20-4

Mark each statement true (**T**) or false (**F**).

A. ☐ Becoming familiar with the signs and symptoms of a heart attack and knowing the effective first aid could save many lives.

B. ☐ The victim of a heart attack often dies a short time after the first indications and before medical aid has been obtained.

C. ☐ Once a heart attack has occurred, there is little a First Aider can do.

D. ☐ The most important aim of first aid for a heart attack victim is to obtain immediate medical aid.

20-4   A. T   B. T   C. F   D. T

20

20-5

There are some **RISK FACTORS** over which one has little control that make a person more susceptible to heart attacks, e.g. -

- Family history of heart disease
- Previous heart attack
- Diabetes

However, **UNHEALTHY LIFESTYLES** are a major cause of heart attack.

The risk of heart attack can be **REDUCED CONSIDERABLY** by adopting **HEALTHY LIFESTYLES**, e.g. -

- No smoking
- Avoiding stress
- Exercising regularly (in moderation)
- Maintaining a recommended body weight
- Keeping a balanced diet
- Reducing the intake of food high in saturated fat to help maintain reasonable levels of cholesterol
- Having regular blood pressure checks

20-6

Check (✔) the habits which would reduce your chances of suffering a heart attack or stroke.

A. ☐ Smoking a pipe instead of cigarettes.

B. ☐ Taking time to relax and rest.

C. ☐ Having regular check-ups by your doctor.

D. ☐ Eating moderately according to good dietary rules.

E. ☐ Starting an exercise programme after consultation with your doctor.

F. ☐ Following your doctor's treatment plan if you have high blood pressure.

20-6

| B. ✔ | C. ✔ | D. ✔ | E. ✔ | F. ✔ |

20

20-7

A **HEART ATTACK** occurs when one of the **CORONARY ARTERIES** feeding the heart muscle is completely or partially **BLOCKED**.

Blood flow to the heart is disrupted. Part of the heart does not get the oxygen it needs. Damage to that part of the heart is **PERMANENT**.

The seriousness of a heart attack depends on the **EXTENT OF HEART DAMAGE**.

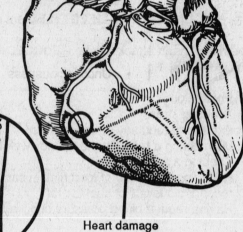

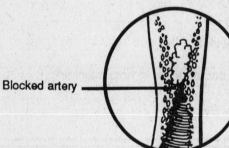

Blocked artery

Heart damage

Diseased Heart

20-8

Mark each statement true **(T)** or false **(F)**.

A. ☐ A heart attack results when part of the heart muscle does not receive any blood supply.

B. ☐ Time and medication can repair the heart tissue affected by a heart attack.

C. ☐ The heart muscle tissue dies without a constant supply of oxygen and nutrients.

D. ☐ A heart attack involving total blockage of a coronary artery and extensive loss of function is considered critical.

20-8   A. T   B. F   C. T   D. T

20

20-9

The casualty may deny that he is having a heart attack but you may note some or all of the following -

SIGNS

You may observe:

- Shortness of breath
- Paleness
- Dizziness
- Unconsciousness
- Profuse sweating
- Vomiting
- Shock

SYMPTOMS

The casualty may complain of:

- Pain, pressure or squeezing sensation in the centre of the chest
- Pain radiating to neck, shoulders and arms
- Feeling of indigestion
- Nausea
- Apprehension and fear
- General weakness

Signs and symptoms will vary according to the severity of the heart attack.

20-10

Which of the following signs and symptoms might assist you in assessing a heart attack?

A. ☐ Tingling sensation in the legs and feet.

B. ☐ Great discomfort in the heart region and above.

C. ☐ White, very moist skin.

D. ☐ Anxiety.

E. ☐ Insisting that it is just a stomach upset.

F. ☐ Flushed face.

G. ☐ Breathing difficulty.

20-10   B. ✓   C. ✓   D. ✓   E. ✓   G. ✓

20

When you suspect that a person is having a heart attack, you should **OBTAIN MEDICAL AID IMMEDIATELY** and -

GET MEDICAL AID!

- **PLACE** the person at rest in the position of most comfort, usually **SEMISITTING** to ease breathing

- **ASK** the conscious casualty if he has any **PRESCRIBED MEDICATION** with him and assist him to take it

- **LOOSEN** tight clothing at the neck, chest and waist

- **REASSURE** the casualty to lessen fear and anxiety

- Monitor **BREATHING** and begin artificial respiration, if necessary

- Monitor **PULSE**. If there is **NO PULSE**, start cardiopulmonary resuscitation (CPR) if trained or call for someone to give **CPR**, but **CONTINUE** artificial respiration until help arrives

An elderly neighbour collapses after running for a bus. He is sweating profusely and clutching his chest. You suspect a heart attack. Which choice of actions would you take?

Choice 1		**Choice 2**
A. ☐ Help him into his house.	OR	A. ☐ Send someone to call for an ambulance.
B. ☐ Prop up his head and shoulders with your heavy coat.	OR	B. ☐ Place your coat under his legs to raise them.
C. ☐ Help him take his pills for his heart condition.	OR	C. ☐ Give him nothing by mouth.
D. ☐ Speak to him gently and tell him help is on the way.	OR	D. ☐ Speak to him in an authoritative voice so he will realize you are in charge.
E. ☐ Give artificial respiration if he stops breathing.	OR	E. ☐ Assume he is dead if he stops breathing.
F ☐ Begin CPR if his heart stops even if you are not trained to do so.	OR	F. ☐ Call for CPR help if his heart stops, but continue with artificial respiration.

A. 2 B. 1 C. 1 D. 1 E. 1 F. 2

20-13

CPR (cardiopulmonary resuscitation) is a combination of two basic life support techniques.

The two techniques consist of -

- **ARTIFICIAL RESPIRATION**

  and

- **ARTIFICIAL CIRCULATION**

CPR is used to maintain the life of a casualty when -

- **BREATHING HAS STOPPED**

  and

- **THE HEART HAS STOPPED BEATING**

The **ABC's** of CPR stand for -

- open the **AIRWAY**

- restore **BREATHING**

- restore **CIRCULATION**

CPR should only be done by rescuers trained to recognized standards.

20-14

Mark each statement true **(T)** or false **(F)**.

A. ☐ CPR should be used in all cases of heart attack.

B. ☐ CPR can keep a casualty alive by supplying oxygen to the lungs and by distributing it to the vital organs.

C. ☐ Rescue breathing is an essential part of CPR.

D. ☐ CPR should be started only when the lungs are not functioning and there is no pulse.

E. ☐ Anyone can do CPR without training.

20-14 A. F B. T C. T D. T E. F

20

20-15

THE BRAIN

The brain controls all activities of the body.
To function normally it requires a continuous blood flow.

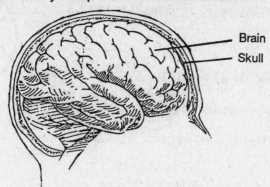

Brain
Skull

The brain receives a rich blood supply from the two carotid arteries.

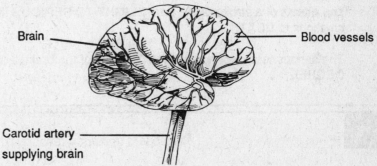

Brain
Blood vessels

Carotid artery
supplying brain

When part of the brain loses its blood supply, that part stops functioning and may be permanently damaged.

20-16

Check (✔) the correct statements.

A. ☐ Insufficient blood to the brain results in "death" of the whole organ.

B. ☐ The brain needs a constant source of blood to do its work.

C. ☐ The two major arteries in the neck are carrying blood to the brain.

D. ☐ Following a stroke, the function of the brain may be forever impaired.

20-16

B. ✓ C. ✓ D. ✓

20

20-17

A **STROKE** occurs when a part of the brain ceases to function because of a shortage of oxygen and food supply.

This may be caused by a -

- **RUPTURED BLOOD VESSEL**

  OR

- **BLOCKED ARTERY**

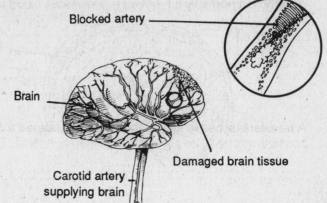

Blocked artery

Brain

Damaged brain tissue

Carotid artery supplying brain

The effects of a stroke range from **SLIGHT TO SERIOUS IMPAIRMENT** of body functions to **DEATH**.

The seriousness depends on **WHAT PART** of the brain is damaged and to what **DEGREE**.

20-18

Mark each statement true **(T)** or false **(F)**.

A. ☐ Damage caused by a stroke may vary from minor to severe.

B. ☐ When blood flow to the brain is stopped, a stroke may occur.

C. ☐ Any of the body's functions may be affected by a stroke depending on which part of the brain is involved.

D. ☐ A stroke seldom affects the brain's function.

E. ☐ The brain needs a continuous blood flow to receive oxygen and nourishment.

20-18

A. T   B. T   C. T   D. F   E. T

20

A **TRANSIENT ISCHEMIC ATTACK** (TIA), also called "Little Stroke", is caused by a short interruption of blood flow to a portion of the brain.

This may result in -

- A sudden, temporary effect on the brain

- Dizziness, unsteadiness or sudden falls

- Recovery without apparent ill-effects

A transient ischemic attack should be considered a **SERIOUS WARNING SIGNAL** of a possible stroke. The person should be advised to seek **IMMEDIATE MEDICAL CARE**.

20-20

Mark each statement as true **(T)** or false **(F)**.

A. ☐ A TIA must be regarded as a danger sign that a stroke is more likely to happen.

B. ☐ Some temporary signs and symptoms of a stroke may be indications of a TIA.

C. ☐ A "little stroke" is a momentary loss of function in a part of the brain.

D. ☐ Persons rarely recover from the damage caused by a TIA.

20-20   A. T   B. T   C. T   D. F

A stroke can occur at any age; however, it usually occurs in people who -

- Are middle-aged

- Are elderly

- Have high blood pressure

It is sometimes difficult to identify a stroke. Suspect a stroke when -

- The casualty is middle-aged or older

- The attack is very sudden

20-22

Mark each statement true **(T)** or false **(F)**.

A. ☐ Strokes are more common in people between 45 - 90 years of age.

B. ☐ A stroke can never occur in a younger person.

C. ☐ An elevated blood pressure is a contributing factor to a stroke.

D. ☐ It is easy to recognize when a stroke has occurred.

E. ☐ A stroke usually occurs unexpectedly.

20-22   A. T   B. F   C. T   D. F   E. T

20

20-23

The signs and symptoms of a stroke differ depending on what part of the brain is damaged. You may note some or all of the following -

SIGNS

You may observe:

- Unequal size of the pupils of the eyes
- Failure of the pupils to react to light
- Paralysis of face muscles
- Difficulty in speaking and swallowing
- Loss of bladder and bowel control
- Paralysis of limbs, particularly on one side
- Changes in the level of consciousness
- Convulsions

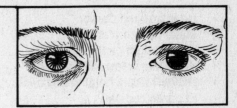

SYMPTOMS

The casualty may complain of:

- Numbness of hands and feet, particularly on one side

20-24

Check (✔) the signs and symptoms which could indicate that a stroke has occurred.

A. ☐ The pupils of the eyes do not change size when a flashlight is shined into them.

B. ☐ The casualty wants to respond to your questions but she cannot seem to get the words out.

C. ☐ The casualty appears overactive and vomits.

D. ☐ The casualty cannot move her left arm or leg.

E. ☐ The person cannot control the need to urinate or move his bowels.

F. ☐ Muscle spasms may occur in a person who has suffered a stroke.

20-24   A. ☑   B. ☑   D. ☑   E. ☑   F. ☑

20

When you suspect that a person has had a stroke, you should **OBTAIN MEDICAL AID IMMEDIATELY.**

While waiting for medical aid, you should -

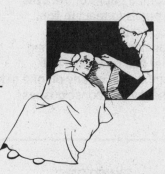

- Reassure the person
- Make him comfortable
- Loosen tight clothing
- Keep him warm with blankets
- **NEVER** apply heating devices to paralyzed parts

If the person is **CONSCIOUS,** you should -

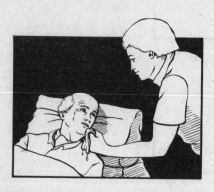

- Place him at rest and support him in a **SEMISITTING** position

- **MOISTEN** his lips and tongue with a wet cloth, if he complains of thirst

If the person is **UNCONSCIOUS,** you should -

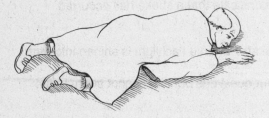

- Give him **NOTHING** by mouth

- Place him in the **RECOVERY POSITION** on the **PARALYZED** side to ease breathing

A stroke victim may also require artificial respiration.

- Maintain an open airway
- If breathing and the heart stop, CPR will be necessary

PROTECT HIM FROM INJURY

An elderly man suddenly becomes paralyzed on his left side and has difficulty speaking.

You suspect he has had a stroke.

Which of the following should you do?

Yes   **No**

A. ☐ ☐ Instruct someone to telephone for an ambulance.

B. ☐ ☐ Speak to the man kindly to relieve his anxiety.

C. ☐ ☐ Unbutton his shirt at the neck and loosen his belt.

D. ☐ ☐ Give him a glass of water to drink.

E. ☐ ☐ Position him to assist his breathing.

F. ☐ ☐ If he becomes unconscious, place him in the recovery position on his right side.

G. ☐ ☐ Take care to avoid further damage to his paralyzed limbs.

H. ☐ ☐ If breathing stops, begin artificial respiration.

I. ☐ ☐ If there is no pulse, begin CPR.

A. Yes B. Yes C. Yes D. No E. Yes F. No G. Yes H. Yes I. Yes

20

20-27

Mark each statement true (T) or false (F).

A. ☐   If part of the heart is without a supply of blood, it will suffer permanent damage.

B. ☐   A heart attack victim has a greater chance of survival if he recognizes the symptoms as soon as they appear and gets medical aid immediately.

C. ☐   CPR should be started when breathing has stopped and the pulse is faint.

D. ☐   Once a heart attack has occurred, there is little a First Aider can do.

E. ☐   Calling medical aid as soon as one recognizes the signs of a heart attack could save many lives.

F. ☐   A stroke occurs when blood flow carrying oxygen and nutrients to the brain is interrupted.

G. ☐   A large number of heart attacks could be avoided if people would adopt a healthy lifestyle.

H. ☐   Careful monitoring of the pulse is necessary when giving first aid to a heart attack victim.

I. ☐   A transient ischemic attack (TIA) is a warning signal of a possible stroke.

20-27 A. T   B. T   C. F   D. F   E. T   F. T   G. T   H. T   I. T

20

For further information on this topic, refer to:
First Aid Safety Oriented, Second Edition, Chapters 5, 8, 25

END OF EXERCISE 20

20

INTRODUCTION TO DIABETIC EMERGENCIES

21-1

The human body requires **ENERGY** to function.

Its energy source is **SUGAR** which comes from food when it is digested.

This sugar is stored in the body to be used when needed.

To regulate the use of sugar, the body produces a substance called **INSULIN**.

Normally, there is a balance between the **SUGAR USED** and the **INSULIN PRODUCED**.

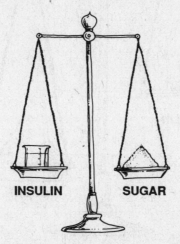

INSULIN   SUGAR

Normal Balance of Sugar and Insulin

21-2

Mark each statement true **(T)** or false **(F)**.

A. ☐   Sugar acts as a fuel for the body.

B. ☐   Most foods contain insulin and supply it to the body.

C. ☐   A body chemical called insulin controls the sugar level of the body.

21-2

A. [T]   B. [F]   C. [T]

DIABETES is a condition in which the body does **NOT** produce enough insulin, causing the sugar level to be **OUT OF BALANCE**.

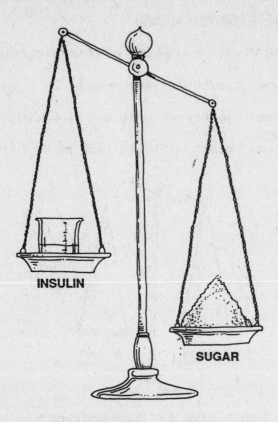

INSULIN

SUGAR

To balance the sugar level, a **DIABETIC** (person with diabetes) may take prescribed amounts of insulin.

21-4

Mark each statement true (**T**) or false (**F**).

A. ☐ A diabetic lacks the required amount of insulin to keep the sugar at a normal level.

B. ☐ Insulin can be taken by anyone without instructions from a doctor.

C. ☐ A diabetic takes insulin to regulate the use of sugar by the body.

21-4

A. T   B. F   C. T

21

An **EMERGENCY** results when a diabetic has in the body -

NOT ENOUGH INSULIN
(DIABETIC COMA)

TOO MUCH INSULIN
(INSULIN SHOCK)

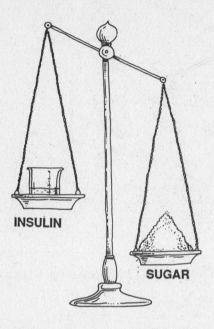

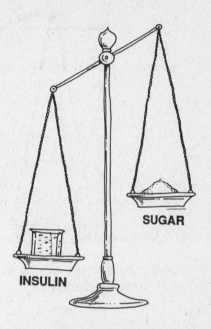

• Accidental underdose	• Accidental overdose • Too much exercise • Insufficient food

21-6

Which of the following situations may lead to a diabetic emergency?

A. ☐ A man forgets to take his prescribed amount of insulin.

B. ☐ An elderly man eats too many sweets.

C. ☐ A diabetic misses dinner.

D. ☐ A teenage diabetic competes in a bicycle race.

21-6

A.   C. ✓ D.

21

21-7

A **CONSCIOUS** diabetic will be able to tell you what is wrong when a diabetic emergency occurs.

However, keep in mind that he may be confused.

An **UNCONSCIOUS** person may be wearing a **MEDIC-ALERT** bracelet or neck tag that will tell you that he has diabetes.

21-8

Which of the following actions would help you to assess a casualty's distress as a diabetic emergency?

A. ☐ Wait 10 minutes to see if his condition improves.

B. ☐ Search him for some information that identifies him as a diabetic.

C. ☐ Ask him about his condition.

D. ☐ Keep asking him questions, even if his response does not make sense.

21-8

B. ✓   C. ✓

21

In a diabetic emergency the casualty either **NEEDS SUGAR** or **NEEDS INSULIN**. You should question the **CONSCIOUS** casualty.

If the casualty cannot tell you what he needs, look for the following -

SIGNS		SYMPTOMS	
NEEDS SUGAR Insulin Shock	**NEEDS INSULIN** Diabetic Coma	**NEEDS SUGAR** Insulin Shock	**NEEDS INSULIN** Diabetic Coma
You may observe: • Full, rapid pulse • Shallow breathing • Pale, sweating skin • Trembling • Aggressive behaviour (sometimes) • Confusion • Unconsciousness developing quickly	You may observe: • Weak, rapid pulse • Deep breathing • Flushed, dry, warm skin • Breath smells musty or like acetone • Gradual onset of unconsciousness	The casualty may complain of: • Headache • Hunger	The casualty may complain of: • Nil

---

21-10

Indicate whether each of the diabetic casualties described below requires sugar **(S)** or insulin **(I)**.

A. ☐ Casualty is unconscious; you have trouble detecting a pulse; his face is red and you notice a strange odour.

B. ☐ Casualty is rapidly becoming unconscious; his pulse is strong; his face is pasty and he starts to shake all over.

21-10

A. $\boxed{I}$ B. $\boxed{S}$

21

21-11

If the conscious casualty knows what is wrong, or you can tell by the **SIGNS** and **SYMPTOMS**, assist him to take what is needed - **SUGAR** or **INSULIN**.

If the casualty is confused about what is required, give him something **SWEET** to eat or drink and get medical aid.

If the casualty becomes **UNCONSCIOUS**, place him in the **RECOVERY POSITION**, monitor his breathing and get medical aid.

21-12

Which of the following actions should you take when a diabetic emergency occurs?

Yes   **No**

A. ☐ ☐   Give a conscious diabetic several glasses of cool water to drink.

B. ☐ ☐   Give a conscious diabetic a cup of sweetened tea if there is any doubt about giving him insulin.

C. ☐ ☐   Send someone to telephone for medical assistance if the sweetened drink did not improve the casualty's condition.

D. ☐ ☐   Place an unconscious diabetic in an appropriate position to ensure adequate breathing.

E. ☐ ☐   Help a conscious casualty to take his insulin if he says he requires it.

21-12   A. No   B. Yes   C. Yes   D. Yes   E. Yes

21

EPILEPSY is a medical condition which is a disorder of the nervous system. It may result in recurring attacks called **EPILEPTIC SEIZURES**. In most cases, this condition is controlled by medication.

An **EPILEPTIC SEIZURE** may come on **SUDDENLY** and be **BRIEF**.

Any or all of the following signs and symptoms will help you to identify an epileptic seizure -

SIGNS	SYMPTOMS
You may observe: • Fainting • Sudden loss of consciousness • Noisy breathing • Frothing from the mouth • Grinding of the teeth • Convulsions (uncontrolled muscle spasms)	The casualty may complain of: • Sensation that a seizure is about to occur (aura)

On regaining consciouness the person will be unaware of recent events and be confused.

21-14

Mark each statement true **(T)** or false **(F)**.

A. ☐   A person with epilepsy usually has incidents without warning.

B. ☐   Epileptic attacks are usually of short duration and may occur any time.

C. ☐   A person who has passed out during an epileptic seizure may not remember the incident on recovery.

D. ☐   During a seizure, a person's limbs may tighten and he may gasp for air.

E. ☐   A person's mouth is usually dry and hangs open during an epileptic attack.

21-14   A. F   B. T   C. T   D. T   E. F

When a person is having an epileptic seizure, you should attempt to **PROTECT** him from injury during the period of convulsions.

You should -

- Clear the area of onlookers to ensure **PRIVACY** for the casualty

- Clear the area of **HARD** or **SHARP OBJECTS** that could cause injury

- Guide but **DO NOT** restrict his movements

- Wipe away saliva but **DO NOT** attempt to force the mouth open

When convulsions have ceased, place him in the **RECOVERY POSITION** and **MONITOR BREATHING.** Obtain medical aid, if necessary, or advise the casualty to seek medical advice.

21-16

A man in a crowded store suddenly falls to the floor and goes into convulsions. What should you do?

Choice 1		Choice 2
A. ☐ Tell all bystanders to form a circle around the man.	OR	A. ☐ Enlist the help of some bystanders to keep people away from the man.
B. ☐ Take away all dangerous objects near the man.	OR	B. ☐ Place a blanket around him to protect him.
C. ☐ Hold his arms firmly to prevent injury.	OR	C. ☐ Watch him closely to ensure he does not hurt himself.
D. ☐ Observe him constantly to ensure that he is breathing.	OR	D. ☐ Hold his jaw apart to open his airway.
E. ☐ Following the seizure, position him to maintain an open airway.	OR	E. ☐ Following the seizure, leave him to himself.

21-16 A. 2   B. 1   C. 2   D. 1   E. 1

21

21-17

When a child has a high temperature, he may go into **CONVULSIONS**.

Fever convulsions can be recognized by any or all of the following signs -

SIGNS

You may observe:

- Uncontrolled muscular contractions of the face and limbs
- Rigid body arched backward
- Blood vessels of the face and neck protruding (congestion)
- Holding of the breath
- Froth at the mouth

21-18

Which of the following may occur when a three-year-old has convulsions brought on by a very high temperature?

A. ☐ His arms and legs hang loosely.

B. ☐ Foam appears around his lips.

C. ☐ He seems to stop breathing for short periods of time.

D. ☐ His body tightens with head and feet pressed back.

E. ☐ The veins on his neck are standing out.

21-18   B. ✓   C. ✓   D. ✓   E. ✓

21

21-19

When a child is having convulsions, you should -

- **PROTECT** him from injury but **DO NOT** restrain him

- Obtain **MEDICAL AID**

Following the convulsions, you should -

- **LOOSEN** clothing

- Maintain an **OPEN AIRWAY**

- Place him in the **RECOVERY POSITION**

- Reassure the person with the child

21-20

Which of the following should you do when a two-year-old boy is having convulsions?

Yes **No**

A. ☐ ☐ Hold him flat on his back.

B. ☐ ☐ Tell his mother to call for medical help.

When the convulsions have ceased, you should -

C. ☐ ☐ Unbutton his shirt at the neck.

D. ☐ ☐ Tell his mother not to worry.

E. ☐ ☐ Ensure that he is breathing.

F. ☐ ☐ Position him flat on his stomach.

21-20 A. No B. Yes C. Yes D. Yes E. Yes F. No

21

21-21

An **ALLERGIC REACTION** is the body's response to a substance to which it has become **HIGHLY SENSITIVE** through a previous contact.

The severity of an allergic reaction varies from minor discomfort to **SEVERE SHOCK**.

ALLERGIC REACTIONS may be caused by substances introduced into the body by -

* Injection (e.g. bee stings, drugs)

* Inhalation (e.g. pollen, dust)

* Ingestion (e.g. foods, medications)

* Absorption (e.g. pesticides, plants)

The history preceding an allergic reaction should be thoroughly looked into.

The casualty should be advised to avoid substances causing allergic reactions and to seek medical advice.

21-22

Mark each statement true **(T)** or false **(F)**.

A. ☐ An allergic reaction may be mild or life-threatening.

B. ☐ Certain drugs may cause allergic reactions.

C. ☐ Allergic reactions are only caused by substances we swallow.

D. ☐ A person may not know that he is allergic to a particular substance.

21-22

A. T   B. T   C. F   D. T

21

An allergic reaction can range from a mildly annoying to a severe, life-threatening condition. It can be recognized by any of the following -

SIGNS

You may observe:

- Red, watery eyes
- Flushed skin
- Hives
- Swelling of face, lining of the nose and tongue
- Coughing, wheezing, sneezing
- Cyanosis (bluish skin)
- Weak and slow pulse
- Vomiting and diarrhea

SYMPTOMS

The casualty may complain of:

- Itching
- Burning sensation in the eyes, face and upper chest
- Dizziness
- Faintness
- Chest pain
- Abdominal cramps
- Nausea

21-24

Which of the following signs and symptoms may assist you to recognize an allergic reaction?

A. ☐ Raised red welts on the body.

B. ☐ Difficulty in breathing.

C. ☐ Puffy face and congested air passages.

D. ☐ Violent shivering.

E. ☐ Irritation of the skin.

F. ☐ Shallow pulse.

G. ☐ Indigestion and loose bowel movement.

H. ☐ Yellowish eyes.

21-24

A. ☑ B. ☑ C. ☑ E. ☑ F. ☑ G. ☑

21

21-25

A person who has a severe allergy usually carries this information on him.

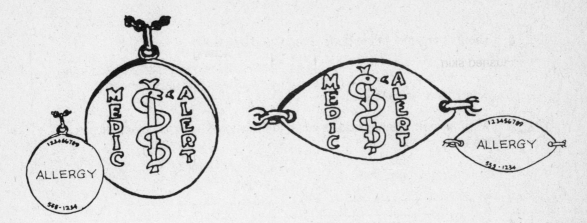

Medic-Alert Devices

He may also carry a kit to counteract the allergic reaction. **ASSIST** him **TO TAKE** his **PRESCRIBED MEDICATION.**

If shock appears, try to reduce its effects and transport the casualty to medical aid **URGENTLY.**

21-26

Check (✓) the procedures you would follow in giving first aid to a person who is suffering from a suspected allergic reaction.

A. ☐ Make him vomit if he has eaten something and he is unconscious.

B. ☐ Check for Medic-Alert information.

C. ☐ If he has an allergy kit, take him and the kit to a doctor.

D. ☐ If he has an allergy kit, help him to administer his medication.

E. ☐ Try to prevent shock from worsening and ensure adequate breathing.

21-26

B. ✓   D. ✓   E. ✓

21-27

Mark each statement true **(T)** or false **(F).**

A. ☐ The use of sugar in the body is regulated by insulin.

B. ☐ A diabetic emergency occurs when there is too little or too much insulin in the body.

C. ☐ A Medic-Alert tag gives detailed information about the first aid to be administered.

D. ☐ Convulsions and noisy breathing are signs of an epileptic seizure.

E. ☐ An allergic reaction may cause a severe shock.

F. ☐ A child with a very high temperature may go into convulsions.

G. ☐ The aim of first aid for an epileptic seizure is to protect the person from injury and maintain an open airway.

21-27 A. ⊤ B. ⊤ C. F D. ⊤ E. ⊤ F. ⊤ G. ⊤

21

For further information on this topic, refer to: *First Aid Safety Oriented*, Second Edition, Chapter 22

END OF EXERCISE 21

NOTES

INTRODUCTION TO ENVIRONMENTAL ILLNESSES AND INJURIES

22-1

The human body normally maintains a temperature of about **37°C** (98. 6°F).

The body has mechanisms, such as sweating and shivering, that help to keep its temperature **CONSTANT**.

- Sweating helps to keep the body cool

- Shivering assists the body to stay warm

However, when the body is subjected **SUDDENLY** or for a **LONG TIME** to very hot or very cold temperatures, its temperature control system may break down causing **HEAT ILLNESSES** or **COLD INJURIES**.

22-2

Mark the following statements true **(T)** or false **(F)**.

A. Normal body temperature is between 36°C (96. 8°F) and 37°C (98. 6°F).

B. The body is able to regulate its temperature when environmental conditions are not too severe.

C. Exposure to extremes of temperature for extended periods is unlikely to cause a person any harm.

D. Perspiring helps to keep the body from getting too hot.

E. Trembling of the body is nature's way of trying to keep a person warm.

22-2

A. T   B. T   C. F   D. T   E. T

22 - 1

22

22-3

Exposure to cold may result in -

- **FROSTBITE** - a local cooling of a part of the body

- **HYPOTHERMIA** - a general cooling of the entire body

The risk of frostbite or hypothermia is increased when -

- You are **EXPOSED** to very low temperatures and strong winds

- Your clothing is **WET** (for example from sweating or if you are immersed in water)

- You are **ALONE** and **EXPOSED** to the cold for **LONG PERIODS OF TIME**

- Your clothing does not keep in **YOUR BODY HEAT**

- You are in a **WEAKENED CONDITION** because of lack of food, fatigue, intoxication or illness

- You are **ELDERLY OR VERY YOUNG**

22-4

TO PREVENT COLD INJURIES -

- **STAY WARM** - wear several layers of loose-fitting clothing, preferably of wool
    - keep the head and neck covered

- **STAY DRY** - avoid getting wet, even by sweating

- **EAT WELL** - eat high energy foods at regular intervals

- **STAY SAFE** - limit the time spent in the cold
    - stay with a partner so you can check each other for signs of cold injuries

- **AVOID USE OF TOBACCO AND ALCOHOL** - these contribute to heat loss by decreasing blood circulation

22

Listed below are dangerous situations that could result in cold injuries.

Match each situation with a safety practice that could prevent the injury.

Dangerous Situations

Safety Practices

A. ☐ Limited nourishment.

1. Wear warm clothing and protect your head, hands and feet.

B. ☐ Weakened condition

2. Eat foods such as chocolate, nuts or raisins frequently when you are in the cold.

C. ☐ Poor clothing.

3. Carry an extra pair of woollen socks so you can keep your feet dry.

D ☐ Long exposure.

4. Abstain from becoming over-tired or taking large amounts of alcoholic drinks when you are in the cold.

E. ☐ Wet clothing.

5. Use the "buddy system" to ensure safety in the cold.

F. ☐ No partner.

6. Stay outside for only short periods of time when the temperature is very low.

FROSTBITE may be -

- **SUPERFICIAL** - when it affects only the surface of the skin

OR

- **DEEP** - when it affects the skin and underlying tissues

SUPERFICIAL FROSTBITE usually affects ears, face, fingers and toes.

Watch for any of the following signs and symptoms -

SIGNS	SYMPTOMS
You may observe: • White skin • Skin firm to the touch	The casualty may complain of: • Numbness in the affected

Superficial frostbite may develop into **DEEP FROSTBITE**.

DEEP FROSTBITE is far more serious. It usually involves an entire hand or foot. It may be recognized by these signs and symptoms -

SIGNS	SYMPTOMS
You may observe: • White, waxy skin • Skin feels cold and hard	The casualty may complain of: • Lack of feeling in affected area

Indicate with the appropriate letter whether a person with the following signs and symptoms may be suffering from -

DEEP FROSTBITE (D) or SUPERFICIAL FROSTBITE (S).

A. 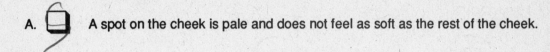 A spot on the cheek is pale and does not feel as soft as the rest of the cheek.

B 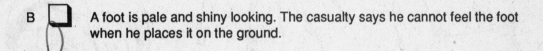 A foot is pale and shiny looking. The casualty says he cannot feel the foot when he places it on the ground.

C. One ear is white and the casualty complains of a dull feeling in the ear lobe.

D. The tips of the fingers of one hand are colourless and cold. The surface of the skin feels firm but you can feel soft tissue underneath.

E. 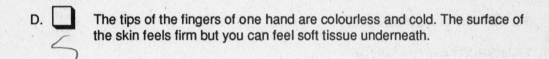 There is no reaction when you touch the casualty's hand. The skin feels cold and very firm and looks shiny.

When **FROSTBITE** is **SUPERFICIAL** -

- **REWARM** the frostbitten part **GRADUALLY** with the heat of your body

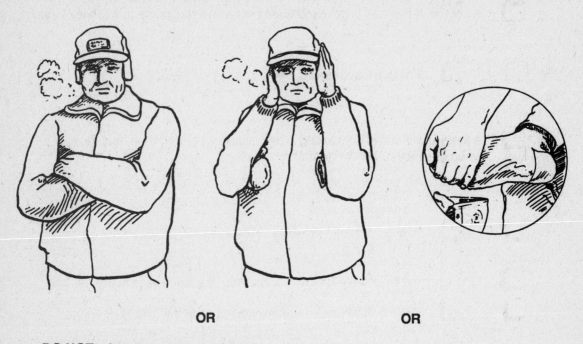

OR   OR

- **DO NOT** rub or put snow on a frostbitten part

A casualty with **DEEP FROSTBITE** requires medical attention -

- **DO NOT THAW** the frozen part

- **TRANSPORT** him by stretcher

If the casualty must walk to medical aid -

- **DO NOT THAW THE FROZEN PART**
  (Walking on a frozen foot is not likely to cause more serious damage.)

- **ASSIST** the casualty to make walking easier

> **TREAT** the frozen part **GENTLY** to **PREVENT FURTHER TISSUE DAMAGE**

Which of the following actions are correct first aid for frostbite?

	Yes	No	
A.	☑	☐	Place your frostbitten hands in your armpits to warm them.
B.	☐	☒	Warm a frozen foot quickly by using a heating pad.
C.	☑	☐	If your ears become numb in the cold, cover them with your hands.
D.	☐	☒	Briskly massage frostbitten toes with your hands.
E.	☐	☒	Hold a handful of soft snow against a frostbitten cheek.
F.	☑	☐	A casualty with a frozen leg should be carried, if possible, to the nearest medical facility.
G.	☑	☐	If a casualty with a severely frostbitten foot cannot be carried to medical aid, do not rewarm his foot but help him to walk.
H.	☑	☐	Handle the casualty with care to avoid aggravating his injury.

A. |Yes| B. |No| C. |Yes| D. |No| E. |No| F. |Yes| G. |Yes| H. |Yes|

22

Thawing of a frozen body part will cause pain and should **ONLY** be attempted when -

- Medical aid is **NOT** available

- The casualty is in a **WARM, SAFE** environment

- There is **NO** danger of refreezing

If you **MUST** thaw a frozen part, you should -

- Place the frozen part in **WARM WATER** at 40°C (104°F) until tissues become soft to the touch. Warmer water will cause extreme pain

- **DRY** the injured part and apply clean dressings to any broken skin

- **COVER** the frozen part lightly

- Keep the casualty **WARM** and **MONITOR** his condition

Your friend has severe frostbite of both hands and forearms. You are in a remote region and cut off from medical aid.

Which of the following procedures should you carry out?

	Yes	No	
A.	☐	☑	Rub his hands and arms briskly.
B.	☐	☑	Place the frostbitten areas under a fast-running cold-water tap.
C.	☑	☐	Soak his hands and arms in a tub of water at a temperature of not less than 39°C (103°F) and not more than 40°C (104°F).
D.	☑	☐	When you have thawed his hands and arms, cover any blisters or wounds with sterile gauze.
E.	☐	☑	Leave his hands and arms exposed to the air for rewarming.
F.	☑	☐	Watch him carefully and make sure he does not become cold again.

22-11   A. No   B. No   C. Yes   D. Yes   E. No   F. Yes

22

HYPOTHERMIA is body temperature below normal and usually results from being in cold water or being exposed to abnormally cold air for prolonged periods of time.

Hypothermia may progress from **MILD** to **MODERATE** to **SEVERE** if first aid is not given.

The following table lists the changes in the signs that may occur as the casualty's condition worsens during the stages of hypothermia -

SIGNS	PROGRESSIVE STAGES OF HYPOTHERMIA		
	MILD	MODERATE	SEVERE
Body temp.	35°C (95°F)	below 32°C (89. 6°F)	below 27°C (80. 6°F)
Pulse	normal range	slow and weak	weak, irregular or absent
Breathing	normal range	slow	slow or absent
Appearance	shivering, slurred speech	shivering may stop	shivering has **stopped**
Mental State	conscious, withdrawn	confused, sleepy	unconscious

22-13

Mark each statement true **(T)** or false **(F)**.

A. ☐   A person who is wet and in the cold may develop hypothermia.

B. ☒   A person in mild hypothermia will have a temperature of below 32°C (89. 6°F).

C. ☑   Hypothermia becomes more serious as the casualty's temperature falls.

D. ☒   A person in moderate hypothermia may have a rapid pulse and laboured breathing.

E. ☑   A person suffering from very long exposure to cold may appear to have no signs of life.

F. ☑   A person in severe hypothermia will cease to tremble.

22-13   A. T   B. F   C. T   D. F   E. T   F. T

22

22-14

When a casualty is suffering from **HYPOTHERMIA**, you should -

- Handle him **GENTLY** with the **LEAST** possible movement (rough handling can result in life-threatening problems)

- **REMOVE** wet clothing and place him under warm covers, such as a warmed sleeping bag

- Apply **BODY HEAT** or place the casualty near a **SOURCE OF HEAT**

- Give him a **WARM, SWEET DRINK**, if he is **CONSCIOUS**

- Monitor **BREATHING** and **PULSE**

22-15

A man is pulled from an icy lake. He is conscious and shivering.

The following are possible actions you could take. Number them in the best order of performance.

2 A. ☑ Wrap him in blankets.

5 B. ☐ Watch him closely.

4 C. ☐ Give him some tea and sugar.

3 D. ☐ Lay him near an open fire.

1 E. ☑ Take off his soaked clothes with care.

22-15

A. 2   B. 5   C. 4   D. 3   E. 1

22

If breathing stops when a casualty is in **SEVERE HYPOTHERMIA** and it is necessary to give artificial respiration -

- Reduce the rate of ventilation to **ONE BREATH EVERY 12 to 15 SECONDS**

- Check the carotid pulse for **UP TO 3 MINUTES** to ensure that a slow, weak pulse will not go undetected

If a carotid pulse is **NOT** present, you should -

- **GET MEDICAL AID AS QUICKLY AS POSSIBLE AND START CPR**

- Give ventilations at a reduced rate (see above)

- Perform chest compressions at a slightly slower rate

> **IF CPR CANNOT BE MAINTAINED WITHOUT INTERRUPTION UNTIL HAND-OVER TO MEDICAL AID, IT SHOULD NOT BE STARTED. CONTINUE VENTILATING UNTIL MEDICAL AID ARRIVES**

Which of the following actions would be considered correct first aid for a non-breathing casualty suffering from severe hypothermia?

Yes **No**

A. ☑ ☐ Open the airway and reassess breathing.

B. ☐ ☑ Allow 3 seconds to check the pulse at the neck after giving the initial two breaths.

C. ☐ ☑ Blow air into his mouth at a rate of one breath every 5 seconds.

D. ☑ ☐ If there is no heartbeat, CPR is required.

E. ☑ ☐ If necessary, begin CPR if you are qualified and can continue until help arrives.

A. Yes   B. No   C. No   D. Yes   E. Yes

22-18

HEAT CRAMPS, HEAT EXHAUSTION and **HEATSTROKE** are heat illnesses that are caused by -

- **LONG EXPOSURE** to hot conditions

- **OVEREXPOSURE** to the sun

- **LACK OF FLUIDS** to replace lost body fluids

- **VIGOROUS EXERCISE** or hard labour in a hot environment

To prevent heat illnesses, you should -

- Expose the body **GRADUALLY** to a hot environment

- Protect the **HEAD** from direct sunshine

- Drink **SUFFICIENT WATER** to replace body fluids lost from sweating

- Avoid **LONG PERIODS** of work or exercise in a hot environment

22-19

Which of the following precautions would help you to avoid illness from exposure to heat?

Yes   **No**

A. ☐   ☐   Take drinks to prevent your body from drying out when you are working in the heat.

B. ☐   ☐   Avoid wearing a hat on a hot sunny day to allow excess body heat to be lost through the head.

C. ☐   ☐   If you are not used to a hot climate or workplace, stay in the heat for only a short time.

D. ☐   ☐   Take frequent breaks and sit in a cool place when you are working or playing on a hot day.

22-19   A. Yes   B. No   C. Yes   D. Yes

22

22-20

Either or both of the following signs and symptoms may indicate that a person has **HEAT CRAMPS** -

SIGNS

You may observe:

- Excessive sweating

SYMPTOMS

The casualty may complain of:

- Painful muscle spasms in the limbs and abdomen

22-21

Which of the following signs and symptoms would help you to assess a casualty's condition as heat cramps?

A. ☑ Very moist skin.

B. ☐ Loss of feeling in the limbs and lower body.

C. ☐ Very dry skin.

D. ☑ Great discomfort and tightening of the muscles of the arms and legs.

22-21   A. ☑   D. ☑

When a person is suffering from heat cramps, you should -

- Place him at rest **IN A COOL PLACE**

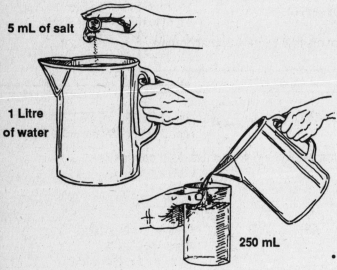

5 mL of salt

1 Litre
of water

250 mL

- Give him a glass (250mL) of **SLIGHTLY SALTED** water to drink (Mix 5mL of salt to 1L of water - 1 tsp of salt to 1 quart of water = 0. 5%.)

- Give **ONE MORE** glass of salted water in **10 MINUTES**

- **DO NOT** give any more salted water even if cramps persist

- Obtain medical aid if muscle pains continue

A man who is playing soccer on a hot day complains of pain in his legs and arms.

Which of the following should you do?

Choice 1		Choice 2
A. ☑ Lay him down in the shade of a tree.	**OR**	A. ☐ Lay him down on the playing field until the pain disappears.
B. ☑ Make a salted drink by mixing 5 mL of salt with 1 L of water (1 tsp. salt to 1 quart water).	**OR**	B. ☐ Make a salted drink by adding 5 mL of salt to 2 L of water (1 tsp. salt to 2 quarts of water).
C. ☐ Give him 250 mL of cool water to drink.	**OR**	C. ☑ Give him 250 mL of slightly salted water to drink.
D. ☑ Give him a second glass of salted water if spasms continue for more than 10 minutes.	**OR**	D. ☐ Give him sips of cool water if spasms continue for more than 10 minutes.
E. ☐ Give him a third glass of salted water if the cramps persist.	**OR**	E. ☑ Take him to medical aid if the cramps persist.

HEAT EXHAUSTION is a more serious heat illness than heat cramps.

Any or all of the following signs and symptoms may indicate that a casualty is suffering from heat exhaustion.

SIGNS

You may observe:

- Excessive sweating
- Cold, clammy, pale skin
- Weak and rapid pulse

- Rapid, shallow breathing
- Vomiting
- Unconsciousness

SYMPTOMS

The casualty may complain of:

- Blurred vision
- Dizziness
- Headache

- Nausea
- Painful muscle cramps in arms, legs and abdomen

22-25

When a casualty is suffering from heat exhaustion, which of the following signs and symptoms may be present?

A. ☑ His skin is whitish, cool and damp.

B. ☐ His pulse and breathing are very slow.

C. ☑ He tells you that he cannot see clearly, has a sore head and he feels sick to his stomach.

D. ☑ He has difficulty walking because his legs hurt.

E. ☑ He collapses and does not respond.

22-25

A. ☑   C. ☑   D. ☑   E. ☑

22

The first aid for heat exhaustion is a combination of the first aid for heat cramps and shock.

If the casualty is **FULLY CONSCIOUS** -

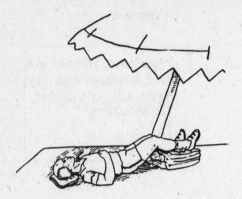

- Place him at rest **IN A COOL PLACE**, with feet and legs **ELEVATED**

- **LOOSEN TIGHT CLOTHING** at neck and waist, and remove excessive clothing

- Give **SLIGHTLY SALTED WATER** (0. 5% solution) to drink, as much as the casualty will take

If casualty becomes **UNCONSCIOUS** -

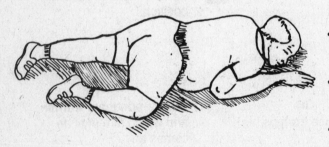

- Place him in the **RECOVERY POSITION**

- Monitor **BREATHING** and give artificial respiration, if necessary

- Obtain medical aid

A man working in a hot assembly plant complains of muscle spasms and is beginning to show signs of shock.

If he is fully conscious, you should -

Choice 1   **Choice 2**

A. ☑ Help him to lie down in a well ventilated area and place a support under his ankles and legs.   **OR**   A. ☐ Help him to sit down in a well ventilated area and place a support behind his shoulders.

B. ☐ Give him nothing to eat or drink so that he will not feel ill.   **OR**   B. ☑ Give him as much of a weak salt solution as he will drink.

C. ☐ Ensure his clothing is snug and warm.   **OR**   C. ☑ Untie his collar and belt.

If the man loses consciousness, you should -

D. ☐ Place him on his back.   **OR**   D. ☑ Place him in the recovery position.

E. ☑ Ensure adequate breathing and send someone for medical assistance.   **OR**   E. ☐ Ensure adequate warmth and watch him until he comes to.

22-27

A. [1]   B. [2]   C. [2]   D. [2]   E. [1]

22

22-28

HEATSTROKE is **LIFE-THREATENING** and is far more serious than heat cramps or heat exhaustion. The following signs and symptoms may indicate heatstroke -

SIGNS

You may observe:

- Body temperature as high as 44°C (111°F)
- Rapid and full pulse
- Flushed, hot, **DRY** skin

- Noisy breathing
- Vomiting
- Restlessness
- Convulsions
- Unconsciousness

SYMPTOMS

The casualty may complain of:

- Headache
- Dizziness

- Nausea

Elderly persons or those in poor health are more likely to experience heatstroke.

22-29

When a person has heatstroke, he may -

Choice 1		Choice 2
A. ☐ Be in no danger.	**OR**	A. ☑ Be in grave danger.
B. ☑ Appear red in the face and breathe with difficulty.	**OR**	B. ☐ Appear white in the face and breathe quietly.
C ☐ Feel cold to the touch and be covered with droplets of sweat.	**OR**	C. ☑ Feel extremely warm to the touch and show no sign of sweating.
D. ☑ Complain that his head hurts and that he is about to vomit.	**OR**	D. ☐ Complain that his back hurts and that his fingers are numb.
E. ☑ Have a temperature of 43°C (109°F) and a fast pulse.	**OR**	E. ☐ Have a temperature of 35°C (95°F) and a slow pulse.
F. ☐ Feel weak as a result of internal bleeding.	**OR**	F. ☑ Pass out and fall to the ground.

22-29

A.	2	B.	1	C.	2	D.	1	E.	1	F.	2

22

A person suffering from heatstroke is in a **VERY SERIOUS CONDITION** because the body is overheated and **CANNOT** reduce its temperature without assistance.

SEND FOR MEDICAL AID IMMEDIATELY

To prevent permanent damage or death, you must **REDUCE BODY TEMPERATURE QUICKLY.**

To cool the body, you should -

- **REMOVE CLOTHING**

    AND

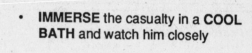

- **IMMERSE** the casualty in a **COOL BATH** and watch him closely

    OR

- **SPONGE** the casualty with **COOL WATER**, particularly in the armpit, neck, head and groin areas

    OR

- **COVER** him with **WET SHEETS** and direct **COOL AIR** over him by fanning

When the body feels cooler to the touch (38°C or 100. 4°F), place him in the **RECOVERY POSITION** and cover him with a dry sheet.

Monitor the casualty and if his **TEMPERATURE RISES, REPEAT** the cooling procedure.

A long distance runner collapses at the finish line of a race.

He has hot, dry, flushed skin and is breathing noisily.

Which three of the following cooling techniques could you use to reduce his body temperature quickly?

A. ☑ Apply a cold towel to his forehead.

B. ☑ Place cold, wet cloths on his forehead, the back of his neck, under his arms and around his lower abdomen.

C. ☐ Place his feet in a pail of cool water.

D. ☑ Soak him in a large tub filled with cool water.

E. ☑ Place a cool, wet bath sheet over his body and circulate air around him.

F. ☐ Wrap cold towels around his wrists and ankles.

You have reduced the body temperature of a casualty suffering from heatstroke.

Which of the following actions should you take while awaiting medical aid?

A. ☐ Place a wet towel over him and elevate his feet.

B. ☑ Position him to ensure an open airway and place a large, dry towel over him.

C. ☐ Cover him with a light blanket and leave him alone to ensure his privacy.

D. ☑ Watch him carefully and take measures to cool him, if he becomes hot again.

| 22-31 | B. ✓ | D. ✓ | E. ✓ | 22-32 | B. ✓ | D. ✓ |

22-33

Mark each statement true **(T)** or false **(F)**.

A. ☑ Heat illnesses may be caused by vigorous activities in a hot, humid environment.

B. ☒ Heat exhaustion is more serious than heatstroke.

C. ☑ Hypothermia may result when a casualty is wet and exposed to a cold environment for a prolonged period.

D. ☒ Normal body temperature is about 41°C.

E. ☑ Frostbite that extends into the body tissues is more serious than frostbite to the skin surface.

F. ☒ A casualty with heat cramps is in a life-threatening condition.

G. ☑ The aim of first aid for heatstroke is to reduce the body temperature as quickly as possible.

H. ☑ To prevent injuries from the cold, wear layered protective clothing and avoid getting wet or tired.

I. ☑ The aims of first aid for hypothermia are to prevent further loss of body heat and increase body temperature.

22-33

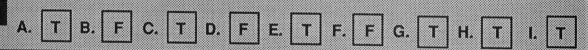

A. T B. F C. T D. F E. T F. F G. T H. T I. T

22

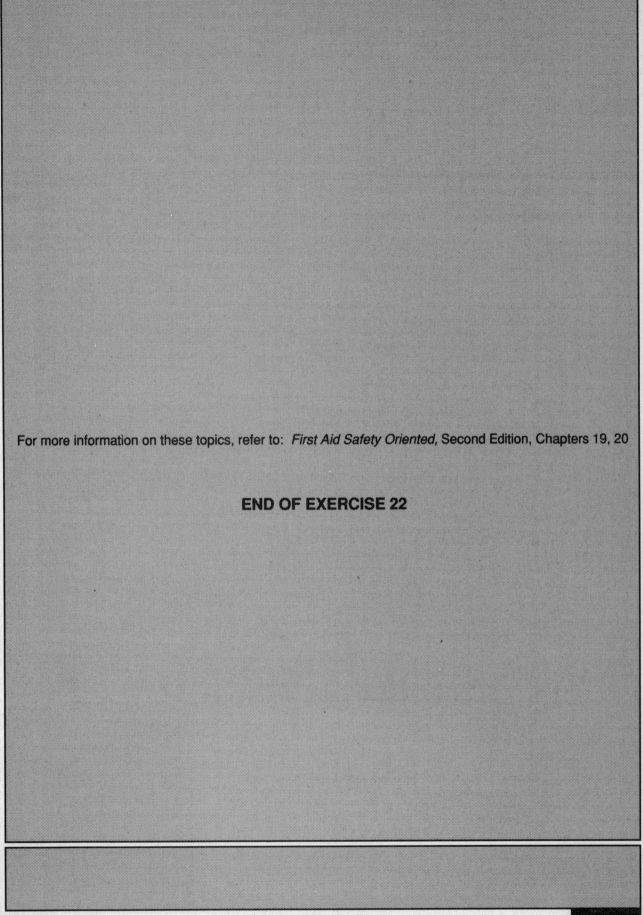

For more information on these topics, refer to: *First Aid Safety Oriented,* Second Edition, Chapters 19, 20

END OF EXERCISE 22

22

INTRODUCTION TO EMERGENCY CHILDBIRTH

23-1

A basic knowledge of the female reproductive system and its relationship to the unborn child will help you to give assistance during an emergency delivery.

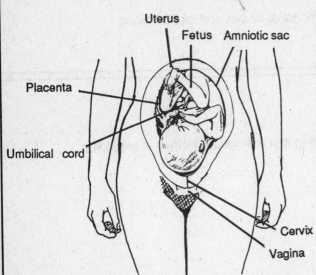

The Female Reproductive System

FETUS	-	The developing baby
UTERUS	-	The organ inside which the fetus develops
CERVIX	-	The neck of the uterus
AMNIOTIC SAC	-	A fluid filled membrane which protects the fetus
PLACENTA	-	A large, flat organ which supplies the fetus with nutrients and oxygen
UMBILICAL CORD	-	The cord which connects the fetus and the placenta
VAGINA	-	The birth canal leading from the uterus to outside the body

23-2

Mark each statement true (**T**) or false (**F**).

A. ☐ The fetus is the unborn infant which lies inside a thin bag filled with a water-like substance.

B. ☐ The fetus takes in oxygen and nourishment from the amniotic fluid.

C. ☐ During delivery the fetus enters the birth canal through the opened cervix.

D. ☐ The placenta is attached to the fetus by the umbilical cord.

23-2

A. T   B. F   C. T   D. T

23-3

LABOUR is the process through which a baby is delivered.

The BEGINNING OF LABOUR is signalled by -

- Labour pains (contractions of the uterus)

- Breaking of the amniotic sac and release of the fluid through the vagina

- Appearance of a "bloody show" (a small amount of mucus and blood flowing from the vagina)

23-4

Which of the following are normal signs indicating that a pregnant woman is beginning labour?

A. ☐   Frequent urination.

B. ☐   A gush or trickle of watery fluid from the vagina.

C. ☐   Sharp pains felt in the abdomen.

D. ☐   A steady flow of blood from the vagina.

E. ☐   A pinkish discharge from the vagina.

23-4

B. ✓   C. ✓   E. ✓

23

23-5

In the **EARLY STAGES OF LABOUR,** transport the mother to the hospital.

In some cases this may not be possible.

INDICATIONS OF IMMINENT DELIVERY ARE -

- Long, strong contractions (pain) at frequent and regular intervals

- Mother's desire to move her bowels

- Mother's previous experience and feelings of imminent birth

- Bulging of the vagina (crowning) or appearance of the baby's head through the vagina

23-6

Mark each statement true **(T)** or false **(F)**.

A. ☐ The urge of the mother to have a bowel movement is a symptom that the baby is about to be born.

B. ☐ Intense pain every two minutes usually indicates that the baby will be delivered within minutes.

C. ☐ When the baby's head can be seen through the vagina, there is still adequate time to transport the mother to the hospital.

D. ☐ A mother who has given birth before can usually assess accurately when delivery is about to occur.

23-6   A. T   B. T   C. F   D. T

23

23-7

To **PREPARE** for an emergency delivery -

- Locate an assistant (female if possible)
- Assemble materials (e.g. clean towels, sheets, baby blanket, absorbent material, container for placenta)
- Provide soap, water and towels for washing your hands

In assembling your emergency supplies, keep in mind that the **AIMS** of first aid in an emergency delivery are to -

- **PROTECT** the mother and baby
- **KEEP** the baby dry and warm
- **PROTECT** the umbilical cord and placenta

23-8

Which of these items and people would be most useful in an emergency childbirth situation?

A. ☐ Adhesive bandages.

B. ☐ Clean cloths.

C. ☐ Sanitary pads.

D. ☐ The pregnant woman's sister.

E. ☐ Boiling water.

F. ☐ Clean sheeting.

G. ☐ The family from next door.

H. ☐ A plastic bag.

I. ☐ Clean wraps for the baby.

23-8

B. ✓   C. ✓   D. ✓   F. ✓   H. ✓   I. ✓

23

To **PREPARE THE MOTHER** for delivery -

- Provide reassurance, comfort and **PRIVACY**

- **POSITION** her on her back with her knees bent and her head propped up

- **PLACE** clean towels under her buttocks and between her legs

- **COVER** her with sheets or towels

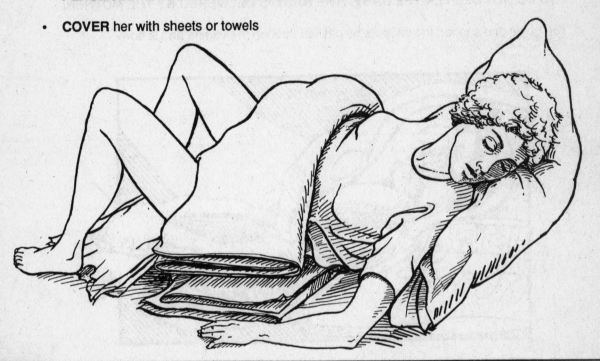

23-10

Mark each statement true **(T)** or false **(F)**.

A. ☐ A large number of assistants will speed up the birth.

B. ☐ The mother should be kept as calm and relaxed as possible.

C. ☐ Every attempt must be made to ensure that the mother and child are exposed to as few germs as possible.

D. ☐ The mother will be most comfortable with a few pillows under her head.

E. ☐ Clean materials should be placed under and over the mother to prepare for the birth.

23-10   A. F   B. T   C. T   D. T   E. T

23-11

The role of the First Aider in emergency childbirth is to -

- **ASSIST** the mother in the delivery of the baby
- **PROTECT** the baby and the mother during and after delivery

YOU DO NOT DELIVER THE BABY. THE BABY IS DELIVERED BY THE MOTHER.

You guide and support the baby as he passes through the vagina and is born.

Cross-sectional View of Delivery of the Head

23-12

Check (✔) the correct statements regarding first aid during an emergency delivery.

A. ☐ The baby must be pulled by the First Aider from the birth canal.

B. ☐ Delivery is a natural process accomplished by the mother's body.

C. ☐ Mother and child both require care after delivery.

D. ☐ The role of the First Aider in emergency childbirth is to ensure the safety of the mother and the infant.

23-12

B. ✔   C. ✔   D. ✔

23

23-13

The baby's head will usually be born first. If the head is pushed out too quickly, the baby may be injured.

To prevent this -

- Tell the mother to **CONTROL** her **PUSHING**

- Apply a **VERY GENTLE RESTRAINT** on the baby's head to slow delivery

- Once the head is delivered, ask the mother to **PUSH HARDER**

As the baby is being delivered, carefully support the head and body.

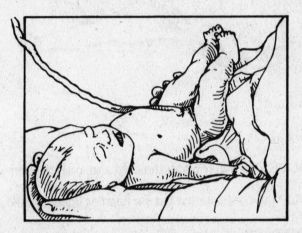

23-14

Mark each statement true **(T)** or false **(F)**.

A. ☐   Rapid emerging of the head can be dangerous to the infant.

B. ☐   Use a very light control with the palm of your hand to ease the baby's head out of the vagina.

C. ☐   Once the top of the head is visible, tell the mother to increase her efforts.

D. ☐   Place both hands around the baby's head and pull it out of the vagina.

E. ☐   Gently and securely hold the newborn when it is emerging from the birth canal.

23-14   A. T   B. T   C. F   D. F   E. T

A baby may be born with the **UMBILICAL CORD** around his neck.

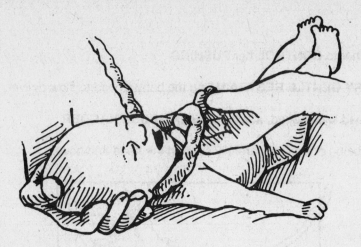

To ensure an open airway -

- **SLIDE** your finger under the cord and loosen it gently

- **SLIP** the cord over the baby's head or upper shoulder

Which of the following procedures should be carried out if a baby is born with the umbilical cord around his neck?

A. ☐ Cut the cord immediately.

B. ☐ Stretch the cord gently.

C. ☐ Pull the baby's head through the cord.

D. ☐ Ease the cord away from the baby's neck.

E. ☐ Wait for medical aid.

F. ☐ Avoid exerting force on the cord.

23-16

B. ✓   D. ✓   F. ✓

23

Newborns are covered with a very **SLIPPERY** material that makes them difficult to hold.

Handle the baby **FIRMLY, CAREFULLY AND GENTLY.**

- **WIPE** the baby's face to clear the nose and mouth
- Hold the baby with the head lower than the body to **CLEAR FLUIDS FROM THE AIRWAY**
- Begin **ARTIFICIAL RESPIRATION** if the baby does not breathe
- **DRY** the baby and keep him **WARM**
- **POSITION** the baby on the mother's **ABDOMEN**

LAY THE BABY ON HIS SIDE WITH HIS HEAD DOWN AND FACING THE FIRST AIDER. THIS WILL ASSIST DRAINAGE AND ALLOW YOU TO MONITOR BREATHING

Choose the correct procedures for caring for a newborn baby immediately after birth.

Choice 1		**Choice 2**
A. ☐ Use both hands and hold the baby with extreme care.	**OR**	A. ☐ Use one hand to hold the baby and the other to comfort the mother.
B. ☐ Rub the infant gently immediately following delivery.	**OR**	B. ☐ Clean the infant's mouth and nose immediately after delivery.
C. ☐ To ensure a clear airway, position the baby with the lower body and feet slightly elevated.	**OR**	C. ☐ To ensure a clear airway, hold the baby upside down by the ankles.
D. ☐ If the baby isn't breathing, blow into his mouth and nose.	**OR**	D. ☐ If the baby isn't breathing, slap him between the shoulder blades.
E. ☐ Dry the baby and wrap him in a cool sheet.	**OR**	E. ☐ Dry the baby and wrap him in a warm towel.
F. ☐ Lay the baby sideways on top of the mother's stomach with his head lowered and turned toward the First Aider.	**OR**	F. ☐ Place the baby lengthwise on the mother's chest with his head turned toward her.

A. 1   B. 2   C. 1   D. 1   E. 2   F. 1

23-19

The **UMBILICAL CORD** connects the baby to the **PLACENTA** (afterbirth).

The **PLACENTA** will usually be delivered within 20 minutes following the baby's birth.

> **NEVER ATTEMPT TO FORCE DELIVERY OF THE PLACENTA BY PULLING ON THE CORD**

To assist -

- Gently massage the mother's lower abdomen to hasten the delivery
- Catch the placenta in a clean towel
- Ensure that all parts of the placenta are saved
- Keep the placenta at the same level as the newborn
- Place the placenta in a plastic bag and wrap it with the infant for transportation to the hospital

> **DO NOT CUT OR TIE THE UMBILICAL CORD**

23-20

Mark each statement true **(T)** or false **(F)**.

A. ☐ Once the baby has been born, tug on the umbilical cord to speed up delivery of the placenta.

B. ☐ After delivery of the placenta, you should cut the umbilical cord with sterile scissors.

C. ☐ All pieces of the placenta must be kept for examination by a doctor.

D. ☐ Normally the baby and placenta will still be joined by the umbilical cord when they are transferred to the hospital.

E. ☐ If the placenta is not expelled within five minutes of the baby's birth, it will have to be removed by a doctor.

F. ☐ Once the placenta is outside the birth canal, its position in relationship to the newborn is unimportant.

23-20

A.	B.	C.	D.	E.	F.
F	F	T	T	F	F

23

If there is obvious **BLEEDING** from the **PLACENTA, ACT QUICKLY!**

TIE the umbilical cord 15 to 30 centimetres (6 to 12 in.) from the baby's abdomen. Use a clean tape or heavy string.

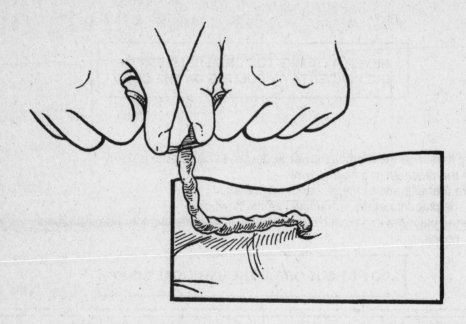

> **TAKE CARE NOT TO CUT THE CORD WITH THE TIE**

Mark each statement true **(T)** or false **(F)**.

A. ☐ Bleeding from the placenta is a normal occurrence during an emergency delivery.

B. ☐ If the placenta is bleeding, a thin string or thread should be used to tie the umbilical cord.

C. ☐ Tie the umbilical cord as close as possible to the baby's navel.

D. ☐ Adhesive tape or thick twine could be used to tie the umbilical cord without damaging it.

E. ☐ If there is no bleeding from the placenta, the umbilical cord should be left alone.

A. F   B. F   C. F   D. T   E. T

23

To **CARE FOR THE MOTHER** after delivery of the placenta -

- APPLY SANITARY PADS OVER THE VAGINA TO ABSORB BLEEDING

- CONTROL BLEEDING BY FIRMLY MASSAGING THE LOWER ABDOMEN

- TRANSFER TO MEDICAL AID AS SOON AS POSSIBLE

- IF TRANSFER IS DELAYED, LET THE BABY SUCK FROM HIS MOTHER'S BREAST

23-24

Mark each statement true **(T)** or false **(F)**.

A. ☐ Some bleeding can be expected after the expulsion of the placenta.

B. ☐ Bleeding can be stopped by packing the vagina with sterile pads.

C. ☐ Mother and child should be moved to the hospital as soon as delivery is complete.

D. ☐ Allow the mother to feed the newborn if you are unable to take them to a medical facility immediately.

23-24   A. [T]   B. [F]   C. [T]   D. [T]

23-25

There will be some bleeding from the mother after the delivery of the placenta.

If **BLEEDING** from the vagina does not stop -

- Continue **MASSAGING** the **ABDOMEN** over the uterus

- Place the mother in the **SHOCK POSITION**

- Transport **IMMEDIATELY** to the closest medical facility

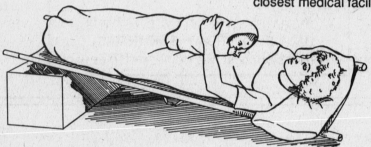

23-26

Check (✓) the actions you should take to deal with excessive bleeding from the mother after the delivery of the placenta.

A. ☐   Pack the vagina tightly with sterile pads.

B. ☐   Continue your efforts to stop bleeding by gentle but firm stroking of the area over the uterus.

C. ☐   Position the mother with the legs and feet elevated to 15-30 cm (6-12 in.).

D. ☐   Bring the mother as fast as possible to the nearest hospital.

23-26

B.   C. ✓   D.

23

23-27

Mark each statement true (T) or false (F).

A. ☐ The placenta must always be delivered after the birth of the baby.

B. ☐ The baby will require considerable assistance from you to help extract him from the mother.

C. ☐ During the early stages of labour, the mother should be transported to the hospital.

D. ☐ A mother's feeling that she needs to move her bowels often means delivery is about to occur.

E. ☐ The baby's feet are usually delivered first.

F. ☐ All newborns have fluid in the nose and throat which must be cleared immediately after delivery.

G. ☐ If the baby doesn't breathe on his own, begin artificial respiration.

H. ☐ When an infant is born with the umbilical cord around his neck, you should ease the cord away from the neck and slide it over his head.

23-27 A. T B. F C. T D. T E. F F. T G. T H. T

23

For further information on this topic, refer to: *First Aid Safety Oriented*, Second Edition, Chapter 24

END OF EXERCISE 23

ADDENDUM A
BASIC ANATOMY AND PHYSIOLOGY

Addendum A, Basic Anatomy and Physiology, is not required study for certification in Standard First Aid course. Therefore, you will not be tested on this material.

This workbook exercise is included for your interest and home study and to assist you in enriching your first aid knowledge.

NOTES

Certain **TOPOGRAPHIC TERMS** are used in first aid. The terms are used to describe the human body in the anatomic position - **standing erect**, with **palms forward** and **facing the First Aider.**

Use of these terms is necessary to give **PRECISE** and **ACCURATE** information about a casualty's condition.

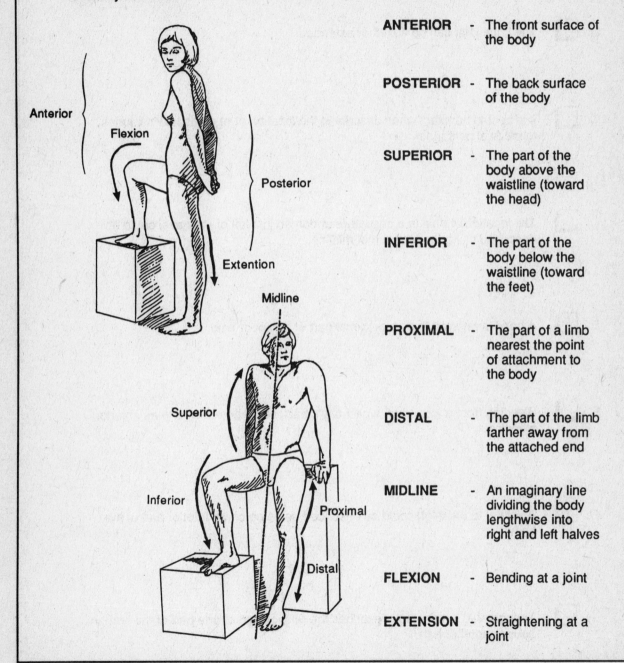

ANTERIOR - The front surface of the body

POSTERIOR - The back surface of the body

SUPERIOR - The part of the body above the waistline (toward the head)

INFERIOR - The part of the body below the waistline (toward the feet)

PROXIMAL - The part of a limb nearest the point of attachment to the body

DISTAL - The part of the limb farther away from the attached end

MIDLINE - An imaginary line dividing the body lengthwise into right and left halves

FLEXION - Bending at a joint

EXTENSION - Straightening at a joint

Mark each statement true **(T)** or false **(F)**.

A. ☐ An injury to the shin would be described as being distal to the knee.

B. ☐ The knee joint can be flexed or extended.

C. ☐ It is best to be exact when describing the location of of a casualty's injuries to medical personnel.

D. ☐ The location of pain in a casualty's abdomen just left of the navel could be described using the term left of midline.

E. ☐ A hand is referred to as a proximal part of an upper limb.

F. ☐ Bleeding from a wound on a casualty's back could be referred to as anterior bleeding.

G. ☐ A wound to the thigh could be described as being on an inferior part of the body.

H. ☐ Topographic terminology describes the relationship of one part of the human body to another part.

A-2

A. T   B. T   C. T   D. T   E. F   F. F   G. T   H. T

A

A-3

A **SYSTEM** is a group of body organs which together perform one or more **VITAL FUNCTIONS**.

The systems we are concerned with are -

- **Musculoskeletal**
- **Nervous**
- **Digestive**
- **Circulatory**
- **Respiratory**
- **Urinary**
- **Reproductive**

A First Aider should have the basic knowledge of -

- What makes up each system
- How each system functions
- What happens when a system is damaged

TO ALLOW THE BODY TO FUNCTION, ALL SYSTEMS WORK TOGETHER. INJURY TO ONE SYSTEM ALMOST ALWAYS RESULTS IN INJURY TO ONE OR MORE OF THE OTHER SYSTEMS

A-4

Check (✓) the correct statements.

A. ☐ Each of the body's working parts is self-contained and operates independently of each other.

B. ☐ There are several parts to each body system.

C. ☐ An understanding of the bodily functions will help a First Aider when assessing a casualty's condition.

D. ☐ When one system of the body does not function properly because of illness or injury, expect malfunctions in other systems as well.

A-4

B. ☑   C. ☑   D. ☑

A

A-5

The **MUSCULOSKELETAL SYSTEM** forms the **FRAMEWORK** of the body. Injury to any part of the system usually affects another part. It also protects organs and allows movement.

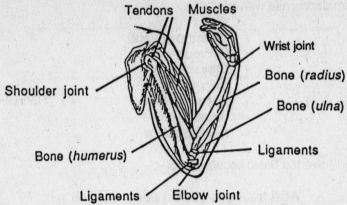

Following is a short description of each component of the musculoskeletal system:

MUSCLES - A tissue that shortens as a result of nerve stimulation and results in movement.

TENDONS - Tough ropes of tissue which attach the muscles to the bones and are the muscles points of action to a bone.

BONES - The hard tissue that forms the skeleton.

JOINTS - The place where two or more bones meet. Joints interacting with tendons and muscles make movement possible.

LIGAMENTS - Bands of strong supporting tissue which connect bone to bone about a joint or support any organ.

A-6

Mark each statement true (T) or false (F)

A. ☐ Damage to a bone may involve muscles, tendons and joint movement.

B. ☐ Muscles are connected to bones by ligaments.

C. ☐ The bones of the skeleton make up the musculoskeletal system.

D. ☐ When we move a body part, nerves, muscles, bones and tendons act together.

A-6

A. T   B. F   C. F   D. T

A

The bones of the **SKELETON** give the body **SHAPE AND FIRMNESS**.

SKELETON

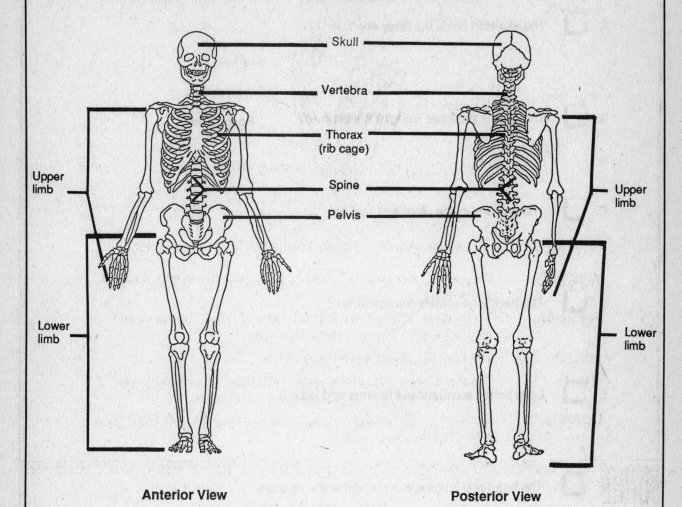

Anterior View

Posterior View

- The **SKULL** surrounds and protects the brain.

- The **SPINE** (backbone) protects the spinal cord.

- The **THORAX** (rib cage) protects the heart, lungs, liver, spleen and partially the kidneys.

- The **PELVIS** protects the ureters, bladder, urethra, intestine, rectum and reproductive organs.

- The long bones of the **UPPER AND LOWER LIMBS** afford some protection for the

Mark each statement true (T) or false (F).

A. ☐ The skeleton holds the body erect.

B. ☐ The skull is the inner lining of the brain.

C. ☐ The pelvis is made up of soft tissues.

D. ☐ The backbone shields the spinal cord.

E. ☐ Long bones are found in the arms and legs.

F. ☐ The heart and lungs are contained in the rib cage.

G. ☐ The intestines are protected by the bony structure of the pelvis.

A. T B. F C. F D. T E. T F. T G. F

The Cranium
(The Skull)

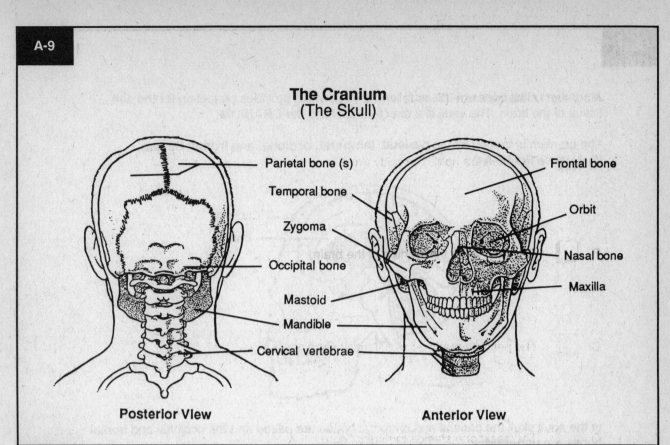

Parietal bone (s)

Temporal bone

Zygoma

Occipital bone

Mastoid

Mandible

Cervical vertebrae

Frontal bone

Orbit

Nasal bone

Maxilla

Posterior View

Anterior View

Label the bones of the cranium where indicated.

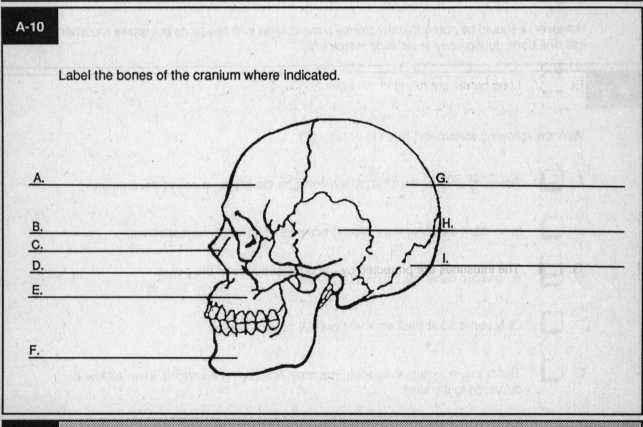

A.

B.
C.
D.
E.

F.

G.

H.

I.

A. Frontal	D. Zygoma	G. Parietal
B. Orbit	E. Maxilla	H. Temporal
C. Nasal	F. Mandible	I. Occipital

A number of flat bones of the skull form a vault which provides protection for the soft tissue of the brain. The vault like structure is called the **CRANIUM**.

The cranium is formed by the **parietal, temporal, occipital** and **frontal bones**. (Reference Frame A-9.)

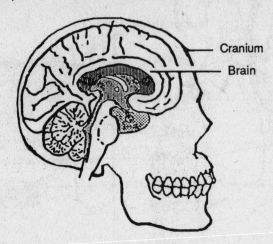

Cranium

Brain

In the adult skull the parietal and temporal bones are paired and the occipital and frontal bones are **unpaired**.

However, it should be noted that the frontal bone at birth is in two parts but grows together into one bone during early skeletal development.

Mark the following statements true **(T)** or false **(F)**.

A. ☐ The bony shell of the skull, which contains the brain, is called the cranium.

B. ☐ In an adult skull there are two (2) occipital and two (2) frontal bones.

C. ☐ A newborn baby has two frontal bones.

D. ☐ Only in the adult skull are there two (2) parietal bones.

E. ☐ The cranium assists in keeping the brain from being damaged when a blow is delivered to the skull.

A-12

A. ☐T   B. ☐F   C. ☐T   D. ☐F   E. ☐T

A

The Vertebral Column

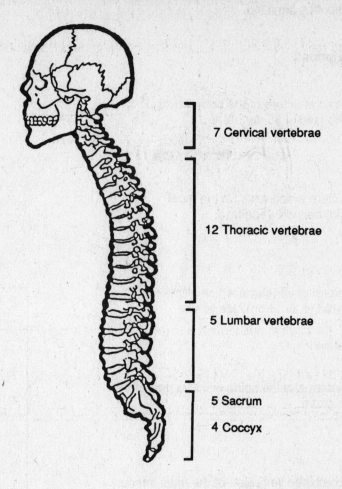

7 Cervical vertebrae

12 Thoracic vertebrae

5 Lumbar vertebrae

5 Sacrum

4 Coccyx

The **VERTEBRAL COLUMAN** (spine) is the foundation structure of the body. The other bony structures of the body are attached to the spine directly or indirectly.

The spine is a strong, flexible structure made up of 33 bones called **VERTEBRAE**.

These are -

    7 - Cervical (neck)
  12 - Thoracic (rib cage)
    5 - Lumbar (lower back)
    5 - Sacrum (fused together to form
            the back of the pelvis)
    4 - Coccyx (fused together to form
            the tailbone)

A

Match the word to the statement which best describes it by placing the appropriate numbers into the boxes provided.

Descriptions

A. ☐ The main structure of the body which is comprised of 33 vertebrae.

B. ☐ A structure which rests on the most superior cervical vertebrae.

C. ☐ The group of vertebrae which allows the head to turn from side to side.

D. ☐ The flat area of the spine which is part of the pelvic girdle.

E. ☐ The combined vertebrae of the most inferior part of the spine.

F. ☐ The portion of the spine which contains the greatest number of vertebrae.

G. ☐ The portion of the spine which is flexible and contains five (5) vertebrae.

Words

1. Skull

2. Cervical

3. Thoracic

4. Lumbar

5. Sacrum

6. Coccyx

7. Vertebral column

The Vertebrae

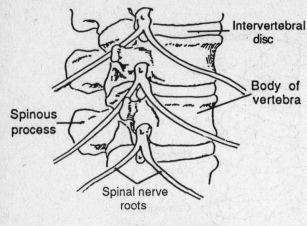

Lateral View of Two
Thoracic Vertebrae

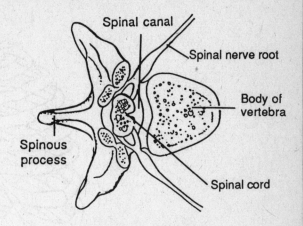

Cross Section of a
Thoracic Vertebra

The vertebrae are held to each other by **LIGAMENTS**.

Between each cervical, thoracic and lumbar vertebra is an **INTERVERTEBRAL DISC**. It is made up of a tough substance called **CARTILAGE**. These discs allow the body to move comfortably and act as shock absorbers for the spine.

Lying on the posterior side of the vertebra is the uneven bony **SPINOUS PROCESS** which, with the body of the vertebra, forms the **SPINAL CANAL**. The spinal canal gives protection to the very delicate **SPINAL CORD**.

The spinous process also acts as an attachment point for muscles.

A-16

Check (✓) the correct statements.

A. ☐   Each vertebra of the lumbar region of the spine is separated by a protective pad.

B. ☐   The cervical and thoracic vertebrae are held together by tendons.

C. ☐   The spinous process and the body of the vertebra create an opening through which the spinal cord runs.

D. ☐   Back muscles are connected to the bony protrusions on the spine.

A-16

A. ☑   C. ☑   D. ☑

A

The Thorax

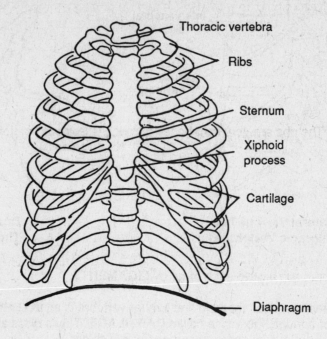

Thoracic vertebra

Ribs

Sternum

Xiphoid process

Cartilage

Diaphragm

Anterior View of the Thorax

The thorax is formed by the -

- **STERNUM**
- **12 PAIRS OF RIBS**
- **12 THORACIC VERTEBRAE**

The floor of the thorax is a large, flat skeletal muscle called the **DIAPHRAGM**.

The **STERNUM**, a narrow flat bone, forms the central part of the thoracic cage. At its most inferior point is a small prominent tip called the **XIPHOID PROCESS**.

The semi-flexible **RIBS** are attached posteriorly to the thoracic vertebrae by strong ligaments.

Anteriorly the most superior pairs of ribs are attached to the sternum by cartilage. The following 3 pairs are attached to the ribs above them by cartilage; and the two most inferior and shortest pairs of ribs are only attached to the thoracic vertebrae. These short pairs are referred to as the **FLOATING RIBS**.

A

Mark each statement true **(T)** or false **(F)**.

A. ☐ The xiphoid tip is the lowest portion of the sternum.

B. ☐ The ribs are very rigid bones allowing little movement of the chest.

C. ☐ All the ribs are attached to the sternum and the thoracic vertebrae.

D. ☐ The floating ribs are connected to the thoracic vertebrae.

E. ☐ In total there are 24 arched rib bones.

F. ☐ The diaphragm is a large organ which covers and protects the rib cage.

A. T   B. F   C. F   D. T   E. T   F. F

A

The pelvis forms the lower part of the abdominal cavity.

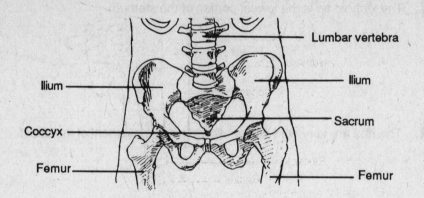

Anterior View of Pelvis

Attached to the fifth lumbar vertebra of the spine is the **PELVIS**. The pelvis is a bowl-shaped ring formed by the two fused parts of the spine, the **SACRUM** and **COCCYX** and a large, curved bone on each side called the **ILIUM**.

The upper end of the femur bone is shaped like a ball and fits into the pelvis to form the hip joint. This bone is held in position by ligaments and muscles.

Mark each statement true **(T)** or false **(F)**.

A. ☐   The pelvis is the bony structure with saucer-like bones on each side called the ilium.

B. ☐   The pelvis is made up of two long, flat bones which are fused together in a basin shape.

C. ☐   The pelvic bones form a socket into which the thigh bones fit.

D. ☐   All the bones that form the pelvis help to support and protect the abdominal and pelvic organs.

E. ☐   The skin holds the pelvis and its bony attachments together and allows movement.

A-20   A. T   B. F   C. T   D. T   E. F

A

Bones of the Upper Limb

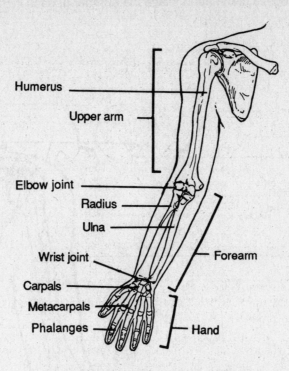

Anterior View of the Right Arm

The upper limb is divided into three parts -

- **UPPER ARM**
- **FOREARM**
- **HAND**

The upper arm has one large, long bone - the **HUMERUS**.

The forearm, distal to the upper arm, has two bones -

- **RADIUS** (the larger bone of the forearm lying on the thumbside)
- **ULNA** (the smaller bone of the forearm lying on the little finger side)

The wrist and hand have many bones. These bones are -

- **CARPALS** (8 in number in one hand)
- **METACARPALS** (5 in number in one hand)
- **PHALANGES** (14 in number in one hand)

Label the bones of the upper limb by writing the anatomical name in the space provided. When labelling the bones of the hand, place the number of each in the bracket ( ).

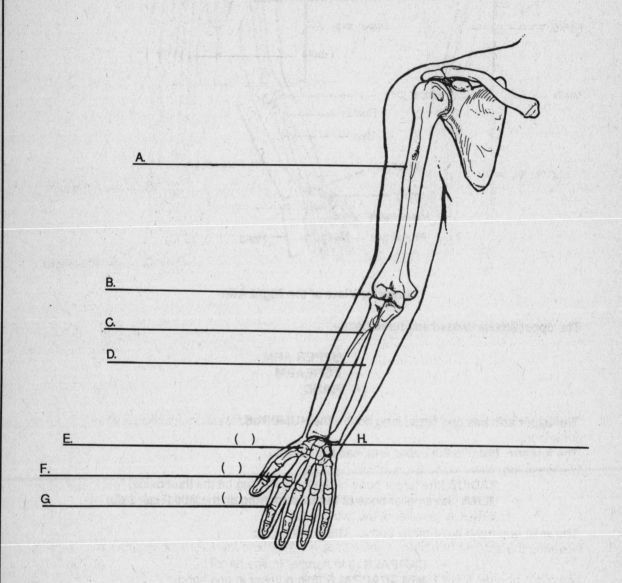

A.

B.

C.

D.

E.   ( )   H.

F.   ( )

G.   ( )

A. Humerus   D. Ulna   G. Phalanges (14)
B. Elbow joint   E. Carpals(8)   H. Wrist joint
C. Radius   F. Metacarpals(5)

A

Bones of the Lower Limb

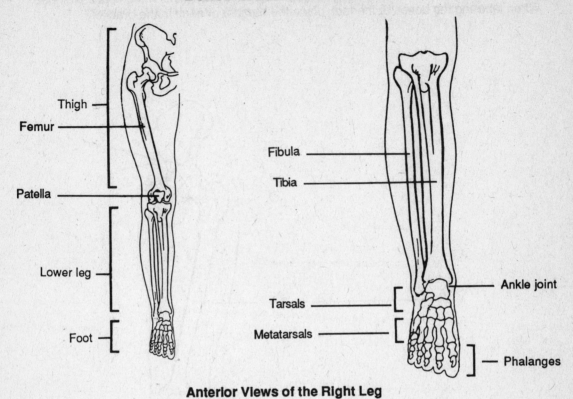

Anterior Views of the Right Leg

The lower limb is divided also into three parts -

- **THIGH**
- **LOWER LEG**
- **FOOT**

The thigh has one large, long bone, the **FEMUR**. It is the longest and strongest bone of the body.

The lower leg, distal to the thigh, has two bones -

- **TIBIA** (larger of the two bones; commonly called the shin bone)
- **FIBULA** (smaller of the two bones)

Covering the anterior part of the knee joint is a triangular bone called the **PATELLA**.

The ankle and the foot have many bones. These are -

- **TARSALS** (7 in number in one foot)
- **METATARSALS** (5 in number in one foot)
- **PHALANGES** (14 in number in one foot)

A

Label the bones of the lower limb by writing the anatomical name in the space provided. When labelling the bones of the foot, place the number of each in the bracket ( ).

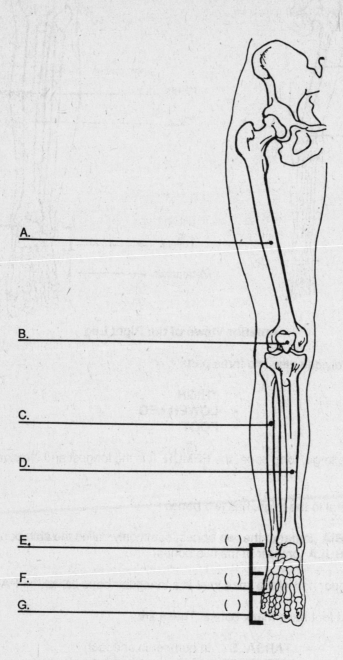

A. _____

B. _____

C. _____

D. _____

E. _____ ( )

F. _____ ( )

G. _____ ( )

A. Femur	D. Tibia	G. Phalanges (14)
B. Patella	E. Tarsals (7)	
C. Fibula	F. Metatarsals (5)	

A

The Joints of the Body

A **JOINT** is formed where two or more bones come together.

The bones of a joint
are held in place by
LIGAMENTS.

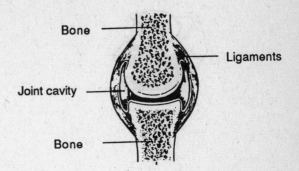

Bone

Ligaments

Joint cavity

Bone

There are three types of joints -

FREELY MOVABLE

(hip)

SLIGHTLY MOVABLE

(spine)

IMMOVABLE

(head)

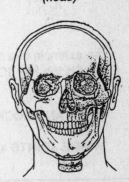

Mark each statement true **(T)** or false **(F)**.

A. ☐   A joint is a structure of the body where several bones meet.

B. ☐   There are joints of the body that allow no movement of their bony parts.

C. ☐   Ligaments prevent movement of a joint.

D. ☐   Tissues surrounding a joint help the joint in performing its function.

E. ☐   The hip joint is classified as a slightly movable joint.

A-26   A. [T]   B. [T]   C. [F]   D. [T]   E. [F]

A

Joints in the limbs are either -

BALL AND SOCKET JOINTS OR **HINGE JOINTS**

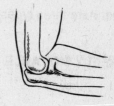

An example of a ball and socket joint is the **HIP JOINT**.

An example of a hinge joint is the **ELBOW JOINT**.

BALL AND SOCKET JOINTS allow movement in more than one direction.

HINGE JOINTS allow for free movement in one plane only.

Mark each statement true **(T)** or false **(F)**.

A. ☐ The elbow and knee are joints that allow movement in more than one direction.

B. ☐ The finger and thumb joints bend in only one direction.

C. ☐ Movement of the hip joint is very limited.

D. ☐ The shoulder joint is designed to allow a good range of movement.

E. ☐ The wrist joint allows a waving action.

A-28

A. F   B. T   C. F   D. T   E. T

A

Both the **SHOULDER** and **STERNOCLAVICULAR** joints are relatively unstable. Therefore, when any sudden or severe force is directed at these joints they are easily dislocated (bones pushed out of place).

The shoulder joint is the most frequently dislocated of all the large joints of the body.

The **SCAPULA** (which lies on the upper posterior side of the ribs) and the **CLAVICLE** form the **SHOULDER GIRDLE.**

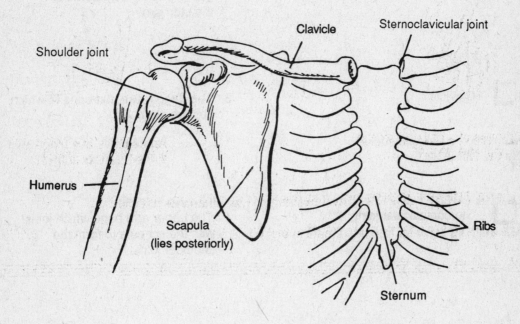

Anterior View of the Shoulder and Sternoclavicular Joints

Knowing the structure of the **shoulder** will assist you in assessing a casualty with a shoulder injury.

Mark in the box provided the number of the statement which best describes the terms given.

A. ☐ Humerus

1. A triangular, flat bone which forms the back part of the shoulder girdle.

B. ☐ Scapula

2. A narrow bone of the shoulder girdle which is connected to the sternum.

C. ☐ Clavicle

3. The dagger-like, flat bone to which ribs are attached.

D. ☐ Sternoclavicular joint

4. The upper arm bone which joins with the scapula to form the shoulder joint.

E. ☐ Shoulder joint

5. The joint which is dislocated more commonly than any other joint of its size.

F. ☐ Sternum

6. The joint which is formed by the dagger-like bone and the narrow, slightly curved bone.

A-30 A. 4 B. 1 C. 2 D. 6 E. 5 F. 3

A

The elbow and the knee joints are **HINGE JOINTS** and allow movement in one plane only **FLEXION** and **EXTENSION**.

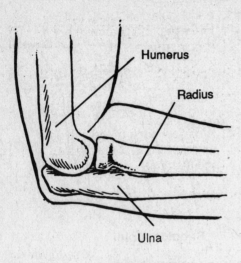

Elbow Joint

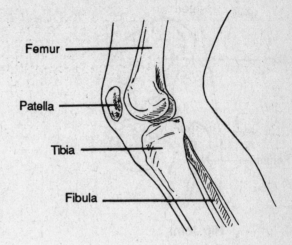

Knee Joint

The elbow joints allow **forward movement**.
The knee joints allow **backward movement**.

The knee joints are considered to be the most unstable joints in the body. The **PATELLA** provides protection for the knee joint.

A-32

Mark each statement true **(T)** or false **(F)**.

A. ☐ The elbow and knee joints flex in many directions.

B. ☐ Any injury to the elbow could involve the humerus, tibia and radius.

C. ☐ The elbow joint lacks a protective cap like the patella.

D. ☐ An injury to the knee could involve the femur, tibia and patella.

E. ☐ A hinge joint moves only in one direction.

A-32   A. F   B. F   C. T   D. T   E. T

Joints which allow the greatest range of movement are the **BALL-AND-SOCKET** type joints.

The hip and shoulder joints are examples of this type of joint.

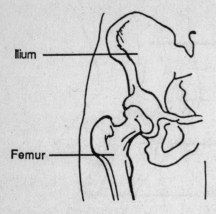

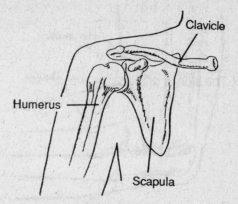

Hip Joint

Shoulder Joint

The third type of joint which also allows movement, though more limited than the hinge and ball-and-socket joints, is the **PIVOT JOINT**. An example of a pivot joint is where the radius and ulna rotate at the wrist. The rotation of these bones permits the hands to be either palm up or palm down.

Match each statement with one of the three types of joints given.

A. ☐ The meeting of the ulna and the humerus.

B ☐ The meeting of the ulna and radius distal to the elbow joint.

C. ☐ The meeting of the humerus and scapula.

D. ☐ The meeting of the tibia and femur.

E. ☐ The meeting of the femur and the ilium.

Choices

1. Hinge joint

2. Ball-and-socket joint

3. Pivot joint

A. ☐1   B. ☐3   C. ☐2   D. ☐1   E. ☐2

A

A-35

The **SKIN** is the largest and one of the most important organs of the body.

The **SKIN** -

- helps to **PROTECT** the body from bacteria, injury and extremes of temperature
- assists to **CONTROL** the temperature of the body
- helps to **RETAIN** body fluids
- assists in the **ELIMINATION** of waste products (perspiration)

The skin is made up of two layers -

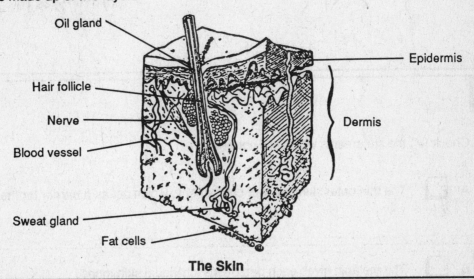

The Skin

A-36

Mark each statement true **(T)** or false **(F)**.

A. ☐ Although the skin covers the whole body, its role is meaningless in relationship to body functions.

B. ☐ The skin prevents the body temperature from dropping quickly in cold weather.

C. ☐ Germs are kept out of the body by the skin.

D. ☐ The top layer of the skin contains no blood vessels or nerve endings.

E. ☐ The epidermis is the thin outer layer of the skin.

F. ☐ Sweat glands originate in the dermis layer and open onto the surface of the epidermis.

A-36   A. F   B. T   C. T   D. T   E. T   F. T

A

The **EPIDERMIS** has several layers of cells.

The top two layers are renewed frequently and are replaced by the new cells from below. In extreme heat, the evaporation of perspiration on the outer skin assists in keeping the body cool.

The pigmentation of the skin is determined by **MELANIN** which is found in the deepest layer of the epidermis.

Check (✓) the statements which are correct.

A. ☐ The thin outer skin has four components which act as a barrier for the body.

B. ☐ The melanin gives each person his individual skin tones.

C. ☐ The colour of the skin is determined by a chemical in the dermis.

D. ☐ The replacement of the outer skin is a continuous process.

E. ☐ The epidermis is part of the cooling system of the body.

A. ☑ B. ☑ D. ☑ E. ☑

The **DERMIS** contains -

- Blood vessels
- Hair follicles
- Sweat and oil glands
- Sensory nerves

Below the dermis is the **SUBCUTANEOUS** or fatty tissue. This varies in thickness depending on what part of the body the skin is covering.

The subcutaneous tissue acts as an insulator to retain body heat.

Mark each statement true **(T)** or false **(F)**.

A. ☐ Through the nerves in the skin you are able to distinguish between hot and cold.

B. ☐ The layer of cells below the dermis helps the body to cool down.

C. ☐ The subcutaneous cells are often exposed and damaged when a person receives a severe acid burn to the palm of the hand.

D. ☐ Each hair on the body is rooted in a follicle.

E. ☐ The water which is secreted through the skin is collected in a vessel in the epidermis.

F. ☐ There are many veins and arteries in the dermis.

A-40   A. T   B. F   C. T   D. T   E. F   F. T

A

A-41

The **NERVOUS SYSTEM** is made up of the **BRAIN, SPINAL CORD** and **SPINAL NERVES.**

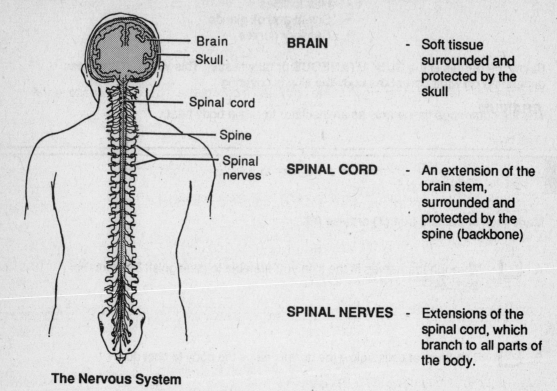

Brain
Skull
Spinal cord
Spine
Spinal nerves

The Nervous System

BRAIN - Soft tissue surrounded and protected by the skull

SPINAL CORD - An extension of the brain stem, surrounded and protected by the spine (backbone)

SPINAL NERVES - Extensions of the spinal cord, which branch to all parts of the body.

ALL BODILY FUNCTIONS (e.g. respiration, circulation, digestion, taste, touch, etc.) **ARE CONTROLLED BY THE NERVOUS SYSTEM.**

A-42

Mark each statement true **(T)** or false **(F).**

A. ☐ Spinal nerves are paired.

B. ☐ Nerves extend from the spinal cord throughout the body.

C. ☐ The nervous system is very delicate and the body provides no protection for it.

D. ☐ The spinal cord is attached to the brain.

A-42

A. T   B. T   C. F   D. T

A

Central Nervous System

The **CENTRAL NERVOUS SYSTEM** consists of the -

- **BRAIN**
  and
- **SPINAL CORD**

The brain is the controlling organ of the body and it occupies almost all the space in the **CRANIUM.**

The brain -

- Carries on internal functions, e.g. memory and thought processes
- Receives information
- Sends out nerve impulses (voluntary and autonomic activities)

The spinal cord -

- Transmits the impulses from the brain through its long tracts of nerves to the **PERIPHERAL NERVOUS SYSTEM**

Mark each statement true **(T)** or false **(F).**

A. ☐ The brain is the command centre of the body.

B. ☐ The spinal cord is the auxiliary command centre of the body.

C. ☐ The peripheral nervous system receives commands through the spinal cord.

D. ☐ The skull is the housing for the brain.

A-44 | A. [T] B. [F] C. [T] D. [T]

A

Peripheral Nervous System

The **PERIPHERAL NERVOUS SYSTEM** is made up of the nerves which lie outside the brain and spinal cord. They go from the spinal cord to all parts of the body.

There are two types of peripheral nerves -

- **MOTOR NERVES** - impulses **from** the brain

and

- **SENSORY NERVES** - impulses **to** the brain

Motor nerves carry messages (impulses) that create movement.

Sensory nerves carry sensations of touch, taste, heat, cold and pain to the brain.

Peripheral nerves are controlled by the will of an individual and, therefore, are called **VOLUNTARY NERVES**.

The **AUTONOMIC NERVOUS SYSTEM -** nerves that function involuntarily and supply the -

- Involuntary muscles of the body
  e.g. - Muscles of respiration
        - Muscles of digestion

The autonomic nervous system also provides the nerve supply for glands, the cardiac muscle and regulates the temperature of the body.

Match the word listed to the best description by placing its number in the appropriate box.

A. ☐ These nerves supply the stomach and intestine.

B. ☐ The complete network of nerves which acts under the control of the will of a person.

C. ☐ Stimuli are carried by this network to the muscles which control breathing and absorption of food.

D. ☐ When you wish to bend your arm, these nerves are activated by the brain.

Choices

1. Peripheral Nervous System

2. Autonomic Nervous System

3. Voluntary nerves

4. Involuntary nerves

A. 4   B. 1   C. 2   D. 3

A

The **CIRCULATORY SYSTEM** carries blood throughout the body.

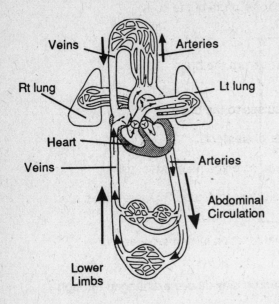

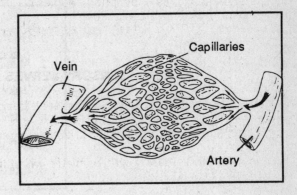

Oxygen and Carbon Dioxide Exchange

The Circulatory System

The closed circulatory system is made up of the -

- **HEART** - A strong, 4-chambered muscular pump which sends blood throughout the body

- **ARTERIES** - Tubular vessels which carry blood from the heart to all body cells

- **CAPILLARIES** - Extremely small tubular vessels which allow the exchange of fluids and gases in the cells of the body

- **VEINS** - Tubular vessels which transport the blood containing the waste products from the cells back to the organs of excretion and the heart

- **LUNGS** - Paired organs that effect ventilation and facilitate the oxygenation of the blood. The exchange of gases (carbon dioxide for oxygen) is done through very thin-walled tissues in the lungs called **ALVEOLI**

Constant circulation of the blood is necessary to -

- **Carry** oxygenated blood and the nutrients picked up by the blood to all body cells

- **Collect** waste products (i.e. fluids and carbon dioxide) from the body cells and return them to the organs of excretion and the heart.

Match each numbered part of the circulatory system with the correct description by placing a number in the box provided.

Choices

1. Heart
2. Alveoli
3. Veins
4. Capillaries
5. Lungs
6. Arteries

A. ☐ Two large organs in which oxygen and carbon dioxide are exchanged through the delicate walls of tiny blood vessels.

B. ☐ A muscular organ which rhythmically forces blood to all parts of the body.

C. ☐ The smallest carriers of blood through which various gaseous elements and substances are transferred from the body tissues to the blood and from the blood to the body tissues.

D. ☐ Hose-like structures through which blood flows from all parts of the body back to the heart.

E. ☐ Hose-like structures through which blood flows from the heart to all parts of the body.

F. ☐ Thin-walled air sacks in the lungs which allow exchange of gases.

The **CARDIOVASCULAR SYSTEM** is a closed system in which blood circulates through the -

- **HEART**
- **ARTERIES**
- **CAPILLARIES**
- **VEINS**

The blood carried by the arteries to the tissues contains:

- oxygen (in the haemoglobin of the blood)
- food (in a digestible form for the cells)
- chemical elements

The blood carried away from the tissues by the veins contains:

- carbon dioxide
- waste products from the cells

The **LYMPHATIC SYSTEM** is another liquid transportation system which works in conjunction with the cardiovascular system to help the body to -

- collect tissue fluids
- filter the fluids and return them to the cardiovascular system through a series of lymphatic vessels

The **SPLEEN** is an organ associated with the lymphatic system. It lies under the diaphragm, posterior to the stomach and under the lower portion of the left rib cage.

This fragile, blood filled organ has three functions -

- Storage of blood cells
- Production of blood cells
- Destruction of blood cells

The spleen is not as vital an organ as the heart and if removed, the liver and bone marrow assume its function.

A-50

Match each word numbered and listed with the correct statement by placing a number in the box provided.

A. ☐ The auxiliary system that provides drainage of fluids from body cells.

B. ☐ Vessels of the circulatory system which carry blood from the heart.

C. ☐ The four-part organ which forces the blood to the lungs and limbs.

D. ☐ Blood vessels which carry the blood back to the heart from the extremities.

E. ☐ Hair-like vessels of the circulatory system which allow the exchange of gases, food and waste products in the cells of the body.

F. ☐ A very delicate organ which makes and gets rid of blood cells.

G. ☐ Collecting tubes which give back fluids into the cardio-vascular system.

H. ☐ The entire series of vessels through which the blood flows.

Choices

1. Cardiovascular System
2. Lymphatic System
3. Lymphatic Vessels
4. Heart
5. Veins
6. Capillaries
7. Arteries
8. Spleen

A-50

A. 2 B. 7 C. 4 D. 5 E. 6 F. 8 G. 3 H. 1

A

A - 34

The **HEART** is a muscular organ which lies anteriorly and slightly left of centre in the thoracic cavity and is protected by the sternum and the ribs.

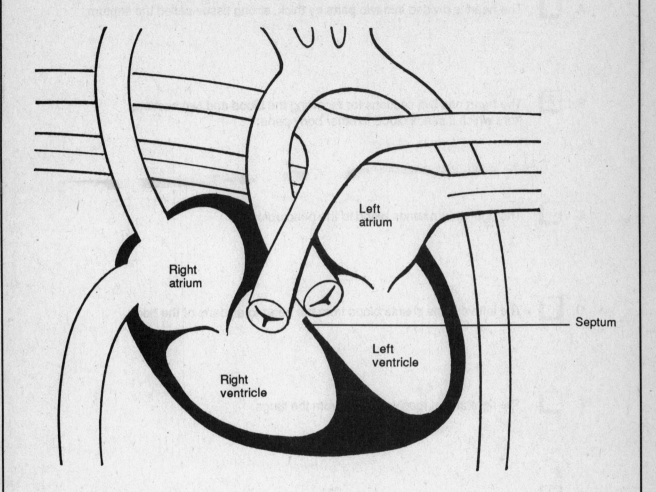

The Heart

The right side and the left side of the heart are separated by a muscular wall - the **SEPTUM.**

The right and left sides of the heart are again divided into two chambers each -

- The **ATRIUM** (the upper, collecting chamber)
- The **VENTRICLE** (the lower, pumping chamber)

The heart is a double pump encased in a double-walled sac - the **PERICARDIUM.** The outer wall gives support to the heart and the inner wall protects the heart and prevents friction from the heart movement.

A

Mark each statement true **(T)** or false **(F)**.

A. ☐   The heart is divided into two parts by thick, strong tissue called the septum.

B. ☐   The heart has two sections for receiving the blood and two sections from which it sends blood to other body parts.

C. ☐   The right atrium sends blood to the pericardium.

D. ☐   The left ventricle shunts blood from the heart to all parts of the body.

E. ☐   The right atrium receives blood from the lungs.

F. ☐   The heart is protected by a double-lined bag-like structure.

G. ☐   The dagger-like flat bone of the chest alone keeps the heart safe in the thoracic cavity.

The Right Side of the Heart and its Associated Blood Vessels

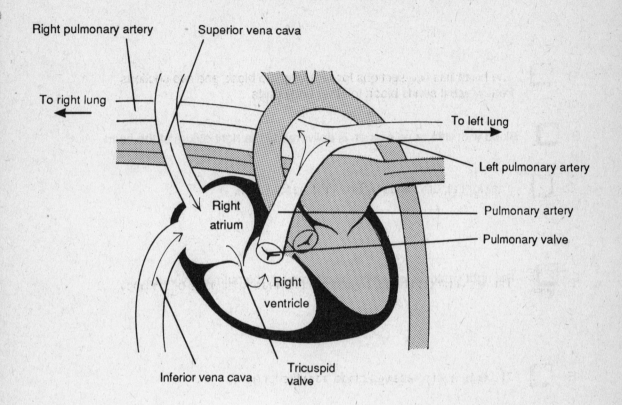

Right pulmonary artery Superior vena cava

To right lung

To left lung

Left pulmonary artery

Right atrium

Pulmonary artery

Pulmonary valve

Right ventricle

Inferior vena cava

Tricuspid valve

The **SUPERIOR VENA CAVA** and the **INFERIOR VENA CAVA** bring blood from the head and neck and the lower parts of the body respectively. These two large blood vessels enter the **RIGHT ATRIUM**, the collecting chamber of the heart for **deoxygenated blood.**

The blood goes from the right atrium through the **TRICUSPID VALVE**, which allows a certain amount of blood into the **RIGHT VENTRICLE**, (a lower pumping chamber).

The blood is then pumped through the **PULMONARY VALVE** by the right ventricle into the **PULMONARY ARTERY** and then into the **RIGHT AND LEFT PULMONARY ARTERIES**. These arteries carry the deoxygenated blood to the **LUNGS.**

Valves of the heart, when healthy, allow blood to flow in one direction only.

A

Mark each statement true **(T)** or false **(F)**.

A. ☐   The pulmonary artery which leaves the heart divides into two parts, one going to the right lung and the other to the left lung.

B. ☐   Blood with little or no oxygen is delivered to the right atrium of the heart.

C. ☐   The right ventricle forces the blood through the pulmonary valve.

D. ☐   The tricuspid valve allows the blood to flow from the right atrium into the pulmonary artery.

E. ☐   The superior vena cava and the inferior vena cava bring deoxygenated blood into the right ventricle.

A. ☐ T   B. ☐ T   C. ☐ T   D. ☐ F   E. ☐ F

A

The Left Side of the Heart and Its Associated Blood Vessels

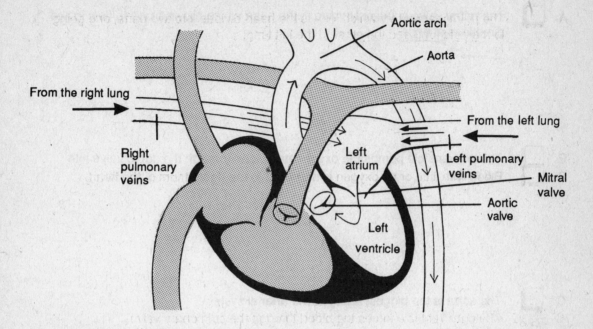

After the blood has been oxygenated in the lungs, it returns to the **LEFT ATRIUM** through the **LEFT AND RIGHT PULMONARY VEINS.**

The **MIITRAL VALVE** between the left atrium and the **LEFT VENTRICLE** opens allowing a certain amount of blood into the left ventricle. Like all the valves of a healthy heart, it allows blood flow in one direction only.

The left ventricle, the strongest and most muscular portion of the heart, pumps the oxygenated blood through the **AORTIC VALVE** into the **AORTA**. The aorta is the largest artery of all the arteries of the body.

The aorta divides and sends the oxygenated blood to the areas of the body above and below the heart.

The blood circulation system is a closed loop. It begins and ends at the heart and includes -

The **PULMONARY CIRCULATION** which begins on the right side of the heart where the deoxygenated blood is sent to the lungs.

The **SYSTEMIC CIRCULATION** which begins at the left side of the heart where the blood is pumped into the aorta and to other parts of the body.

Mark each statement true **(T)** or false **(F)**.

A. ☐ The mitral valve is the only valve in the heart which allows blood to flow in two directions at once.

B. ☐ The left ventricle pumps the oxygenated blood through the aortic valve into the aorta.

C. ☐ The aorta is the biggest artery of the arterial system.

D. ☐ The main function of pulmonary circulation is to rid the blood of oxygen.

E. ☐ Systemic circulation delivers the blood to the cells of the body.

A. F   B. T   C. T   D. F   E. T

A

Label the parts of the heart and its blood vessels where indicated.

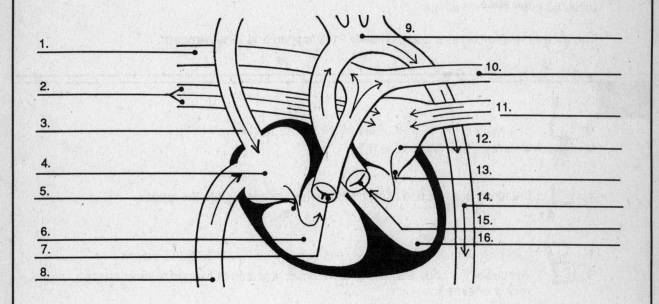

1.
2.
3.
4.
5.
6.
7.
8.

9.
10.
11.
12.
13.
14.
15.
16.

1. Right pulmonary artery	5. Tricuspid valve	9. Aortic arch	13. Mitral valve
2. Right pulmonary veins	6. Right ventricle	10. Left pulmonary artery	14. Aorta
3. Superior vena cava	7. Pulmonary valve	11. Left pulmonary veins	15. Aortic valve
4. Right atrium	8. Inferior vena cava	12. Left atrium	16. Left ventricle

A

A-58

The function of the respiratiory system is to exchange **OXYGEN** and **CARBON DIOXIDE** within the body.

The exchange of these gases is performed in two ways -

1. **EXTERNAL RESPIRATION** - the exchange of oxygen and carbon dioxide in the lungs.

2. **INTERNAL RESPIRATION** - the exchange of oxygen and carbon dioxide between the bloodstream and the cells of the body.

The body can store only enough oxygen for a few minutes. The oxygen in our bodies is replaced every time we inhale.

The air we breathe contains approximately 21% oxygen and 79% nitrogen.

A-59

Mark each statement true (T) or false (F).

A. ☐   Breathing is a function of respiration which brings air into the lungs.

B. ☐   Tissues of the body are able to store small amounts of oxygen to function for a very short time.

C. ☐   The giving off of nitrogen and the absorption of oxygen into the blood is called internal respiration.

D. ☐   Brain cells continually require a new supply of oxygen.

A-59

A. T   B. T   C. F   D. T

A

The Organs of Respiration

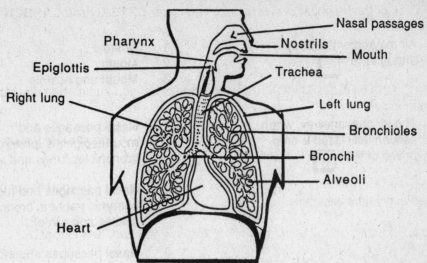

NASAL PASSAGES	- Air enters the nasal passages through the two nostrils. The air is warmed, moistened and filtered as it passes over the damp, mucous membrane of the passages.
PHARYNX	- The pharynx is the communal passage for both the nutrients and the air from the mouth and the nasal passages to pass to the stomach and lungs respectively. It divides into the:

- **ESOPHAGUS** (food passageway to stomach)
  and
- **TRACHEA** (airway to the lungs)

The **LARYNX** (Adam's Apple—voice box) is the uppermost part of the trachea.

EPIGLOTTIS	- A flap of tissue which automatically closes off the trachea when food is swallowed and remains open at other times to allow air to enter the bronchi.
BRONCHI	- The trachea divides into the left and right bronchi which enter the left and right lung respectively.

In the lungs, the bronchi further divide into smaller passages. They are the:

- **BRONCHIOLES**
  and
- **ALVEOLI** (gas exchange sac at the end of the bronchioles)

A

Select the best response to complete the statement and place its number in the box provided.

A. Air may enter the body through the - ☐

1. Nostrils
2. Mouth
3. Mouth and nostrils

B. The air passageway, when sequentially listed is comprised of the - ☐

1. Nasal passages and mouth, epiglottis, pharynx, bronchioles, lungs and alveoli
2. Nasal passages and mouth, pharynx, trachea, bronchi, bronchioles and alveoli
3. Nasal passages and mouth, esophagus, pharynx, bronchi, bronchioles and alveoli

C. The cap which prevents food from entering the trachea is the - ☐

1. Esophagus
2. Larynx
3. Epiglottis

D. The left and right bronchi become smaller airways called - ☐

1. Bronchioles and alveoli
2. Epiglottis and alveoli
3. Bronchioles and trachea

E. The airway ends at the - ☐

1. Epiglottis
2. Alveoli
3. Bronchi

F. When we breathe, the epiglottis allows air to go directly into the - ☐

1. Bronchioles
2. Bronchi
3. Trachea

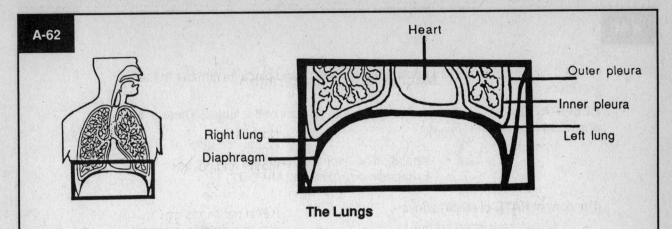

The Lungs

The lungs lie in a double-layered sac called the **PLEURA.** The thin, inner layer of the pleura lies against the lungs. The thicker, outer layer is more muscular and lies against the chest wall. These two layers are separated by the **INTRAPLEURAL SPACE.**

The pleura has two functions -

- **Allows** the lungs to expand
- **Provides** a lubricant for lung movement

Separating the organs of respiration in the thorax from the abdominal cavity is a strong, flat muscle - the **DIAPHRAGM.** The diaphragm changes its shape (from flat to dome-shaped) and in doing so makes the thoracic cavity **larger** or **smaller.** This variance of space is essential to the **MECHANISM OF RESPIRATION.**

A-63

Mark each statement true **(T)** or false **(F).**

A. ☐ Each lung is encased in two layers of tissue.

B. ☐ The pleura has two walls which are identical.

C. ☐ Without the pleura, the lungs would rub against the rib cage when air is drawn into them.

D. ☐ The diaphragm separates the upper organs for breathing from the lower organs of digestion.

E. ☐ The diaphragm changes shape to allow room for the stomach to expand after food has been eaten.

F. ☐ The diaphragm has an important function in the process of respiration.

A-63   A. [T]   B. [F]   C. [T]   D. [T]   E. [F]   F. [T]

A

Mechanism of Respiration

RESPIRATION is the passage of air going into and out of the lungs. There are two phases of respiration -

- Inhalation or inspiration (**AIR IN**)
- Exhalation or expiration (**AIR OUT**)

The normal **RATE** of respiration is -

- 10 to 18 times per minute for adults
- 18 to 28 times per minute for children
- 41 to 55 times per minute for infants

Normal breathing is -

Regular
Quiet
Moderately deep

The rate and depth increase with activity, stress, etc.

The **RESPIRATORY CENTRE** is located in the brain at the base of the skull. The respiratory centre reacts to various forms of chemical stimulation. The most important of these is the reaction of the centre to:

- **INCREASING AMOUNTS OF CARBON DIOXIDE** in the blood

  or

- **DECREASING AMOUNTS OF OXYGEN** in the blood

Place the flat of your hand on the upper part of your chest. Using a watch or clock with a second hand, count the number of breaths taken in a minute.

Does your breathing rate fall within the normal range? ☐ yes ☐ no

Repeat this exercise after running on the spot for one minute.

Did your breathing rate ☐ increase or ☐ decrease?

Match the term given with the best description by placing the appropriate number in the box provided.

A. ☐ The physiological act of taking in and letting out of air into our lungs.

B. ☐ The act of breathing in.

C. ☐ The number of times an adult, child or infant breathes in a minute.

Choices

1. Normal breathing

2. Rate of respiration

3. Respiratory centre

4. Respiration

D. ☐ Respiration that is at regular intervals, almost silent and with a fairly good chest expansion.

5. Inhalation

6. Exhalation

E. ☐ The act of breathing out.

F. ☐ The portion of the brain affected by chemical changes in the blood.

When the levels of carbon dioxide in the body **INCREASE**, the respiratory centre is affected and sends a message through the appropriate nerves to stimulate the diaphragm and the **INTERCOSTAL MUSCLES** which lie between the ribs. The message received is to -

- Increase the **rate of breathing**
- Increase the **depth of breathing**

INHALATION PHASE (INSPIRATION)

The intercostal muscles tighten and the diaphragm **CONTRACTS**. The ribs are pulled upward and outward and the diaphragm flattens downward.

The thoracic cavity is increased in size and a negative pressure (vacuum) is created and air is drawn into the lungs. Now the amount of carbon dioxide in the blood is reduced and the level of oxygen is increased. The stimuli going to the respiration centre of the brain stop.

EXHALATION PHASE (EXPIRATION)

When the amount of carbon dioxide in the blood is reduced, the intercostal muscles and the diaphragm relax.

The ribs drop and the diaphragm resumes its dome-shaped state. These muscular reactions reduce the size of the thoracic cavity and force the flow of air out of the lungs.

The larynx opens to release the air from the bronchi, while the abdominal muscles contract. The contraction of these muscles pushes the abdominal contents up against the diaphragm. This helps to -

- further decrease the capacity of the thoracic cavity

AND

- assist the forcing out of the same volume of air that was taken in during the inhalation phase

Mark each statement true **(T)** or false **(F)**.

A. ☐ When there is too much carbon dioxide in the blood, breathing automatically becomes faster and the chest expansion is greater.

B. ☐ Breathing in is assisted by the elastic tissues between the ribs and the diaphragm making the rib cage larger.

C. ☐ The chest cavity only changes shape when a person is running or under stress.

D. ☐ Breathing out is accomplished by the relaxation of the same muscles that assisted in bringing in the air to the lungs.

A-67   A. T   B. T   C. F   D. F

A

A-68

The **DIGESTIVE SYSTEM** acts on the food we eat so that it can be used to **NOURISH** all the cells of the body. It also **COLLECTS** and **DISPOSES** of **SOLID WASTE**.

The digestive system is composed of:

- An **ALIMENTARY TRACT** (food passageway). This tract goes from the mouth, through the body and terminates at the rectum.

- The **ORGANS OF DIGESTION**, which contain glands that secrete digestive juices and transform food into a usable form of nourishment.

The organs of digestion are either **SOLID** or **HOLLOW**.

A-69

Check (✔) the correct statements.

A. ☐ To be able to digest the food we eat, it has to be changed into a simple form for absorption by the body.

B. ☐ The alimentary tract allows the food and waste to pass through the body.

C. ☐ All the organs of digestion are open tubes.

D. ☐ Glands of digestion secrete fluids which assist in the breakdown of foods.

A-69

A. ☑   B. ☑   D. ☑

A

DIGESTION has two distinct processes -

- **Mechanical**   and   - **Chemical**

The **MECHANICAL PROCESSES** are -

- Chewing (digestion begins in the mouth)
- Swallowing
- Movement of food through the gastrointestinal tract (peristalsis)
- Elimination of solid waste materials (defecation)

The **CHEMICAL PROCESS** is the breakdown of food by enzymes (digestive juices) secreted from glands of the digestive organs. This transforms food into an acceptable form for the body.

The enzymes act on the food to change -

Carbohydrates	Into	simple sugars
Fat	Into	fatty acids
Proteins	Into	amino acids

Mark in the box provided the number of the statement which best describes the terms given.

A. ☐ Fatty Acids

B. ☐ Chemical process

C. ☐ Carbohydrates

D. ☐ Mechanical process

E. ☐ Alimentary tract

F. ☐ Mouth

G. ☐ Enzymes

H. ☐ Peristalsis

1. Eating, pushing food through the body and evacuation are parts of this process.

2. A digestible form of fat.

3. The hollow passageway through which food and drink pass through the body.

4. The pushing movement of food through the alimentary canal.

5. Where the process of digestion begins.

6. This particular type of food group produces simple sugars.

7. The changing of the individual food groups into acceptable substance for the body.

8. Secretions which act on foods to change them into simpler substances for the body to digest.

A-71   A. 2   B. 7   C. 6   D. 1   E. 3   F. 5   G. 8   H. 4

A

Digestive System

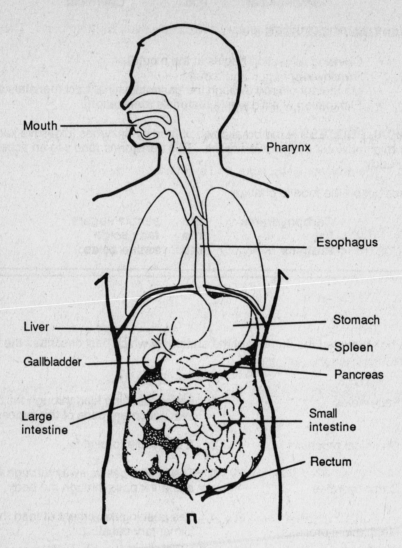

Mouth

Pharynx

Esophagus

Liver

Stomach

Spleen

Gallbladder

Pancreas

Large intestine

Small intestine

Rectum

The **MOUTH, PHARYNX** and **ESOPHAGUS** form the initial part of the alimentary canal. Through this canal, foods and liquids pass. The digestion process begins in the mouth.

The **STOMACH** receives the food and liquid from the esophagus. The stomach acts as a reservoir for the food. The food and liquid are -

- **STORED;**
- **WARMED;**
- **SOFTENED;** and
- further **BROKEN DOWN CHEMICALLY.**

Select the correct answer to each question and indicate your answer in the box provided.

A. ☐ The beginning of the alimentary canal is divided into three parts. They are:

  1. The colon, esophagus and mouth.

  2. The mouth, stomach and pharynx.

  3. The mouth, pharynx and esophagus.

  4. The pharynx, esophagus and stomach.

B. ☐ After the food leaves the mouth, it is passed directly into:

  1. The stomach.

  2. The pharynx.

  3. The esophagus.

  4. The rectum.

C. ☐ The food or liquid passed into the stomach is:

  1. Further digested, kept in a solid state and eliminated from the body.

  2. Worked on by the enzymes of the stomach, brought to body temperature and kept until it is ready to be further processed.

  3. Chemically acted upon, cooled below body temperature and fully absorbed through the walls of the stomach.

  4. Turned into a cool, liquid mass by the enzymes of the stomach and stored until it is required by the cells of the body.

A. ☐ 3   B. ☐ 2   C. ☐ 2

A

The stomach passes small amounts of partially digested food into the intestine which measures 8.5 to 9 metres in length in the adult.

The **INTESTINE** is divided into two sections -

- **SMALL INTESTINE**
- **LARGE INTESTINE**

The intestines are suspended loops which lie in the abdominal cavity. The main functions of the intestines are to allow the -

- **ABSORPTION** of nutrients through the intestinal wall into the blood stream which carries them to the cells of the body.

- **COLLECTION** of waste material for excretion through the rectum.

Check (✓) the correct statements.

A. ☐   The intestines are coils of hollow tubes which lie in the abdominal cavity.

B. ☐   The body cells receive nutrients directly from the small intestine.

C. ☐   The large intestine is the collecting area for solid waste materials to be excreted through the rectum.

D. ☐   The intestinal tubes can be anywhere from 8 to 9 metres in length for a person who is 25 years of age.

E. ☐   The digested food is passed through the wall of the intestine into the blood stream.

A-75

| A. ✓ | C. ✓ | D. ✓ | E. ✓ |

A

Organs which assist in the digestion of food are the -

- **LIVER**
- **GALLBLADDER**
- **PANCREAS**

The **liver** lies just beneath the diaphragm on the right side of the body. The liver produces a substance called **BILE** which aids in digestion.

The **gallbladder**, connected to the underside of the liver, stores the bile until it is required for the process of digestion.

The **pancreas** also lies in the abdominal cavity in front of the spine and behind the stomach. The pancreas produces insulin and pancreatic juices which also aid in digestion.

The stomach, intestines and gallbladder are classified as hollow organs.

The liver and pancreas are classified as solid organs that have an abundant supply of blood vessels.

Match the organ to the statement which best describes it.

A. ☐ The organ where bile is stored.

B. ☐ The liver and the pancreas are organs that are filled with many blood vessels.

C. ☐ The stomach, intestines and gallbladder are organs that produce substances which aid in digestion.

D. ☐ The organ which produces insulin.

E. ☐ The organ in which bile is manufactured.

Choices

1. Liver
2. Hollow organs
3. Pancreas
4. Solid organs
5. Gallbladder

A-77

A. | 5 | B. | 4 | C. | 2 | D. | 3 | E. | 1

A

Organs of the Urinary System
(anterior view)

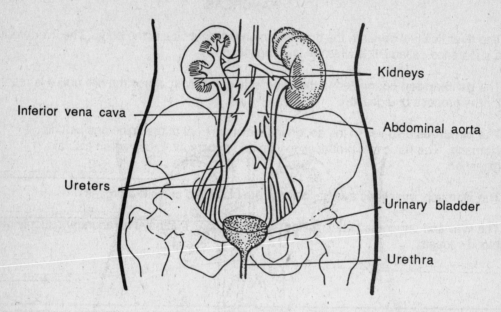

KIDNEYS

Inferior vena cava

Abdominal aorta

Ureters

Urinary bladder

Urethra

KIDNEYS	- Located posteriorly in the upper, mid segment of the abdominal cavity. They are partially protected by the lower ribs and are classified as **SOLID ORGANS** of this system. The two kidneys filter the blood and manufacture urine.
URETERS	- Paired tubes that extend from each kidney to the urinary bladder. The ureters pass the urine from the kidneys to the urinary bladder.
URINARY BLADDER	- A sac located in the lower, central portion of the pelvic cavity when empty. When filled with urine, it extends into the lower part of the abdominal cavity. The urinary bladder stores the urine until it is excreted through the urethra.
URETHRA	- A muscular tube that extends from the urinary bladder to the exterior of the body.

The ureters, urinary bladder and urethra are classified as **HOLLOW ORGANS** of the urinary system.

Branches of the **ABDOMINAL AORTA** take oxygenated blood **TO** the kidneys.

Branches of the **INFERIOR VENA CAVA** collect deoxygenated blood **FROM** the kidneys.

A

Write in the anatomical terms for the organs of the urinary system where indicated on the diagram provided.

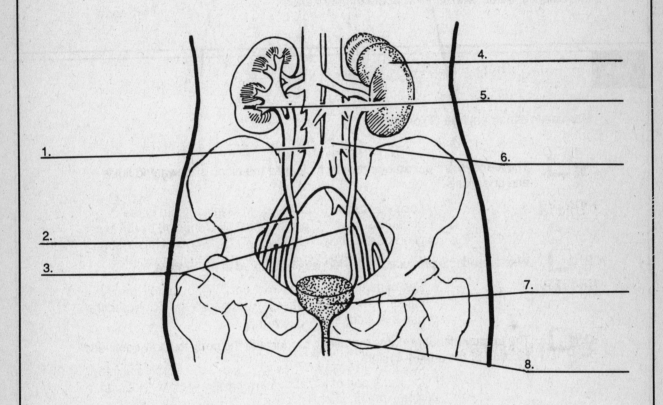

1.

2.

3.

4.

5.

6.

7.

8.

1. Inferior vena cava   3. Left ureter   5. Right kidney   7. Urinary bladder
2. Right ureter   4. Left kidney   6. Adominal aorta   8. Urethra

A

The urinary system **REMOVES, FILTERS, COLLECTS** and **EXCRETES** waste from the body in the form of urine.

Blood which flows through the kidneys is filtered. During this process -

- urine is formed
- wastes are removed
- useful elements are returned to the blood

The urinary system maintains the balance of water and chemicals in the body. Without this balance, health and survival would be threatened.

Mark each statement true **(T)** or false **(F).**

A. ☐ The kidneys are paired organs which cleanse the blood of unwanted fluids and chemicals.

B. ☐ Waste products produced in the kidneys are stored in the urethra.

C. ☐ The urinary bladder returns the useful products to the body to allow continued function of the urinary system.

D. ☐ Malfunction of the urinary system is a life-threatening condition.

E. ☐ The ureters carry the urine from the kidneys to the urinary bladder.

A. T B. F C. F D. T E. T

A

The Female Reproductive System
(Lateral View)

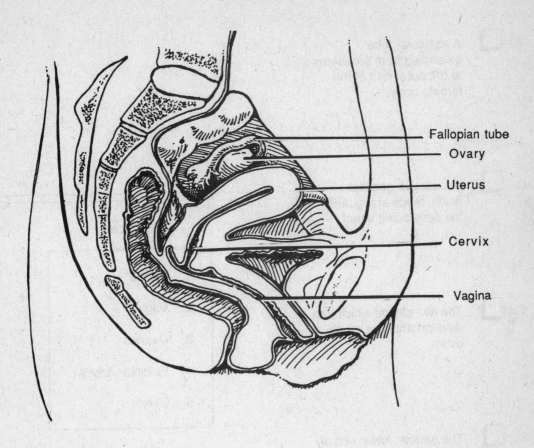

- Fallopian tube
- Ovary
- Uterus
- Cervix
- Vagina

The female reproductive system consists of:

OVARIES — These paired organs produce the ovum (egg). Both ovaries seldom produce and expel an ovum at the same time.

FALLOPIAN TUBES — Along these paired tube-like structures, the ovum travels from each ovary to the uterus.

UTERUS — The muscular structure that holds, protects and nourishes the fetus (unborn child). The uterus opens into the vagina. The neck of the uterus is called the **CERVIX**.

VAGINA — The muscular canal which connects the uterus to the external genitalia of the female. It is more commonly known as the birth canal during the delivery of an infant.

Match each numbered part of the female reproductive system with the best description by placing the appropriate number into the box provided.

A. ☐ A muscular tube extending from the uterus to the outer part of the female body.

B. ☐ A muscular sac that holds, feeds and guards the developing infant.

Choices

C. ☐ The two glands which can develop and give off an ovum.

1. Uterus

2. Vagina

3. Ovaries

4. Fallopian tubes

5. Cervix

D. ☐ The narrow, lower end of the uterus.

E. ☐ The two long, slender vessels which extend from the area of the ovaries and open into the uterus.

A. 2   B. 1   C. 3   D. 5   E. 4

A

The Male Reproductive System
(Lateral view)

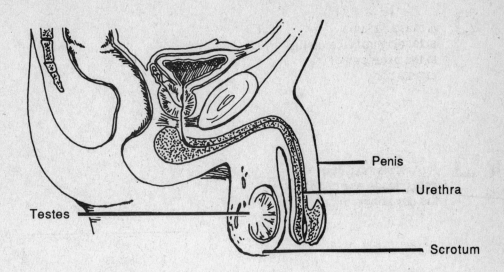

Penis

Urethra

Testes

Scrotum

The external male reproductive organs are:

TESTES - Paired external glands which store spermatazoa.

PENIS - The external, muscular organ through which urine is eliminated from the urinary bladder and through which the spermatazoa are expelled from the body. The urethra is the passageway which allows fluid to flow through the penis to the exterior of the body.

A-85

Mark each statement true **(T)** or false **(F)**.

A. ☐ The testes are the organs which produce spermatazoa.

B. ☐ The penis is used by both the urinary and reproductive systems to eliminate liquid products from the body through the urethra.

C. ☐ The testes are encased in the scrotum.

A-85   A. F   B. T   C. T

A

THE END OF ADDENDUM A.

NOTES

NOTES

NOTES

NOTES